Escape Routes
Published in the United Kingdom in 2011 by
Punk Publishing Ltd
3 The Yard
Pegasus Place
London
SE11 5SD

www.punkpublishing.co.uk
www.escape-routes.co.uk

A catalogue record of this book is available
from the British Library.

ISBN 978-1-906889-10-4

10 9 8 7 6 5 4 3 2 1

CONTENTS

INTRODUCTION

HAVE YOU EVER DREAMT of escaping to those beautiful, barely populated countryside corners of England? Of swinging your leg over the saddle and setting off along narrow lanes, gliding through spectacular scenery in your own sweet time, and pausing wherever you wish? When you're out on your bike, nothing can stop you. No queues, no parking spaces, no petrol required – just pure and simple pedal power is all you need. So where do you fancy going today?

The back roads of England are sprinkled with idyllic villages, hidden pubs, and secret country gardens just waiting to be discovered, and this book will show you exactly where to find them. I've found some real gems – in the unlikeliest of places: a sun-soaked vineyard in a valley less than an hour from London (see p98), a hamlet deep in the Norfolk lanes where the clocks seem to have stopped back in the 18th century (see p136), and a gourmet chocolate shop in the middle of the Lake District's moors (see p234). This, however, is just scratching the surface...

Take a trip through the book and you'll find 60 glorious bike rides that will lead you far away from the madding crowds, to a county's most intimate landscape secrets; places where time slows down to a luxurious crawl. It's not about how many miles you do, the number of calories you burn, or how quickly you can go; it's all about being out in the fresh air, with the sun on your face and the breeze blowing through your hair. And who cares if you ride up that hill, or decide to push? Sometimes it's nice just to stop for a second and enjoy the view…

Whatever you're riding – a second-hand jalopy you bought through the free-ads, the latest road bike with all the trick bits, or a 'sit-up-and-beg' with a basket on the front – there are routes in here to suit everyone and their chosen wheels.

You'll find Jaw-dropping Views, Magical History Tours, and rides that take you Beside the Seaside – or perhaps you'd prefer a journey that's Best for Pubs, or one that will take you Down by the River?

See pages 8–19 for more tips on where to find a route to perfectly match your mood.

One of my favourites is the ride from Freshford to Avoncliff (see p54), taking you through a lush valley, where you can stop off for a stroll round an Italianate garden, before calling in at a riverside pub and making your way along a canal. You can count on one hand the number of cars you'll see all day. Actually, the ride that starts at a swish hotel and leads you through the Yorkshire Dales to a set of dramatic waterfalls at Aysgarth (see p220) might just pip it to the post… It's difficult to tell really – every one is a corker that uncovers something special.

These are much more than just bike rides, they're Escape Routes. Tried and tested recipes for fabulous stress-busting weekends away (or longer breaks?), with suggestions about where to stop and what to see along the way.

Having pedalled my way through the network of narrow lanes that criss-crosses England, and poked my nose into rustic nooks and crannies from Cornwall to Northumberland, I've personally selected each of the rides in this book (and made all the wrong turns so you don't have to).

Each of the rides begins (and ends) at a smart B&B, bijou independent hotel, or cosy self-catering cottage, because fluffy towels and comfy beds are important, too. And, aside from the sights you'll see when you're out in the saddle, I've outlined things you might want to do when you're not cycling.

Every ride is brought to life with a personal account of all the sights, sounds, and experiences you'll encounter; a gorgeous hand-drawn map to help you find your way around; and detailed directions, too (always useful). One more thing before I go: all the mileages mentioned are approximate (to the nearest few hundred metres or so); so don't shout at me if they're a bit out on occasion. Besides, you won't be worrying about that when you see the views.

So what are you waiting for?

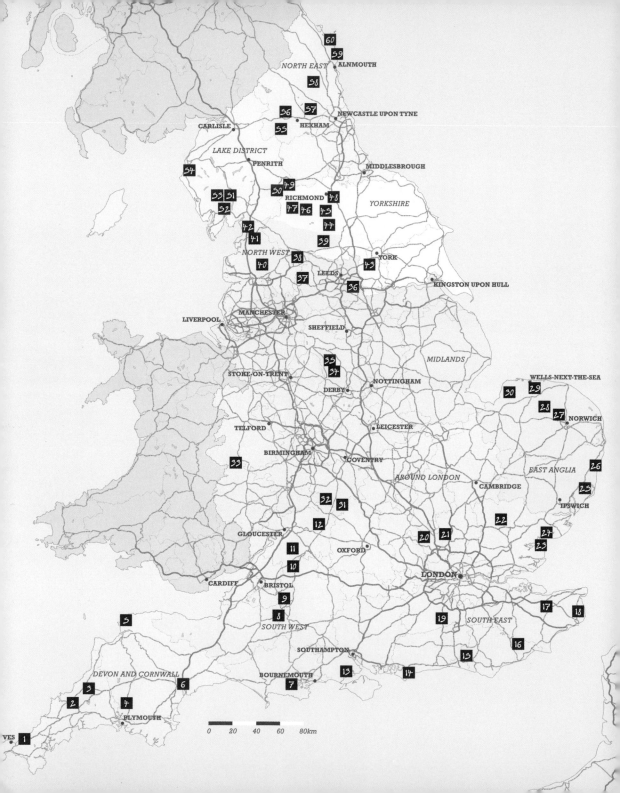

No	Ride	Page	Magical History Tour p8	Down by the River p10	Beside the Seaside p12	Jaw-dropping Views p14	Best for Pubs p16	Taste Tour p18
1	Gwithian to Coombe	22			☆	☆		
2	Tredethy to Pencarrow	26						☆
3	Camelford to Delabole	28				☆		☆
4	Tavistock to Horndon	32				☆	☆	
5	Mortehoe to Croyde	36			☆	☆		
6	Kenton to Topsham	40		☆				
7	Wareham to Corfe Castle	46	☆			☆		
8	Mells to Frome	50	☆	☆				☆
9	Freshford to Avoncliff	54		☆		☆	☆	
10	Tetbury to Sherston	58					☆	☆
11	Minchinhampton to Nailsworth	62				☆		☆
12	Guiting Power to Broadway	66			☆	☆		
13	East End to East Boldre	72	☆				☆	
14	Pagham Harbour to West Wittering	76			☆		☆	
15	Ditchling to Wivelsfield Green	82				☆		
16	Staplecross to Bodiam Castle	86	☆					
17	Old Wives Lees to Faversham	88					☆	☆
18	Deal to Ringwould	92	☆		☆			
19	Dorking to Coldharbour	98				☆		☆
20	Aldbury to Frithsden	102		☆			☆	
21	Ayot St Lawrence to 'Old' Welwyn	106					☆	
22	Finchingfield to Great Bardfield	110				☆	☆	
23	Tillingham to Bradwell Waterside	112	☆	☆		☆	☆	
24	West Mersea to Cudmore Grove	118			☆	☆		
25	Butley to Orford	124	☆			☆		
26	Westleton to Walberswick	128			☆		☆	
27	Honingham to Lyng	132				☆	☆	
28	Foulsham to Heydon	136	☆					
29	Wells-next-the-Sea to Wighton	140	☆		☆		☆	
30	Sedgeford to Snettisham	144				☆		
31	Oxhill to Braines	150				☆	☆	☆
32	Clifford Chambers to Hidcote Gardens	154				☆		☆
33	Ashford Bowdler to Pipe Aston	158	☆					☆
34	Shottle to Carsington Water	162		☆		☆		
35	Bonsall to Winster	166				☆		
36	Whitwell to Normanton	170		☆		☆		
37	Hebden Bridge to Todmorden	176		☆			☆	
38	Laneshawbridge to Black Lane Ends	178				☆	☆	
39	Sawley to Bolton-by-Bowland	182				☆		
40	Cow Ark to Bashall Town	186				☆		☆
41	Lancaster to Crook O'Lune	190		☆		☆	☆	
42	Arnside to Leighton Hall	194				☆		
43	Colton to Bolton Percy	200					☆	☆
44	Kirkby Malzeard to the Drovers Inn	204				☆	☆	
45	East Witton to Jervaulx Abbey	210	☆			☆		☆
46	West Witton to Melmerby	214				☆	☆	☆
47	Bainbridge to Aysgarth Falls	220				☆		☆
48	Brompton-on-Swale to Gilling West	224	☆			☆		
49	Brough to Sandford	230	☆	☆		☆		
50	Ravenstonedale to Orton	234				☆		☆
51	Far Sawrey to Wray Castle	238		☆		☆		
52	Lakeside to Near Sawrey	240	☆			☆		
53	Coniston to Little Langdale	244				☆	☆	
54	Moresby to Dean	250				☆		
55	High Keenley Fell to Allendale	256				☆		☆
56	Carraw to Simonburn	260	☆			☆		☆
57	Matfen to Belsay Hall and Castle	264	☆			☆	☆	☆
58	Alnham to Thropton	268	☆			☆	☆	
59	Craster to Alnmouth	272			☆	☆		
60	North Sunderland to Bamburgh	278	☆		☆	☆		

Find history at every turn en route to Corfe Castle, p46

THIS COMMEMORATES THE MILLENNIUM OF THE MURDER OF EDWARD KING OF ENGLAND AND MARTYR 18TH MARCH 978

1978

Great sea views from 15th-century Deal Castle, p92

The Master Builder's hotel at Buckler's Hard – aflutter with history, p72

Bodiam Castle: love this place! Over 600 years old and still standing strong, p86

DUDLEY AND ETHEL MILLS DROKES 1912–1928 FROM THEIR FRIE...

Explore the New Forest's history with a trip down the river, p72

MAGICAL HISTORY TOUR

The English countryside is peppered with old stone castles, half-timber cottages, and ancient battlefields. As you pootle along through the back roads and empty lanes, you'll come across quirkily named villages that give yet more clues to a county's colourful past. Like the Norse-sounding Askrigg in Yorkshire, the hamlet of Cow Ark in Lancashire, or Old Wives Lees in Kent. Whether you're a history buff or just plain curious, there are things you'll see when you're cycling that would be little more than a blur seen from a car…

Colourful characters behind every door en route to Ludlow, p158

Check out the antique collection at Norfolk Courtyard B&B, near Foulsham, p136

The houses near Heydon village are like an architectural time warp, p136

Corfe Castle: you can see the 1,000-year-old ruins from miles away, p46

Stay at the imposing Augill Castle and take a trip to the weathered walls of the fortress at Brough, p230

Boats, bikes, and water birds by the Exe Estuary, near Exeter, p40

Rent a boat at Carsington Water in Derbyshire, p162

Accompany the river to Frome and pause for a cuppa along the way... p50

Cream Teas
12 pm-4pm

→

Iford Manor: stop for a stroll around the Italianate gardens, p54

Swap your bike for a boat at Bradwell Waterside, p112

Wildlife and water vistas from the track around peaceful Rutland Water, p170

DOWN BY THE RIVER

What better way to spend a day when the sun's blazing down and the rest of the world is stuck in a queue somewhere, than cycling by the water's edge – whether it's a river, canal, lake, or tiny babbling brook. Boats chug along slowly, bound for nowhere in particular, ducks hang about on the banks, chatting, and the pace of life slows to a luxurious crawl. Stick a blanket in your bag and you could stop off for a picnic wherever you fancy, or even take a quick dip…

CYCLISTS DISMOUNT

p190

Gucie
BOAT TRIPS
07966-808717

It's just a flat pootle along the canal at Hebden Bridge, p176

Toe-dipping temptations en route to Sandford, p230

Godrevy Point lighthouse: inspiration for the Virginia Woolf novel, p22

Lined up for inspection: the beach huts at Southwold, p128

The view across West Itchenor's waterfront – the perfect spot for a break, p76

Make some footprints in the miles of golden sand at Mortehoe, p36

The old-fashioned fishing boats at Deal, p92

Beach huts on Mersea Island – less than two hours from London... p118

p118

Stop for fresh lobster at Craster, p272

JILL ANNE
LOWESTOF

p128

The beach huts of Wells-next-the-Sea in all their glory... p140

BESIDE THE SEASIDE

Fish and chips and fresh salty air. There's nothing quite like the English seaside – especially when you're out on your bike. You can freewheel through fishing villages in Suffolk, stop off at surf shacks in Cornwall, and cruise along a cliff-top path on the Northumberland coast, all with some good honest pedal power. Throw a towel in your backpack, whack on a dollop of sun cream, and off you go. Ah, yes... it's good to be by the sea.

JAW—DROPPING VIEWS

From the vast open skies of East Anglia, to the drama of the Lake District peaks, it's amazing what you'll see when you're not trapped behind the wheel. Whether you want chocolate-box Cotswold villages, undulating fields of golden corn, or 50 miles of Yorkshire Dales in a single glance, you can pick a ride to match any mood. Simply swing your leg over the saddle and point the bike where you'd like to go. Just don't forget the camera…

Fragrant fields of lavender in Gloucestershire, p66

Stare out across Dartmoor's entrancing countryside, p32

See what you can spot on the way to Snettisham, p144

The Stroud Valley in all its glory, p62

If it's big landscapes you're after, take the bike to Oxfordshire, p150

Tree 'tunnels' on the way to Camelford – amazing to ride through! p28

Low tide at Arnside, p194

The rolling fields of Lancashire, p178

p178

Leighton Hall: one of my favourite country houses, p194

Stop for a pint of Jail Ale at the Trout and Tipple, near Tavistock, p32

PLYMOUTH CAMRA COUNTRY PUB OF THE YEAR 2009

TROUT & TIPPLE

p82

p58

ENGLISH SPOKEN H

p88

Rose &

PLEASE ENJO

BUT REMEMBER:

★ PARENTS ARE RESPONS
CHILDRENS SAFETY

★ NO BALL GAMES PLEA

★ KEEP YOUR DOG ON A

★ ONLY FOOD & DRINK PURCHASED H
CONSUMED ON THESE PREMISES

p112

BBQ & Garden Bar Open

Drink a toast to Henry Adams at Buckler's Hard - former master ship-builder for Lord Nelson p72

BEST FOR PUBS

What do you fancy, a Headless Peg, half a Golden Bolt, or maybe a drop of Tally Wacker? When you've been pedalling through the lanes with the breeze against your cheeks, a pint of bizarrely named English ale (unless you're a cider drinker, of course) is just the ticket. But whatever your tipple, there's a lot to love about the Great British pub. Those wonky walls, that ancient fireplace – and, of course, the beer garden… From the Elephant's Nest in Devon, to the Twice Brewed Inn way up on the Scottish border, you'll see all sorts of idiosyncratic boozers – many with unfathomable names – on these routes. How about one more for the road?

No traffic to worry about in West Itchenor, p76

Bulmers
koppaberg of Sweden
Savanna

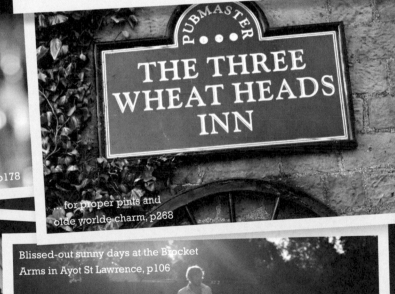

BARM POT

p178

PUBMASTER

THE THREE WHEAT HEADS INN

…for proper pints and olde worlde charm, p268

C.A.M.R.A.
EAST ANGLIA
UB OF THE YEAR 1988
TILLINGHAM
& FEATHERS

MAY BE

Blissed-out sunny days at the Brocket Arms in Ayot St Lawrence, p106

ON-ONE

OLD MILL HERBARY

HONEY FOR SALE

Delicious local produce around every Cornish corner, p26

Mmm... meringues – help yourself in Tetbury, p58

Try a chocolate snowball or two, some of the tasty old-school treats from the Old Bakehouse, p50

The Old Bakehouse
HOMEMADE
SNOW BALL
86p.

HUMBU
CONFECTIONE

TONGUE PAINT
LOLLIPOPS.
15 each

Favours for the sweet-toothed in Faversham, p88

TASTE TOUR

One of the best things about cycling is that it gives you a licence to eat as much as you like. Which is a good job, really, because there's so much to tempt the palate out there on the open road – whatever your taste. A farm shop here, a tea room there; an ice cream café, pick-your-own fruit farm, a few microbreweries and vineyards, and even a cider orchard or two... you'll find plenty of reasons to stop and sample along the way.

Acres of vineyards just an hour from London... p98

Winstones Ice Cream shop in Rodborough: home to the best cornets in the west, p62

'Who said mint sauce?' A couple of locals near Clifford Chambers, p154

p150

Ripe for the picking in Hertfordshire, p102

The Wensleydale Heifer does the best fish and chips in England – fact! p214

DEVON AND CORNWALL

1

GWITHIAN TO COOMBE

Blue sea, green fields, and quiet country lanes...

A WORD OF WARNING about staying at Calize Country House: it's rather tempting to spend all day staring at the ocean view instead of riding your bike.

Perched on a hill above the tiny village of Gwithian, near St Ives, Calize puts you in pole position for some spectacular sunsets. Not only that, but just off the coast, at Godrevy Point, you can also see the eponymous lighthouse that featured in Virginia Woolf's novel.

If that's not enough to get you packing your bags for the weekend, the cycle ride around here certainly will. It begins with an easy cruise down through the village and then a minute or so later you're riding along a little B-road that skirts the coast, with snack-seeking gulls hovering on the sea breeze for company.

As the road bends to the right you pedal up to higher ground on the promise of more sea views – and the return favour of a downhill stretch at some point. There's moorland on your left, which erupts with yellow gorse flowers every April; on your right, gorgeous little pastures full of cows nonchalantly grazing the days away. And when you reach the top there's a real treat over your shoulder: the Atlantic stretching out as flat as a millpond – and the outline of arty St Ives appearing below.

Enjoy a few downhills as well as more glimpses of the sea as you pedal along the top towards Tehidy Country Park. It's National Trust land all along here, so if you fancy taking a closer look, hop off the bike and head along one of the many pedestrian paths vying for your footfall.

Once you've finished any extra-curricular exploration on foot, cycle on a couple of miles to Tehidy's entrance and make your way to the path leading down into the woods. There's a map at the start of the trail, making it easy to find your way to Coombe via a flat dirt-track bordered by ancient trees. Down in the woods it feels like you've escaped the rest of the world; the only sounds are birdsong echoing off the gnarly old trunks and the distant gurgle of water from a nearby stream.

A mile or so later you emerge back on to tarmac, turning right at Coombe and climbing uphill for another mile before weaving your way back down to the coast, where you'll need the camera handy.

The views are staggering, and they get better as you descend – St Ives Bay opening out before you, the turquoise water and immaculate stretch of fudge-coloured sand looking like something straight out of a holiday brochure.

This lane brings you back out at the coast road you climbed earlier (payback time), so turn left and it's downhill all the way to the beach. But don't go back to the village just yet; turn right and take the dirt track down to the waterfront. There's a great beachside café (Sunset Surf) along here, where you can grab a pint of Skinner's ale, sit out on the deck, and watch the sun stain the sky pink as it drops below the horizon. A fitting end to a beautiful day.

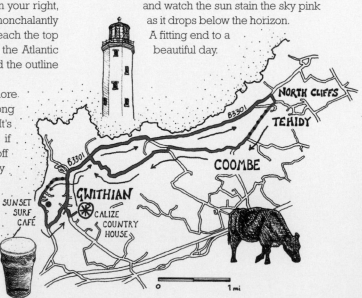

THE ROUTE

DISTANCE 11 MILES

DIFFICULTY ◑◑◑

START Calize Country House
Gwithian, Cornwall, TR27 5BW

» Turn right out of Calize Country House drive, on to the road leading into Gwithian.

» Cruise past the Red River Inn and at the junction next to it bear right on to Churchdown Road (effectively straight on).

» Leave the village and keep following the B3301 round to the right and up along the cliff-top, to the entrance of Tehidy Country Park: turn right into the car park and join the trail ahead – leading into the woods.

» Take the first right, then first left, and head down into the woods.

» Turn right before the little bridge, towards Coombe, and continue for a mile before emerging beside some cottages and turning right, on to the tarmac road.

» Climb for about a mile on to rolling fields and take the first left; then (after 70 metres) the first right.

» Stay on this road until you reach the B3301. Turn left at the junction and head downhill back towards Gwithian and the coast.

» At the bottom of the hill, where the road bends left, you bear right – taking a path towards the beach.

» As you reach the seafront, bear left and head along to the Sunset Surf Café.

» Carry on past the Sunset Surf Café, and follow the tarmac lane up to the main road: turn left at the junction.

» Follow the road downhill, back into Gwithian.

» Turn right at the Red Dragon Inn and head back up Prosper Hill to Calize Country House.

STOP AND SEE

EN ROUTE

Godrevy Point *Hayle, Gwithian, Cornwall*
This beautiful peninsula, where the Atlantic has been pounding the cliffs for centuries,
is a great place for birdspotting, and if you cast your eyes out from the cliffs you'll see the lighthouse featured in Virginia Woolf's novel, *To the Lighthouse*.

Seal Cove *Hayle, Gwithian, Cornwall*
Just along the coast from Godrevy Point, Seal Cove is a renowned hang-out for colonies of seals. Visit between October and January, and you'll see pups, too.

Sunset Surf Café *10 Gwithian Towans, Gwithian, Cornwall, TR27 5BT; 01736 752575; www.sunsetsurfshop.co.uk*
A laid-back café serving Skinner's ales, award-winning local haddock and chips, and cream teas. There's an adjoining surf shop and school, too, if you fancy hitting the waves.

OFF ROUTE

St Ives Bay *St Ives, Cornwall*
Although not exactly on the route, this strip of golden sand will have been teasing you all day. It lies right next to the ride and is patrolled by lifeguards, too, so if the sun's out, spend the afternoon catching rays.

EAT, DRINK, SLEEP

Red River Inn *Prosper Hill, Gwithian, Cornwall, TR27 5BW; 01736 753223; www.red-river-inn.co.uk*
A friendly local pub within walking distance of Calize Country House. Landlord Aaron is a bit of a character and serves a mean burger. There's a garden opposite – ideal on a fine summer's day.

The Jam Pot *Gwithian Towans, Gwithian, Cornwall, TR27 5BT; 01736 779190; www.jampotcafe.co.uk*
This kooky, whitewashed café is right on the beach, just a short walk from the Sunset Surf Café. Cream teas, sandwiches, and smoothies are the orders of the day, served with lashings of sunshine, if your luck's in.

Calize Country House *Gwithian, Cornwall, TR27 5BW; 01736 753268; www.calize.co.uk*
Perched on top of a hill overlooking Godrevy Lighthouse, Calize is bright and airy and serves tasty breakfasts. There's space to lock up bikes, and a two-bed, self-contained apartment in the grounds if you fancy a longer stay.
Doubles from £80 per night.

Driftwood Beach Chalet *Gwithian Towans, Gwithian, Cornwall, TR27 5BU; 01209 832042; www.driftwoodbeachchalet.co.uk*
Cute little 1930s cabin with two double bedrooms, a bunkroom, flat-screen TV, Blu-ray player, private garden with BBQ, tons of books – and surfboards! All just a happy skip away from the beach. Ranging from £350 to £1150 (depending on season) for a week.

Treglisson *Wheal Alfred Road, Hayle, Cornwall, TR27 5JT; 01736 753141; www.treglisson.com*
A lovely old farmhouse in Hayle, just a few miles down the road from Gwithian. There are three smart en suite rooms, a heated indoor pool, and the house is surrounded by manicured gardens. Oh, and if you're saving the pennies then bring a tent – there's a campsite here, too.
Doubles from £55 per night.

RENT

Hayle Cycles *36 Penpol Terrace, Hayle, Cornwall, TR27 4BQ; 01736 753825; www.haylecycles.com*
This place offers a good range of bikes for both adults and children – even tandems if you feel like sharing the work. Hire from £10 a day.

HELPFUL HINT

You'll need a mountain bike for the section through Tehidy Country Park.

2

TREDETHY TO PENCARROW

Tiny lanes, lots of tea, and a bit of birdlife...

I WASN'T SURE whether to tell you about Tredethy House in Cornwall. Tucked away in a criss-cross of lanes that lace the Cornish hills, it's the kind of place you want to keep to yourself – one of those home-away-from-home bolt-holes where it feels more like staying with friends than in a hotel.

This 11-room country pile was once home to illustrious pre-war racing driver, Prince Bira of Siam, and there are still echoes of those heady, idyllic days echoing around the place – the children's antique pedal car found in one of the rooms, old books lining the shelves, and other quirky leftovers. This special atmosphere is helped along by the super-friendly Italian owners, Marco and Cristina, who live here with their young family; Marco whipping up hand-made pasta dishes, fresh breads, and locally caught fish in the trattoria…

It's tempting to just lie out on the lawn with a good book and soak up the sun all weekend, but if you can manage to tear yourself away from the hotel, there's a great little ride that leaves straight from the front gates. Heading out over the brow of a hill, you cruise along to the main road, where a quick right and left has you pedalling along an undulating lane that leads to St Mabyn. Don't be surprised if the occasional frisky pheasant bursts from the bushes en route: there are whole squadrons of these clumsy fliers hidden away in the patchwork quilt of fields accompanying you along to the village, a mile or so away. A row of tiny cottages heralds your arrival at St Mabyn, where you'll come across a Proper Cornish Pub – run by a Proper Cornishman.

Landlord of the St Mabyn Inn, Gary Saundry, isn't interested in exposed brick, untreated wood, and all that other fanciness; this place is about good beer. And lots of it. There's a cosy garden at the back, overlooked by the church, and if anyone's feeling peckish, the menu features kitsch pub classics like chicken in a basket.

Once you've refuelled, the route leads you out past the village shop (which also serves coffee and fresh pastries), climbing gently for a quarter of a mile before you're back out among lush green fields. Next thing, you're gliding downhill through the trees – the wind watering your eyes, hair going everywhere – before it all goes quiet as you pull up at the entrance to Pencarrow.

This rather magnificent country house is surrounded by Italianate gardens with lakes and the whole works, making it ideal for a stroll in the late afternoon sun. More importantly, there's a café serving a mean cuppa and tasty home-made cake, where the resident peacocks strut around on the scrounge for stray crumbs. Whenever you're ready, simply slip out through the car park and along a bumpy farm track that cuts across the fields. The views are gorgeous, with St Mabyn's church tower poking up on your left, a couple of miles away, showing you exactly how far you've come.

Eventually you reach the main road and make a left back towards Tredethy, veering right on to a tiny lane that brings you out by the gates. Just in time for an early evening aperitif on the lawn...

THE ROUTE

DISTANCE 6 MILES

DIFFICULTY ⚪⚪

START Tredethy House

Helland Bridge, Bodmin, Cornwall, PL30 4QS

» Turn right out of the hotel and at the junction ¼ mile later turn right, then immediately left – signposted St Mabyn.

» Follow this lane for 1¼ miles to a junction: turn left into St Mabyn.

» Just after the St Mabyn Inn, turn left into Wadebridge Road, passing St Mabyn Store and heading out of the village.

» After ¼ mile, keep following the road as it bends left, signposted Wadebridge.

» Carry on along this road for 1¼ miles to a junction: turn left, then left again to go through the gates of Pencarrow.

» Leave through the car park on to a farm track, and follow it between the fields to the main road (B3266): turn left.

» Follow this road for ½ mile and turn right, for Helland Bridge. Tredethy House is at the end of this lane (½ mile away).

STOP AND SEE

EN ROUTE

The St Mabyn Inn *1 Chapel Lane, St Mabyn, Cornwall, PL30 3BA; 01208 841266*
A 17th-century local inn serving ales like Skinner's Cornish Knocker, Cornish Rattler cider, and a menu including filling meals like pork hock with mash. There's a little beer garden at the back, too.

Pencarrow House & Gardens *Bodmin, Cornwall, PL30 3AG; 01208 841369; www.pencarrow.co.uk*
This majestic Georgian house comes surrounded by 50 acres of woodland and gardens. It's well worth taking a tour of the house (which has been in the same family for over 500 years), or heading to the Peacock Café for some home-made carrot cake before enjoying a leisurely wander around the gardens.

OFF ROUTE

Helland Bridge Pottery *Helland Bridge, Bodmin, Cornwall, PL30 4QR; 01208 75240; www.paul-jackson.co.uk*
Walk or cycle down the hill from Tredethy House and you'll find yourself in a stunning valley with a collection of cottages. Sculptor Paul Jackson has a pottery studio here, with a range of contemporary pieces on show.

The Old Mill Herbary *Helland Bridge, Bodmin, Cornwall, PL30 4QR; 01208 841206; www.oldmillherbary.co.uk*
Three acres of terraced gardens cascading over the hillsides in the valley at Helland Bridge, just below Tredethy House. There's a woodland area awash with flowers in spring, plus butterflies and the occasional otter in summer. Come for a stroll or stock up on unusual plants for the garden.

EAT, DRINK, SLEEP

Tredethy House *Helland Bridge, Bodmin, Cornwall, PL30 4QS; 01208 841707; www.tredethyhouse.com*
This wonderfully peaceful old hotel sits atop a hill, with stunning views out over the Cornish countryside. There are 11 spacious en suite rooms to choose from, fab gardens, bike hire, and delicious Italian food on tap, courtesy of the owner, Marco. Doubles from £90 per night.

Trehellas House *Washaway, Bodmin, Cornwall, PL30 3AD; 01208 72700; www.trehellashouse.co.uk*
Cosy 18th-century courthouse B&B, a mile from Tredethy, with 12 smart rooms. The award-winning restaurant serves tasty local dishes such as dressed Padstow crab. Doubles from £90 per night.

Orchard Restaurant *Polmorla Road, Wadebridge, Cornwall, PL27 7ND; 01208 812696; www.theorchardrestaurant.co.uk*
About four miles from Tredethy House, this modern bistro serves delicious home-made dishes including Cornish scallops, and pan-roasted wild sea bass with three-bean butter sauce, mushrooms, and parsley oil.

RENT

Camel Trail Cycle Hire *Eddystone Road, Wadebridge, Cornwall, PL27 7AL; 01208 813050; www.bridgebikehire.co.uk*
Huge range of bikes including cruisers, tandems, trailers, and hybrids – the latter costing £10 a day. Delivery (and collection) anywhere in the area costs from £20.

HELPFUL HINT

Bring a picnic blanket for spreading out on the lawn at Pencarrow House.

3

CAMELFORD TO DELABOLE

The highs and lows of the Cornish countryside...

A 'JAW-DROPPING' VIEW generally suggests one that stretches on for miles. But in the countryside around Camelford there's a mixture of those expansive, dramatic vistas and intimate little lanes. A combination that had me picking my chin up off the floor.

From Woolland House you head uphill before the road starts undulating along leafy lanes with high grassy banks. Before long you're dropping downhill into the hamlet of Slaughter Bridge – its ominous name a clue to an ignominious past. It's here that King Arthur is said to have fought his final bloody battle and, further up the hill, the Arthurian Centre is located on the site where the fighting that ended Arthur's life allegedly took place. Despite its gory history, this is an incredibly peaceful spot where a little river winds along a small valley. So be sure to bring some snacks along for a picnic.

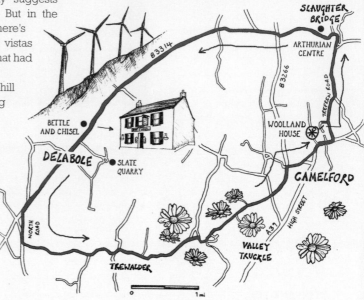

When you're done dosing up on Arthurian legends, it's time to take to the saddle and cycle on towards Delabole. Before long, a collection of wind turbines is revealed on the horizon. Stop for a second and you'll hear them whirring away gently, standing tall like sculptural art installations against a stunning backdrop of sloping hills and mini fields.

Freewheeling down the road to Delabole, you pass a fab fish-and-chip shop (Smugglers) on your left; the takeaway wraps are delicious. Meanwhile, further up the main street, the Bettle and Chisel does a mean ploughman's and other standard pub faves. If you do stop here, head into the back garden, too; the sea is visible in the distance, and according to Sherry, the landlady, sunset views are stupendous.

Another vista you should definitely treat your eyes to is that of the electric-blue 'lagoon' at the bottom of the Delabole Slate Quarry. From your perch at the quarry's edge, the enormous trucks below look like scaled-down versions on an architect's model.

The mine is off to your left as you cycle on from the Bettle and Chisel, and the road out of Delabole is satisfyingly downhill for a while, with glimpses of the sea appearing on your right before you head inland.

In spring, white and yellow blossoms line the lane and the faint sounds of gulls overhead remind you that you're never far from the sea. Ahead, green fields undulate towards a blue sky peppered with fuzzy clouds as you cruise uphill, through more picturesque villages, past bunches of white daisies sprinkled along the verges, and between high old hedgerows sheltering you from the breeze.

The final stretch back to Camelford is almost all uphill, but there's a handily placed bench about halfway up, where you can pause for a photo stop. Don't forget to pick your jaw up off the floor afterwards.

THE ROUTE

DISTANCE   9 MILES
DIFFICULTY   ○○○○
START   Woolland House

Trefrew Road, Camelford, Cornwall, PL32 9TP

» From Woolland House, head right along Trefrew Road, away from Camelford, reaching a fork in the road after 1½ miles: bear left (effectively straight on).

» Less than a mile later, turn left at the junction with the B3314 and follow the road over a little bridge, to the Arthurian Centre (on your right).

» Continue uphill to a staggered crossroads: go right and immediately left – for Delabole.

» Follow this road for 2 miles, reaching the Bettle and Chisel pub at Delabole. (For Delabole Slate Quarry, take the first left after the pub, into Pengelly.)

» Continuing on from the pub, you reach a fork just under a mile later: bear left, on to North Road.

» Turn left at the next junction, signposted Newhall Green.

» Follow the road through Newhall Green then turn left for Lanteglos.

» Keep following signs for Lanteglos and Camelford.

» The road descends sharply to a junction: turn right and drop over a humpbacked bridge to arrive at another junction, next to a church: turn left for Camelford.

» Climb to the main road: go straight on (not left), signposted Boscastle.

» Follow this road for ¼ mile before turning right, into Clease Road.

» Turn left down Chapel Street, and join the main road at the bottom.

» Take the third left, into Trefrew Road, to return to Woolland House.

STOP AND SEE

EN ROUTE

Arthurian Centre *Slaughter Bridge, Camelford, Cornwall, PL32 9TT; 01840 213947; www.arthur-online.co.uk*

Small, family-oriented museum on all things King Arthur, located on the site of the eponymous 6th-century stone commemorating his last battle. It's a beautiful spot – a great place for picnicking.

Delabole Slate Quarry *Pengelly, Delabole, Cornwall, PL33 9AZ; 01840 212242; www.delaboleslate.co.uk*

This could be the deepest man-made hole in Europe; and if that's not enticing enough for you, the scenery should be. Gaze into its depths and you'll see a stunning azure pool akin to an Alpine lake. Take a tour to discover the quarry's 600-year history.

Bettle and Chisel *114 High Street, Delabole, Cornwall, PL33 9AQ; 01840 211402; see www.staustellbrewery.co.uk*
This friendly, no-frills village pub has good beers on tap (such as Tribute and Tinners), stone floors, and a bar made using slate from Delabole's quarry.

OFF ROUTE
Camel Valley Vineyard *Nanstallon, Bodmin, Cornwall, PL30 5LG; 01208 77959; www.camelvalley.com*
British wines have come a long way in recent years, and this place, set on a hillside near the Camel river, is proof. Bob and Annie Lindo have been producing rather delicious vino for over 20 years now – supplying some of London's top eateries. Why not stop here and take an informal tour; soak up the scenery, and (of course) sample some of the good stuff.

EAT, DRINK, SLEEP
Woolland House *Trefrew Road, Camelford, Cornwall, PL32 9TP; 01840 212342; www.woolland-house.co.uk*
This smart Edwardian house on the edge of Camelford has three luxurious en suite rooms with Egyptian cotton linen and various other stylish touches. There's also a secluded garden where you can sit and reward yourself with a cream tea when you've finished your ride.
Doubles from £70 per night.

Warmington House *32 Market Place, Camelford, Cornwall, PL32 9PD; 01840 214961; www.warmingtonhouse.co.uk*
Beautifully restored town house in the centre of Camelford, with four en suite rooms, original fireplaces, and wood beams. After a day spent exploring the lanes, come back and sink into a roll-top bath while you wait for your cream tea.
Doubles from £80 per night.

Pendragon Country House *Davidstow, Camelford, Cornwall, PL32 9XR; 01840 261131; www.pendragoncountryhouse.com*
Gorgeous country-house hotel with seven luxurious rooms named after the Knights of the Round Table – each individually decorated with antiques and original features. Go for Lamorak, which offers restful olive-green walls, a four-poster bed, and views over Bodmin Moor. Meals here are cooked by the owner, Nigel; try the honey-and-mustard-glazed ham and rocket risotto – delicious.
Doubles from £80 per night.

The Masons Arms *Market Place, Camelford, Cornwall, PL32 9PB; 01840 213309*
A good old town pub dating back to the 18th century. You can expect a menu bursting with home-made specials and fresh fish. Order a pint of Tribute or glass of something chilled, and head out to enjoy the riverside beer garden.

Garden Restaurant *Lanteglos Country House Hotel, Camelford, Cornwall, PL32 9RF; 01840 213551; www.lantegloshotel.co.uk*
Grab a table on the terrace overlooking the gardens and savour one of the freshly prepared, locally sourced dishes such as pan-seared fillet of sea bass with garden herb pomme purée and oyster beignet. An extensive wine list tops everything off rather nicely.

RENT
Camel Trail Cycle Hire *Eddystone Road, Wadebridge, Cornwall, PL27 7AL; 01208 813050; www.bridgebikehire.co.uk*
Boasting a huge range of bikes including cruisers, tandems, trailers, and hybrids – the latter costing £10 a day – this place can organise delivery and collection anywhere in the area, from £20.

4

TAVISTOCK TO HORNDON

Big skies, little villages, and narrow moorland lanes...

BEDDING DOWN IN A TRAIN STATION ticket office might not strike you as the height of luxury, but at Old Tavistock Railway Station things have changed. For starters, there are no trains (not since the sixties); secondly, the station buildings, including the porter's cabin and former refreshment hall, have been converted into luxurious self-catering cottages – with stirring views across to Dartmoor and Tavistock's pretty town centre in the valley below.

After cruising down a hill and huffing and puffing up another, you'll be greeted by a quiet lane with views (over your right shoulder) across to the moor.

Eventually a babbling tributary of the River Tavy escorts you to a rather nice pub called the Trout and Tipple, a favourite with cyclists from all over Europe. The Jail Ale they serve here really hits the spot.

Once you hit the road again it isn't long before you're entering the network of narrow lanes that criss-crosses Dartmoor. There's a bit of a climb on the way to nearby Mary Tavy, but it's worth it for the photo opps at the top: 180-degree views of hedge-bordered fields running away to khaki-coloured moorland in the distance.

Passing a picturesque white farmhouse after a mile or so, you head right and arrive in the village after a couple of climbs and a humpbacked bridge. It's like cycling through a life-sized *Postman Pat* world – all intricate lanes and chirpy brooks.

In Mary Tavy you'll find an eponymous pub serving good local grub, perfect for a pitstop before you tackle the lanes on the other side of the village, carrying on to Horndon for the Elephant's Nest.

This has to be the most peculiarly named pub in England – ask the landlord, Hugh, to explain the story behind it (you'll never guess). Tasty dishes like seared Brixham scallops with diced chorizo, and pub favourites like home-made burgers make this place comfort-food heaven after a morning spent labouring up all those hills. And the good news is that it's mainly downhill all the way back to 'Tavvy'.

The Elephant's Nest lies on the threshold of the moor, where the scenery suddenly changes from neatly parcelled pastures to wild, untamed scrubland; littering the roadside further on there's a mysterious collection of ancient stones – nobody's quite sure how they got there. The lanes become impossibly narrow now, with cars – even *Postman Pat* vans – a rarity, and you'll cross the kind of brook that would have Thomas Hardy going weak at the knees.

Cruising down through Cudlipptown and Peter Tavy (no relation to Mary), you'll eventually have to chug up a hill to make the final descent down the twisty-turny lanes into Tavistock. By the time you reach the station, it'll feel like you've spent the day in another world... where the only Dartmoor 'beast' is a black-and-white postman's cat called Jess.

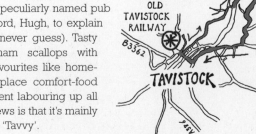

THE
ELEPHANT'S NEST
16TH CENTURY
INN

THE ROUTE

DISTANCE   14 MILES

DIFFICULTY   ○○○○

START   Old Tavistock Railway

Quant Park, Tavistock, Devon, PL19 0JQ

» Head down Kilworthy Hill, turn left, then left again, on to Old Exeter Road.

» Continue for just under a mile, to a crossroads: turn right and drop down to the main road (A386), where you turn left.

» You're on the main road for less than ½ mile (there's a path if you prefer), passing the Trout and Tipple then taking the first left.

» After 1½ miles, bear right at the fork.

» At the junction after ¼ mile, bear right (effectively straight on).

» Follow the lane into Mary Tavy, as it turns into Station Lane and reaches the main road: turn left.

» After 350 metres, turn right (signposted Elephant's Nest).

» Continue for ½ mile, over the bridge, then turn left (signposted Horndon).

» Climb for a mile (passing the Elephant's Nest) after which the road bends sharply right (signposted Peter Tavy).

» Junction shortly after: bear right.

» Cruise along the lane for almost a mile, over the humpbacked bridge and up the other side to a junction: turn right (signposted Peter Tavy).

» Continue on, through Cudlipptown and Peter Tavy.

» Half a mile after Peter Tavy, turn left up Batterbridge Hill.

» Take the first right, and follow the tiny lane (it turns into an unsurfaced road halfway down) until you reach a junction with the B3357: turn right.

» Continue to the junction with the A386: bear left for Town Centre.

» At the mini roundabout, bear left (signposted Town Centre).

» At the next mini roundabout, turn right.

» Straight over the next mini roundabout.

» Take the third right, on to Kilworthy Hill.

STOP AND SEE

EN ROUTE

Trout and Tipple *Parkwood Road, Tavistock, Devon, PL19 0JS; 01822 618886; www.troutandtipple.co.uk*
Cosy old pub specialising in real beers (Jail Ale) and ciders (Sam's Medium), including three or four regularly changing brews.

The Elephant's Nest *Horndon, Mary Tavy, Tavistock, Devon, PL19 9NQ; 01822 810273; www.elephantsnest.co.uk*
Thick stone walls, a worn slate floor, and a higgledy-piggledy collection of bottles on the back bar are waiting for you at this 16th-century pub. The food is excellent and there's a gorgeous garden out the back. Three smart B&B rooms here, too.

OFF ROUTE

Tavistock Pannier Market *Tavistock, Devon, PL19 0AL; 01822 611003; www.tavistockpanniermarket.co.uk*
Five minutes' walk from the railway station cottages, this market has been going since 1105. You can buy everything here from plants to jewellery and books to bags. There's also a great coffee shop (Dukes).

Wheal Betsy *nr Mary Tavy, Tavistock, Devon*
Wheal Betsy is the evocative ruin of an old engine house from the mine that extracted iron, lead, and silver from the land for 137 years. Awesome moor views from here, too.

EAT, DRINK, SLEEP

Old Tavistock Railway Station Cottages *Quant Park, Tavistock, Devon, PL19 0JQ; 01822 610136; www.oldtavistockrailwaystation.co.uk*
Choose from the Ticketing Hall, Porter's Office, or Refreshment Hall – all equipped with 5-star facilities. Ideal for groups. Short breaks (Friday–Monday or Monday–Friday) from £350 per cottage.

Burnville Farm *Brentnor, Tavistock, Devon, PL19 0NE; 01822 820443; www.burnville.co.uk*
This gorgeous old Georgian house B&B on Dartmoor has two luxurious en suite rooms with antique furniture and stunning views. The garden is surrounded by glorious countryside. Evening meals available, too. Doubles from £75.

Mount Tavy Cottage *Tavistock, Devon, PL19 9JL; 01822 614253; www.mounttavy.co.uk*
Dating back 250 years, this lovely cottage is surrounded by 10 acres of English country garden, with two smart rooms in the cottage itself, two self-catering garden studios, and a self-catering cottage just along the road. Doubles from £70 per night.

Peter Tavy Inn *Peter Tavy, nr Tavistock, Devon, PL19 9NN; 01822 810348*
A sweet little 15th-century country pub, 20 minutes' cycle from Tavistock. Expect dishes like game casserole with Stilton dumpling, and a choice of four or five proper ales.

Jack and Jill's *73 West Street, Tavistock, Devon, PL19 8AJ; 01822 617884*
Ask any local and they'll tell you this is the best chippy for miles around. So good that there's another one on Brook Street.

NH Creber *48 Brook St, Tavistock, Devon, PL19 0BH; 01822 612266; www.crebers.co.uk*
Old-school deli selling home-made pâtés, cold cuts, cheeses, wines, and chutneys. Order a hamper for a gourmet picnic.

RENT

Tavistock Cycles *Brook Street, Tavistock, Devon, PL19 0HF; 01822 617630; www.tavistockcycles.co.uk*
Ridgeback mountain bikes to suit all shapes and sizes – with plenty of gears for those hills. Each comes with a helmet, lock, and puncture-repair kit at a hire rate of £15 a day.

5

MORTEHOE TO CROYDE

From one incredible beach to another...

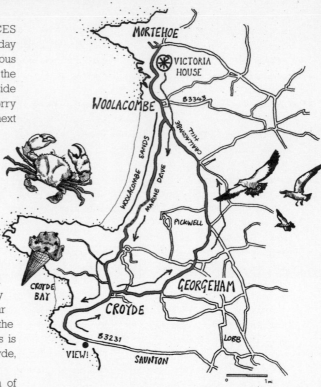

MORTEHOE IS ONE OF THOSE PLACES that instantly makes you forget everyday stress. Looking out to sea, with an enormous electric-blue sky overhead and the contours of the coast wrapped reassuringly around the countryside like the arms of an old friend, it's difficult to worry about anything – except, perhaps, where your next ice cream is coming from.

Beginning at the bright-and-breezy Victoria House, with its cornflower-blue window frames and vanilla walls, you take a left and head down the silky smooth road as the bay stretches out to infinity on your right. Along the way you'll pass rows of petite guest houses with immaculate and colourful rockery gardens – reminiscent of those in photos of 1950s street parties.

The pedalling soon pays off when you get your first glimpse of beachy heaven: golden sand and small white waves foaming excitedly as they race each other up the shore. Allow your eye to follow the line of the coast and you'll see the headland jutting out to sea in the distance; this is Baggy Point, and on the other side of it lies Croyde, and your lunch.

Mortehoe trickles to an end at the bottom of the hill, and you cruise right, around the small bay before reaching Woolacombe, where the grass gives way to black rocks – a great crabbing spot. You'll reach a junction facing a collection of bars and to your right is an expanse of sand that makes you want to kick off your shoes and sprint down to the sea. If you can resist the urge, go right and climb up through heathery scrubland on towards Croyde.

As you pootle along the coast, the breeze carries distant sounds from the beach below – excited barks of a dog, kids' laughter – but these soon fade as the dirt track becomes a path sheltered by brambles.

Every now and again you get a glimpse of gorgeous beach below, entreating you to stop for a swim break, or five, along the couple of miles to Croyde's tiny village, where a row of pubs, café-

bars, and an old-fashioned ice cream shop (rhubarb and custard cone, anyone?) lie between you and the shimmering beach on your right.

If your legs are up to it, carry on for a couple more miles to Saunton Sands, a three-mile sweep of golden sand long enough to land a Hercules on. Otherwise head to Georgeham via rows of pink and white cottages and neatly trimmed hedges. After a well-earned pint at the Lower House, brave the climb out of the village to reach stunning views of fields undulating towards a sea glinting in the afternoon sun.

Now simply coast down the steep hill back into Woolacombe and on to the welcoming arms of Victoria House to watch the sun set over the bay.

THE ROUTE

DISTANCE   22 MILES
DIFFICULTY   ○○○
START   Victoria House

Chapel Hill, Mortehoe, Devon, EX34 7DZ

» Head downhill and left from Victoria House, following the coast along to Woolacombe. When you reach the first junction (in Woolacombe), turn right and head up Challacombe Hill.

» Take the first right, into Marine Drive car park, and follow it along the coast to the end. Eventually it becomes a dirt track, and then a narrow path: continue until you emerge again on to a tarmac road.

» At the junction: turn right, for Croyde.

» Follow this lane into Croyde, arriving at a junction just after a car showroom. (If you're stopping in Croyde or carrying on to Saunton Sands, go straight on.)

» Otherwise, turn left and climb to Georgeham. Pass the Lower House pub, and follow the road towards Woolacombe.

» Pass the sign for Pickwell village, and carry on until you reach a left fork.

» Ignore signs for Woolacombe and Ilfracombe and bear left (effectively straight on), descending the steep hill.

» Arrive back in Woolacombe; at the bottom of the hill turn left to Mortehoe.

» Follow the coast back to Mortehoe, and up the hill to Victoria House.

STOP AND SEE

EN ROUTE

Croyde Bay *Croyde, Devon*
Help yourself to 800 metres of golden sand. When you arrive in the village, look out for Billy Budd's pub on your right. A track alongside it leads you to the sea.

Croyde Ice Cream Parlour *6 Hobb's Hill, Croyde, Devon, EX33 1LZ; 01271 891003*
A proper old-fashioned ice cream shop. Take your pick from a mouth-watering range of flavours including rhubarb and custard.

The Blue Groove *2 Hobb's Hill, Croyde, Devon, EX33 1LZ; 01271 890111; www.blue-groove.co.uk*
Laid-back, light, and airy, this cool bistro-bar serves up quality cocktails (try the Fuzzy Shark) and tasty daytime dishes like citrus chilli salad and meaty burgers courtesy of the local butcher. Head to the terrace and gaze out over the water.

OFF ROUTE

Saunton Sands *Saunton, Devon*
Pedal on past Croyde for a couple of miles until you see the enormous stretch of sand unfold before you. A great place to spend the day catching rays.

EAT, DRINK, SLEEP

Victoria House *Chapel Hill, Mortehoe, Devon, EX34 7DZ; 01271 871302; www.victoriahousebandb.co.uk*
Camera at the ready: this B&B offers a fine spot from which to admire some incredible sunsets. Run by Heather and David Burke, it's tucked into the cliffs just a short walk from the beach. There are two smart rooms (think dark wood and sumptuous bed linen), plus the kooky beach house next door – with its private terrace and day bed. Doubles from £110 per night.

Shuna Guest House *Down End, Croyde, Devon, EX33 1QE; 01271 890537; www.shunaguesthouse.co.uk*
Small family-run B&B minutes from the beach, with breathtaking views. There are seven en suite rooms and home-cooked

breakfasts awaiting you in the morning (go for scrambled eggs and smoked salmon). Doubles from £80 per night.

Rockleigh *The Square, Mortehoe, Devon, EX34 7DS; 01271 870704; www.rockleighhouse.com*
Two bright and airy en suite rooms in the centre of Mortehoe, with cracking views out to sea and a restaurant serving home-made, locally sourced food. Doubles from £60 (minimum two nights).

The Boardwalk *The Esplanade, Woolacombe, Devon, EX34 7DJ; 01271 871115; www.theboardwalkwoolacombe.co.uk*
Modern, informal bistro on the edge of Woolacombe, walkable from Victoria House. Menu includes mouth-watering dishes like locally farmed steak and Cornish sardines drizzled with lemon juice then fried in garlic butter.

The Courtyard *South Street, Woolacombe, Devon, EX34 7BB; 01271 871187; www.courtyardrestaurant.co.uk*
Tucked away and just a short walk from the seafront, this lovely, laid-back restaurant has a retractable roof (perfect for sunny evenings). Run by Noel Corston and his wife Nora, it's refreshingly friendly and serves up some imaginative dishes. Try the pan-fried brill with clams, parsnip purée, wood sorrel, and hazelnuts.

RENT

Otter Cycle Hire *The Old Pottery, Station Road, Braunton, Devon, EX33 2AQ; 01271 813339*
The fleet of mountain bikes on offer here is ideal for the topsy-turvy terrain surrounding Woolacombe and Croyde – each one has plenty of gears, suspension, and big knobbly tyres. Both adult and children's bikes available, for £12 per day.

6

KENTON TO TOPSHAM

A castle, a canal, and a café just for cyclists…

THICK PINK STRIPS of perfectly cooked bacon, fried eggs that were laid just hours earlier, and a proper mug of tea to wash it all down with… The breakfast cooked by Delia at Mill Farm is just what you need for a day of cycling under the Devonian sun – albeit at a pretty relaxed pace.

Once you're on the main road, it's not long before you're turning on to a quiet lane that leads up to the gates of Powderham Castle, and on through an avenue of gnarly old trees to a church where a crowd of noisy crows announces your arrival. Head through the gate and along a path winding its way alongside the River Exe, where boats big and small are puttering up and down, while the houses in the village of Exton on the opposite shore gleam in the bright morning sunlight. On your left, there's marshland, home to dozens of mallards and other water birds busy paddling about among the reeds.

Further along the estuary wall, the Turf pub appears like an optimist's mirage in the heat haze. Thankfully, this particular watering hole is 100 per cent real, and has its very own beer garden and Ferryman ale on tap. In summer you can pre-order BBQ ingredients and find them ready and waiting for the smoking grill on your arrival.

Once you've had your fill of chargrilled meaty local burgers and are ready to ride again, there's a regular ferry that will whip you across to Topsham on the opposite bank – it only takes 15 minutes. And this is where you'll find Route 2 – a café designed specifically with cyclists in mind, so you can order a spare inner tube with your Americano.

Carrying on, up the high street, along a corridor of painted terraced cottages, you'll find the road becomes busier so you might want to take to the path. But it's not long before you dive off and follow the blue National Cycle Network signs on to a trail threading its way through a small housing estate.

You're back alongside the river again in no time, leaving the traffic behind to enjoy the easy towpath.

Its smooth, flat tarmac now draws you back towards temptation, in the form of the Turf. Again.

The area off to the right is protected marshland that's teeming with birds. You can stop to indulge your inner twitcher at one of the info signs along the way: boards show pictures of the local feathered residents, so you'll know who's who in the sky.

From the pub you simply follow the path back along the waterfront to the church (and those noisy crows), rejoining the lane and bearing right, back up towards the entrance to Powderham Castle. If you're lucky there might still be time to sit in the garden back at the farm, and soak up the last of the day's rays.

THE ROUTE

DISTANCE 11 MILES
DIFFICULTY ○○○
START Mill Farm

Kenton, nr Exeter, Devon, EX6 8JR

» Left out of Mill Farm on to the main road.
» Take the first right, ½ mile later, signposted Powderham.
» In 1½ miles you'll reach Powderham Castle.
» Follow the road round to the left, down to the nearby church. Go through the gate on your left, just past the church, on to the path.
» Continue, over a level crossing, to the river and carry on for 1½ miles, until you reach the Turf pub on your right.
» From the Turf, take the ferry across the water and head inland to Topsham, turning left on to the High Street.
» The High Street becomes Exeter Road as you leave the village. Cycle on the footpath if you're uncomfortable with the traffic; but after a short distance you can join the cycle path running alongside.
» Turn left after just over a mile, following the blue NCN signs on to Topsham Road (which runs parallel with the main road) and then left again, into Glasshouse Lane.
» Follow Glasshouse Lane to the end, and round to the right, proceeding up the lane to a small junction on the estate. (The last section of this lane is officially 'No Entry', so hop off and wheel your bike here.) Bear left and continue to follow the river (on your left).
» At the main road, turn left and cross the bridge before reaching the cycle path on your left. Turn left here to join the towpath.
» Follow the towpath for 3 miles until you reach the Turf again.
» Now retrace your earlier route along the river, back to the church at Powderham and turn right to rejoin the tarmac road.
» Cycle back past Powderham Castle, following the lane until you reach the main road: now turn left.
» After ½ mile you'll be back at Mill Farm.

STOP AND SEE

EN ROUTE

Powderham Castle *Kenton, Exeter, Devon, EX6 8JQ; 01626 890243; www.powderham.co.uk*
Magnificent house set in acres of grounds; it's been passed down through generations of the same family since 1391. Take a tour of the house, explore the Secret Garden, and get up close and personal with the Bambi lookalikes roaming the deer park.

The Turf *Exeter Canal, Exminster, Devon, EX6 8EE; 01392 833128; www.turfpub.net*
This friendly family-run pub with sun-kissed garden is only accessible via the canal towpath or riverside path from Powderham. Owner Clive is a local legend, dishing out banter as well as superb food and beers.

Exe Estuary Nature Reserve
01392 824614; see www.rspb.org.uk
You don't have to be a bird nerd to get in a flutter over this place; a pristine marshland reserve, spread over 435 acres in total. It's incredibly peaceful (less so when there are 20,000 birds arriving here for winter).

OFF ROUTE

Lympstone *Devon*
Head to Starcross, take the ferry to Exminster, and follow the cycle path alongside the river to Lympstone. This pretty little village has a cluster of cottages huddled around the harbour, and cute cafés and shops. Buy some fish and chips and watch the boats chug past the quayside.

EAT, DRINK, SLEEP

Mill Farm *Kenton, nr Exeter, Devon, EX6 8JR; 01392 832471; www.millfarmstay.co.uk*
Old-fashioned farmhouse with five cosy en suite rooms. Although the rooms aren't the most modern, the beds are comfy and the back garden is ideal for relaxing outside with a post-ride cuppa or glass of vino.

Lovely owner Delia can point you in the direction of hidden local treasures, too. Doubles from £60. No kids under age six.

The Galley *41 Fore Street, Topsham, Exeter, Devon, EX3 0HU; 01392 876078; www.galleyrestaurant.co.uk*
Run by a Masterchef, this place looks fairly innocuous from the outside. But inside it's all exposed brick and maritime flair. Try the delicately grilled monkfish with Bombay potatoes, coriander, and spiced mango.

Rodean Restaurant *The Triangle, Kenton, Exeter, Devon, EX6 8LS; 01626 890195; www.rodeanrestaurant.co.uk*
Kenton born-and-bred chef, Matthew Lilt, can trace his family history back 300 years, and the delicious food he serves is just as local. The seared Brixham scallops with tempura tiger prawns make a mouth-watering start to a tasty evening.

Route 2 *1 Monmouth Hill, Topsham, Exeter, Devon, EX3 0JJ; 01392 873471; www.route2topsham.co.uk*
Above its rather cool, cyclist-oriented café-bar downstairs, Route 2 has three smart Steam Packet apartments – ideally placed for exploring the surrounding area. Apartments from £100 per night.

The Lively Hope *Ferry Road, Topsham, Exeter, Devon, EX3 0JJ; 0208 241 2725; www.livelyhope.co.uk*
This sunny self-catering cottage sits right on the estuary in Topsham. It boasts a roll-top bath, smart kitchen, and riverside garden where swans nest in the spring. From £400 per week (sleeps up to six).

RENT

Route 2 *(see above; hire – 01392 875085)*
A full range of bikes – including tag-alongs and tandems. Staff will even make you up a picnic for the ride. Adult bike £11 a day.

SOUTH WEST

7

WAREHAM TO CORFE CASTLE

Silky-smooth roads, breathtaking views, and just one hill...

IF I HAD TO CHOOSE, THIS COULD WELL BE my favourite ride. Located just along the road from the Purbeck Hills, Wareham is surrounded by surprisingly flat lanes that make for some smooth cycling. In the town itself, attractive old houses line the main street and an idyllic river runs across its southern end. It's here that you'll find Gold Court House, tucked away on a narrow back street, where Merlin the black Labrador snoozes his days away on the neatly trimmed lawn. He'll probably still be here when you get back, so grab your bike, pull the garden gates to, and head out to the riverfront.

The first half-mile takes you over the bridge and out of town along a dead-straight road, passing cow-littered meadows as you go. Banking left at the King's Arms pub, you slip away down Nutcrack Lane, bordered by knotted brambles and old-fashioned pastures. As you carry on through the hamlet of Ridge, the scenery changes from fields to rugged heathland and marsh; the area is home to over 200 species of birds, including nightjars, ospreys, and the rare Dartford warbler – you can stop and see them at the RSPB reserve at Arne, up ahead.

Meanwhile, the route sees you fork right for Corfe Castle, cruising along an avenue of trees that turns to grassland and bracken as you emerge on to open heath. When the gorse is in blossom during spring, the brown and green landscape is speckled with yellow flowers, creating a beautiful foreground against the Purbeck Hills towering up into the sky.

As the road unravels over the landscape, the ruins of Corfe Castle come into focus up ahead, perched imperiously on a hill overlooking the eponymous village filled with ramshackle stone cottages. If you fancy stopping for longer after a tasty lunch in one of the pubs or cafés, there's a pretty church well worth a snoop, as well as the castle itself.

Retrace your wheel-tracks back out of the village and veer off to Church Knowle, taking one last look behind at the castle, its ruins silhouetted against the sky.

Now comes the only big climb of the day. It's pretty short, though, and before long you're up on the top – gazing down over voluptuous countryside, all the way back to Corfe Castle village. It's downhill the rest of the way home, as you drop off the Purbeck Hills and coast through Furzebrook to arrive back at Wareham for afternoon tea. Who knows, you might even be in time to see Merlin the Labrador rising from his slumber…

THE ROUTE

DISTANCE   12 MILES
DIFFICULTY   ○○○
START   Gold Court House

St John's Hill, Wareham, Dorset, BH20 4LZ
» Leave Gold Court House from the back.
Turn right and head round to the river.
» At the main road turn left and ride over
the bridge to Stoborough, turning left just
after the King's Arms pub.
» Follow this road for 2 miles (through
Ridge), before turning right for Corfe Castle.
» Continue for just over 2 miles to a
junction: turn right and at the roundabout
take the first exit – for Corfe Castle.
» Take the first right, signposted Church
Knowle. (For Corfe village, go straight on).
» Two miles later, after passing through
Church Knowle, turn right and climb the hill.
» Descend the other side and carry on for
nearly 2 miles, passing through Furzebrook
to reach a roundabout, where you go
straight over, taking the Stoborough exit.
» Follow this road back to Wareham.

STOP AND SEE

EN ROUTE

Arne Nature Reserve *Wareham,*
Dorset, BH20 5BJ; 01929 553360;
see www.rspb.org.uk
Haven for over 200 species of birds,
including rare breeds like the Dartford
warbler. Pick up a map and head off on one
of the heathland trails. Daytime and
nocturnal guided walks are on offer, too.

Corfe Castle Village and Castle
www.corfe-castle.co.uk; for castle: 01929
481294; see www.nationaltrust.org.uk
Beautiful old village overlooked by the
ruins of the eponymous fort that dates back
a staggering 1,000 years. Once you've had
a look round the castle, head up the small
hill and stop at Cleals – a great little deli
selling Purbeck ice cream and local beers
with ominous names like Old Thumper.

Wareham Boat Hire *Abbots Quay,*
Wareham, Dorset, BH20 4LW; 01929 550688;
www.warehamboathire.co.uk
What better way to round off a ride than
a relaxing row down the river? Rent a
boat from Russ and spend an hour or
so pottering about with the swans, ducks,
and other river residents.

OFF ROUTE

Studland *nr Swanage, Dorset*
This bonny village has three gorgeous
beaches and a nature reserve nearby.
All just seven miles from Wareham.

EAT, DRINK, SLEEP

Gold Court House *St John's Hill,*
Wareham, Dorset, BH20 4LZ; 01929
553320; www.goldcourthouse.co.uk
Three rooms to choose from – all en suite
– with a peaceful garden out the back.
Owners Michael and Anthea know the area
intimately and will happily suggest some
local hidden treasures.
Doubles from £75 per night.

The Priory Country House Hotel
Church Green, Wareham, Dorset, BH20 4ND;
01929 551666; www.theprioryhotel.co.uk
Expensive, but worth it. Eighteen luxurious
rooms including romantic suites with
Jacuzzis overlooking the river; conveniently
close to Wareham's pubs and eateries.
Four acres of gardens and a great
restaurant make this the perfect base for
a weekend of eating, drinking, and biking.
Doubles from £205 per night.

North Mill *Wareham, Dorset, BH20 4QW;*
01929 555142; www.northmill.org.uk
This former mill on the edge of Wareham
has two rooms (one double, one twin), with a
garden right beside the river. Breakfast eggs
come courtesy of the resident hens; served
with home-made breads and spreads.
Double from £80 per night.

The Old Granary

The Old Granary *The Quay, Wareham,*
Dorset, BH20 4LP; 01929 552010;
www.hall-woodhouse.co.uk
Beautiful old building right next to the river;
sit and watch the swans drift by or head
inside to the light, modern interior. Try the
Hopping Hare ale and delicious lamb shank
shepherd's pie – perfect post-ride fare.

The Castle Inn *63 East Street, Corfe Castle,*
Wareham, Dorset, BH20 5EE; 01929 480208;
www.castleinncorfe.com
You'll find this friendly, family-oriented pub
at the top of the main street. Old stone walls
and a wood-burning stove give the place
lots of character – as does welcoming
landlady Laurice. There's an enormous
garden with chickens wandering about;
look out for the steam train passing nearby.

The Greyhound Inn *The Square, Corfe*
Castle, Dorset, BH20 5EZ; 01929 480205;
www.greyhoundcorfe.co.uk
A medieval pub full of friendly locals and
good-quality food (try the Poole Bay
mussels). The garden has views of the
facing hills and a path leading to the castle.

RENT

Purbeck Cycle Hire *Wareham Station,*
Wareham, Dorset, BH20 4AS; 01929 556601;
www.purbeckcyclehire.co.uk
These guys have a range of mountain bikes
for adults and children and trailers for dogs.
Adult's bike costs £14 for a day.

HELPFUL HINT

Take bathers: the coast is a splash away.

8

MELLS TO FROME

Country pubs, quirky cafés, and foodie shops – get ready to ride off those calories...

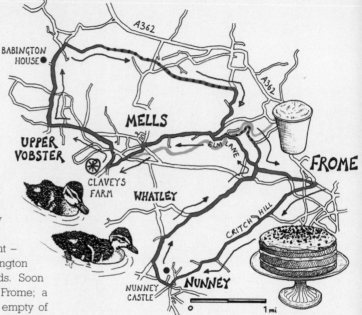

ALTHOUGH YOU MIGHT NOT SEE IT for the first few miles, the River Mells will remain a constant companion for much of this scenic 17-mile route (albeit becoming the River Frome at points).

From Claveys Farm you cruise down the lane towards the centre of Mells, on to an open road that's bordered on either side by tangled hedgerows. A mile or so later you reach a staggered crossroads – the hill on your left leading down to Vobster, where Peta, the landlady of the Vobster Inn (a great little pub), serves up chunky home-made sandwiches and real ales.

The route, however, takes you off right – past 'meedja' and celeb magnet Babington House – and out alongside open fields. Soon you're joining the cycle track towards Frome; a cyclist's dream, with smooth, flat tarmac empty of motorised traffic. On your left you pass an ancient railway car rusting away in the summer sun, and just in case you needed convincing that this is *prahper countreesoide*, the waft of farmyard drifts across from the fields on your right...

Suddenly the lane becomes wilder and more overgrown as you duck beneath a bridge and emerge on to an avenue of trees. It feels like you're discovering a hidden secret; I half expected the Railway Children to come running out of the siding, waving white hankies as I pootled past...

A mile or so later you rejoin the road and make a right into Great Elm, and it's here that you get your first glimpse of the river. Dropping left, down Elm Lane, you encounter a scene straight out of a Constable painting: an idyllic pond with ducklings drifting on the water, overlooked by a gorgeous cottage and rickety old boathouse. The sound of birdsong and trickling water as you cycle past is like a real-life relaxation tape.

It gets better, too. Just over the bridge you join another cycle track and follow the river to the outskirts of Frome, emerging into narrow lanes that take you up a hill into town.

Frome is foodie central, with dozens of independent shops waiting to tempt you inside. Treat yourself to home-made cakes and delicious coffee (you've earned it, after all), then head back out into the country and on to the peaceful village of Nunney.

This is where you'll meet the river again (more of a stream now) and there are benches perched beside it where you can sit, munch a few snacks, and let life drift on by. History buffs will love it here, too: just beyond the river there's a 14th-century castle (with a moat and everything), adding a sense of medieval drama to the scene.

From here you head back to Mells, via that Constable-esque pond again, where those ducklings are still gliding about on the water.

THE ROUTE

DISTANCE   17 MILES

DIFFICULTY   ○○○○

START   Claveys Farm

Mells, Frome, Somerset, BA11 3QP

» Head left from Claveys Farm, then bear left at the fork just along the lane.

» Follow the road downhill to the junction: turn left and climb out of the village.

» Continue along this lane for just under a mile, until you reach a staggered crossroads: turn right. (Go left if you want to call in at the Vobster Inn.)

» Carry on for just over a mile, past Babington House; the road bends left after 200 metres, but you go straight on – signposted Hemington.

» Less than 200 metres later turn right, following the blue NCN sign.

» After ¼ mile you'll reach the start of the cycle track on your right; join it and turn left, signposted Frome.

» Follow the flat, smooth cycle track for just over 2 miles, before it rejoins the road just outside Great Elm.

» Turn right on to the lane and cycle up into the village – following the sign for Frome. At the junction, after ½ mile, bear right and continue up into the village (following the sign for Frome).

» Turn left after 200 metres on to Elm Lane – signposted Frome.

» Drop down the hill, cross the bridge over the pond, and turn left on to the cycle path – following the blue NCN sign for Frome.

» Follow the cycle path alongside the river for almost a mile: you'll have to get off and push at points towards the latter section.

» The path brings you out into a little car park where you rejoin the road and turn left after less than ¼ mile, on to Webb's Hill.

» This becomes Egford Lane at the top of the hill. At the junction with the main road into Frome – Broadway – turn left.

» Follow this towards the town centre for ¼ mile, crossing a roundabout. Drop left,

down Catherine Street, if you want the town; the route turns right just before – on to Nunney Road.

» Gently climb out of Frome and carry on, past the golf course, to Nunney.

» Arriving in Nunney you pass the George on your left, then turn right – over the little bridge – and head out of the village (to visit the castle, turn right on to Castle Street).

» Climb gently along the lane, reaching a junction after ½ mile: turn right, signposted Whatley and Mells.

» After ¼ mile, you'll see Southfield House on your left. Turn right here.

» At the end of this lane, turn right. Then turn left on to Elm Lane after 1 mile.

» Follow Elm Lane back to Great Elm, and down to the village pond you passed earlier.

» Carry on past the pond and up the hill, to the junction at the top: turn left and join the road to Mells.

» When you reach Mells Post Office, go straight over the staggered crossroads, on to Top Lane. At the next crossroads go straight over.

» Keep going straight for less than ¼ mile, until you reach Claveys Farm.

STOP AND SEE

EN ROUTE

The Garden Café *16 Stony Street, Frome, Somerset, BA11 1BU; 01373 454178; www.gardencafefrome.co.uk*
Tucked down an alley with a quiet garden out back, this café's menu is bursting with organic, home-made delights. Try the coffee and walnut cake…

The Little Red Café *16 Catherine Hill, Frome, Somerset, BA11 1BZ; 01373 228806*
Owned by Phil and Liz Chafer, the Little Red Café offers a mouth-watering range of home-made cakes (I love the banana and walnut), organic coffee, and juices. Grab a table on the cobbles outside and watch the world stroll by.

Cheap Street *Frome, Somerset*
The street that time forgot; it's lined with wonky old shop fronts and a stream runs through the middle of the pavement. There's a great café at the top (La Strada) selling freshly squeezed juices and home-made ice cream.

Nunney Castle *Nunney, nr Frome, Somerset, BA11 4LQ; 08703 331181; www.nunneycastle.co.uk*
Dating back to the 14th century, the weathered grey walls of this French-style castle have survived attacks by Cromwell's men, as well as centuries of frost.

OFF ROUTE

Longleat Safari Park *Longleat, Warminster, Wiltshire, BA12 7NW; 01985 844400; www.longleat.co.uk*
Magnificent historic house dating back to 1580, with ornately decorated rooms stacked with artistic treasures. But it's the surrounding 900 acres – home to lions, rhinos, wolves, monkeys, and more – that this place is famous for.

EAT, DRINK, SLEEP

Claveys Farm *Mells, Frome, Somerset, BA11 3QP; 01373 814651*
Run by artist Fleur Kelly, this place is like something out of *The Darling Buds of May*. There are two rooms available in the rambling old farmhouse (built in 1680) with a shared bathroom upstairs. Breakfast is a truly local affair – eggs are fresh from hens that wander the garden and the bacon comes from pigs reared out back. Double room from £70 per night.

The Vobster Inn *Lower Vobster, nr Radstock, Somerset, BA3 5RJ; 01373 812920; www.vobsterinn.co.uk*
A friendly olde worlde pub run by Peta and Rafael Davila, which offers three smart rooms at the back. Head to the huge garden out the front and take your pick from fabulous dishes like ginger-and-honey-marinated pigeon breast with pickled mushroom risotto, and local ales (try the Butcombe). Doubles from £85 per night.

The Talbot Inn *Selwood Street, Mells, Somerset, BA11 3PN; 01373 812254; www.talbotinn.com*
This atmospheric old coaching inn dates back to the 15th century. It has eight rooms to choose from – many with four-poster beds. Best of all, you're only a few steps from the bar, which specialises in top-notch ales. The food is excellent, too; try the sun-dried tomato, basil, and sautéed courgette risotto with crumbled goats' cheese. Tasty. Doubles from £95 per night.

The Grange *Whatley, Frome, Somerset, BA11 3JU; 01373 836579; www.restaurantatthegrange.co.uk*
Bright and airy eatery with an open kitchen and log-fired oven. The restaurant is run by Jane Averill and the menu features mouth-watering dishes like roasted pork fillet on parsnip purée. There are residential cookery courses next door, too, if you fancy having a go in the kitchen yourself.

RENT

Towpath Trail (TT Cycles) *48 Frome Road, Bradford-on-Avon, Wiltshire, BA15 1LE; 01225 867187; www.towpathtrail.co.uk*
Bikes available for all sizes, shapes, and abilities – plus trailers for younger cyclists. One day's adult bicycle hire costs £12.

9

FRESHFORD TO AVONCLIFF

Narrowboats, expansive hillsides, and hidden valleys...

THE FIRST THING YOU NOTICE as you pedal away from Priory Cottage is the aroma of wild garlic in the air. That, and the rich smell of grass wafting up from between the trees lining the hill down to Freshford. Although millions of tourists descend upon the nearby city of Bath year after year, here in the surrounding hills it's just you, the birds, and the clicking of your gears as you cruise down into the village.

Freshford is sprinkled across two small hills and consists of Cotswold-stone houses arranged around a couple of main streets. On your way into the village call in at the community shop (Galleries) to stock up on fruitcake and other snacks for your saddlebag before you reach Freshford. After ascending the High Street you drop down into an impossibly green valley. Meadows bisected by a stream await you, complete with gambolling lambs if you're here in spring; their bleatings echoing off the hillside.

The road leads over a humpbacked bridge and on towards another hill before you continue along the valley floor. There are so few cars along here that the moss is reclaiming the tarmac in places – creating a vivid green carpet zigzagging its way to the tea shop at Iford Manor.

This creamy-coloured Cotswold mansion looks magnificent against the backdrop of trees and blue sky, and its Italian-style gardens, built into the hillside, have terraces and avenues that you could spend days exploring. More importantly, however, the cream teas on offer here are dee-licious.

The climb that follows is a bit of a lung-buster, but if you're too full of scones to pedal, it makes a lovely woodland-bordered walk.

Pretty fields are your companions once you've coasted through Westwood, before a staggered crossroads marks the start of a steep, treelined descent. Sharp switchbacks keep you guessing about what lies at the bottom until the last minute when, suddenly, you burst out into the valley beside an incredible aqueduct crossing the River Avon. Take a break to watch the narrowboats putter past, before heading across the bridge to join the towpath, overtaking canal boats with wholesome names like *Rosie and Lily*. Don't be alarmed if strangers say hello; it's just how it is on the river. Even the ducks are chatty.

After pedalling between steep hillsides covered with trees looking no bigger than broccoli florets, you head on to Limpley Stoke and its Hop Pole Inn for an elderflower pressé that will energise you for the final climb back to Freshford... It may be a hilly ride, but it's probably the prettiest eight miles England has to offer.

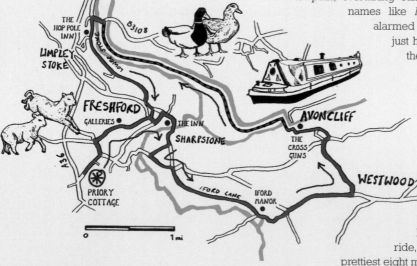

THE ROUTE

DISTANCE   8 MILES
DIFFICULTY ○○○
START   *Priory Cottage Abbey Lane, Hinton Charterhouse, Bath, BA2 7TD*

» Turn right out of Priory Cottage and head downhill into Freshford.

» At the junction at the bottom of the hill turn right (signposted Bradford-on-Avon) and head uphill.

» Follow the road downhill to exit the village, past the Inn, on your right.

» Carry on over the humpbacked bridge and take the first right.

» Turn left at the next junction, ¼ mile later.

» Climb the hill and take the first right.

» Cruise downhill, through the valley for under a mile, to Iford Manor.

» Pass the manor and climb the steep hill and turn right at the top, into Westwood.

» Less than ½ mile later, turn left for Upper Westwood and Avoncliff.

» Continue down the lane for about ½ mile and turn right at the junction – then immediately left, down to Avoncliff.

» At the bottom of the hill join the aqueduct on your right, and follow the towpath for 1¾ miles until you reach the road bridge for Limpley Stoke, which crosses the canal.

» Turn left off the towpath, and double back on yourself to reach the main road. Then turn right and go downhill into Limpley Stoke.

» Go under the road bridge and turn left, on to Lower Stoke.

» Continue on to Crowe Hill, which climbs towards Freshford.

» After ¼ mile you reach a junction: turn left on to New Road.

» Continue, then turn right into Freshford Lane, and up the hill to Priory Cottage.

STOP AND SEE

EN ROUTE

Iford Manor *Bradford-on-Avon, Wiltshire, BA15 2BA; 01225 863146; www.ifordmanor.co.uk*

Beautiful Grade I-listed manor house lying in a stunning tree-covered valley. Arrange a tour of the gardens or stop for a cream tea.

The Cross Guns *Avoncliff, nr Bradford-on-Avon, Wiltshire, BA15 2HB; 01225 862335; www.crossguns.net*

The perfect lunch stop: tucked away on the towpath, this quiet old pub dates back to the 16th century. Sit back and watch the boats chug along past.

The Hop Pole Inn *Limpley Stoke, Bath, BA2 7FS; 01225 723134*

Proper old pub with delicious Bath ales, tasty grub, and a great garden. Just what you need to round off the ride.

OFF ROUTE

Bradford-on-Avon *Wiltshire*

With Bath for a neighbour, Bradford is often overlooked, but it's definitely worth a visit. Just three miles from Freshford, this pretty medieval market town brims with old buildings (like the Tithe Barn at Barton Farm Country Park) and cafés line the river. Try the Fat Fowl or the Lock Inn.

EAT, DRINK, SLEEP

Priory Cottage *Abbey Lane, Hinton Charterhouse, Bath, BA2 7TD; 01225 723321; www.priorycottagebath.co.uk*

Run by super-friendly couple, Martin and Jackie, Priory Cottage boasts en suite rooms with flat-screen TVs and all the trimmings; relax in the guest lounge or the seven-acre garden.
Doubles from £75 per night.

The Grove at Freshford *Station Road, Freshford, Bath, BA2 7WQ; 07798 826684; www.thegroveatfreshford.co.uk*

If you fancy a self-catering break, this place is ideal. A Grade II-listed building in over an acre of gardens, with five bedrooms and a private outdoor pool.

From £300 for a two-night stay (based on two people sharing).

Great Ashley Farm *Bradford-on-Avon, Wiltshire, BA15 2PP; 01225 864563; www.greatashley.co.uk*

Award-winning B&B on a working farm, just two miles from Bradford-on-Avon. Four rooms to choose from, all en suite, which come with breakfasts, teas, and biscuits that have been locally produced. Doubles from £65 per night.

Galleries *Freshford Lane, Freshford, Bath, BA2 7UR; 01225 723249; www.galleriesshop.co.uk*

A community-run shop selling freshly made sandwiches, teas, coffees, and snacks.

The Inn at Freshford *The Hill, Freshford, Bath, BA2 7WG; 01225 722250; www.theinnatfreshford.co.uk*

Idyllic village pub dating back to the 16th century, with views across a babbling brook and green paddocks out the front. Proper ales and ciders, and delicious pub food – from pies to ploughman's.

RENT

TT Cycles *48 Frome Road, Bradford-on-Avon, Wiltshire, BA15 1LE; 01225 867187; www.towpathtrail.co.uk*

Mountain bikes, children's bikes, trailer bikes, and equipment are all available. Adult's bike for £12 a day. Canoes are also for hire, if you fancy a day of messing about on the river.

FANCY A WALK...

Thankyou for joining us for a meal. drink or just a cup of coffee...

Why not now take a lovely walk along the river for a drink at *The Inn at Freshford*...

10

TETBURY TO SHERSTON

Fab pubs, quirky antique shops, and beautiful old houses...

TAKE ANY ROAD OUT OF TETBURY and you'll be cruising along quiet country lanes within five minutes. But if it's pretty pubs and *prahper* ale you're after, head past the church and freewheel your way over centuries-old Bath Bridge.

Coasting along with the summer smell of fresh-cut grass wafting over from the nearby paddock, you duck off left a mile or so later towards Shipton Moyne. Along the way you cross an old humpbacked bridge, the babbling brook below it a tributary of the mighty River Avon that flows all the way to Bristol – over 20 miles away.

Shortly after, you're arriving in the blink-and-you'll-miss-it village of Shipton Moyne, where traffic amounts to nothing more than the occasional tractor. It's also home to the strangely named Cat and Custard Pot pub, which is ideally placed for your first refreshment stop. The ale of choice in these parts is Wadworth 6X – brewed just down the road in Trowbridge – and on a sunny day you can sit on the wall outside and watch horses from the nearby stables clip-clop past; riders sitting straight-backed.

Suitably refreshed, post pit-stop, you pootle down the street past Cotswold-stone cottages covered with climbing roses, and on into a narrow lane. Its bordering hedgerows are so high you could be travelling through a leafy tunnel; squadrons of little birds flit about noisily within, occasionally bursting from the bushes with a frantic flutter of wings.

Easton Grey awaits you, a few miles further – one of the many villages around here that time forgot. A downhill stretch now leads you to a cluster of old cottages huddled around a humpbacked bridge. Leaving the village quiet and heading along a lane towards Sherston, you'll see the scenery open out to reveal gorgeous green fields on either side as you pedal towards lunch – just one short ascent between you and a plate of Malmesbury Gold pork sausages and spring-onion mash at the

16th-century Rattlebone Inn. The wonky walls, nooks, and crannies give this place a cosy feel, and an open fire in winter offers a warming glow.

Head back out of Sherston into smooth, quiet country lanes that thread their way between meadows to Westonbirt Arboretum. Every spring it's awash with pink, white, and purple blossoms.

The Hare and Hounds Hotel isn't far now and serves the best lemon drizzle cake in the world (fact). Take a seat in the garden and order a large slice to energise yourself for the three miles (including some fun downhills) back to Tetbury, where yet more delicious local food and drink await at the Priory Inn.

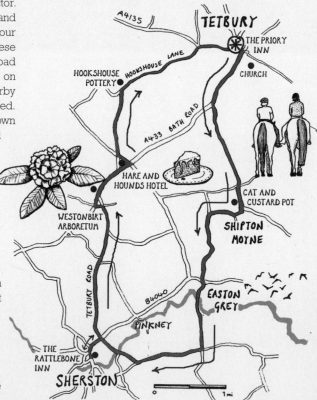

THE ROUTE

DISTANCE   13 MILES
DIFFICULTY   ○○○
START   The Priory Inn *London Road, Tetbury, Gloucestershire, GL8 8JJ*

» Head left from the Priory Inn; follow the road round to the left, until you reach the town hall. Turn right at the mini roundabout and leave the town via Bath Bridge.

» Turn left after a mile, for Shipton Moyne.

» Follow the road for 1½ miles to the Cat and Custard Pot.

» Around 100 metres past the pub, the road forks right, into a narrow lane.

» Take the first left, and pass a couple of farms to reach the main road.

» Turn left, then immediately right and drop down into Easton Grey.

» Go through the village and up a small climb before turning right, for Sherston.

» Follow the road for around 1½ miles and keep an eye out for a small grass triangle, where you turn right.

» Drop downhill to the next junction, then turn right and climb up into Sherston village.

» Turn left at the crossroads into the village – passing the Carpenter's Arms – to arrive at the Rattlebone Inn.

» From the Rattlebone Inn, go back to the crossroads and turn left.

» Continue for 2 miles to the main road.

» Turn right and you'll pass Westonbirt Arboretum, 200 metres along, on the left.

» Continue along the main road, until you reach the Hare and Hounds.

» Just past the Hare and Hounds there's a crossroads: turn left, signposted Leighterton.

» Take the first right, signposted Tetbury.

» Hookshouse Pottery is on your left, after 1½ miles.

» Carrying on past the pottery, you reach a junction with the main road about 1½ miles later.

» Turn right and cruise into Tetbury, passing a little church on your left, before you reach a junction.

» Go straight on, and you'll see the Priory on your right, 50 metres ahead.

STOP AND SEE
EN ROUTE
Westonbirt Arboretum *nr Tetbury, Gloucestershire, GL8 8QS; 01666 880220; www.forestry.gov.uk/westonbirt*
This place is home to one of the biggest collections of trees in the world. In spring the famous rhododendrons burst into bloom, scenting the air with their perfume.

Hookshouse Pottery *Westonbirt, Tetbury, Gloucestershire, GL8 8TZ; 01666 880297; www.hookshousepottery.co.uk*
Ask owner Chris White to show you round (if you're lucky, he might even demonstrate how to throw a pot). If you've got time, check out the colourful garden.

OFF ROUTE
Tetbury's antique shops
There are about 25 to explore, attracting people from around the world. Whether you're after old books, maps, or beautiful garden furniture, you can rummage to your heart's content before wandering around this gorgeous medieval town.

Blue Zucchini Brasserie *7–9 Church Street, Tetbury, Gloucestershire, GL8 8JG; 01666 505852*
Follow the aroma of freshly brewed coffee, pull up a chair, and order a slab of caramel shortbread. It's biscuit-tastic.

EAT, DRINK, SLEEP
The Priory Inn *London Road, Tetbury, Gloucestershire, GL8 8JJ; 01666 502251; www.theprioryinn.co.uk*
Delicious local food, lip-smacking beers (including local brews like Pig's Ear and Banker's Draft), and well-kept comfy rooms greet you here.
Doubles from £59 per night.

Ambleside *Tetbury Upton, Gloucestershire, GL8 8LP; 01666 500857; www.amblesidetetbury.co.uk*
This refurbished cottage, in a hamlet located only about a mile from Tetbury's centre, has two double bedrooms with king-sized beds, flat-screen TVs, and scrumptious organic breakfasts. There's a lovely garden, and good walking to be had in the nearby lanes.
Doubles from £70 per night.

Belgrave House *Market Place, Tetbury, Gloucestershire, GL8 8DA; 07968 083210; www.belgravehousetetbury.co.uk*
A smart townhouse in the centre of Tetbury, with two en suite rooms. Despite the calm, quiet, and convenient location, it's just a stroll away from the town's pubs, antique shops and bookstores. The owner, Carolyn, lays on delicious breakfasts and will put together a tasty picnic for your ride if you book ahead.
Doubles from £65 per night.

RENT
Go-By-Cycle *Tall Trees, Water Lane, Somerford Keynes, Gloucestershire, GL7 6DS; 07970 419208; www.go-by-cycle.co.uk*
Located in nearby Somerford Keynes, Go-By-Cycle offers a variety of bikes for adults and children, and they'll deliver for an extra charge (give them 24 hours' notice). Adult's bike costs £14 for a day.

11

MINCHINHAMPTON TO NAILSWORTH

Views, ice creams, and wandering cows...

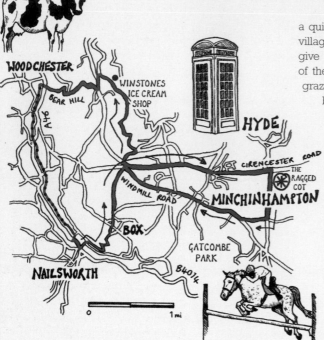

IT'S AN ODD PLACE FOR A PUB, but you'll be glad you found the Ragged Cot. This old coaching inn dates back centuries and is ideal for accessing the Stroud Valley – home to some of Britain's prettiest rides.

Heading left from the pub for about a mile, you cruise down a smooth, treelined road before making a right, towards the gorgeous village of Minchinhampton. Keep an eye out overhead for gliders from the nearby Aston Down flying club as you pedal along past the entrance to Princess Anne's pad, Gatcombe Park; if it's sunny you'll see them silhouetted against the blue sky.

Soon you're bouncing over the cattle grid as you reach Minch', dropping gently downhill and entering a corridor of terraced Cotswold cottages. At the bottom, the marketplace has a great tea room and proper old-fashioned sweetshop – ideal if you need a quick sugar fix before you carry on through the village and out the other side. Tiny terraced houses give way to common land and a stunning view of the Stroud Valley appears on your right. Cattle graze this grassland during the summer, so don't be surprised if you encounter the odd heifer nonchalantly strolling along the road.

After a quick wiggle over a staggered crossroads, you drop down Brimscombe Hill, the wind whistling around your ears as you pick up speed. The Stroud Valley unfolds in all its glory in front of you, but keep an eye out for a red telephone box, the unlikely cue to turn left in the direction of ice cream nirvana… The narrow lane you enter feels like a secret short cut, and after hugging the valley for a mile or so, you cruise up past gnarly old trees and emerge outside Winstones – England's best ice cream shop.*

Having loaded up with a few extra calories for ballast, you freewheel down Bear Hill as more magnificent views of the valley stretch out ahead. You could almost take off and gently glide across to the other side, landing in one of the opposite meadows, but after a grin-inducing two-mile cruise you reach the cycle track at the bottom.

It's an easy run along the valley floor to Nailsworth now – wooded hillsides rising up on either side as your tyres scrunch over small stones. Nailsworth is home to an excellent deli (William's Food Hall) stocking all sorts of goodies like salami and fresh bread – perfect for a picnic on the way back.

But before the Big Eat comes the Big Climb. Known locally as the 'W', the road zigzags up the valley, the scenery getting more expansive the higher you climb. Finally you emerge back on to Minchinhampton Common, where your reward is a cool glass of ale at the conveniently placed Halfway House, just past the summit. It'll go down a treat with the salami and other delicacies you bought back in Nailsworth…

*Source: Matt Carroll – ice cream expert

THE ROUTE

DISTANCE   12 MILES

DIFFICULTY   ⚪⚪⚪⚪

START   The Ragged Cot

Cirencester Road, Minchinhampton, GL6 8PE

» Turn left out of the Ragged Cot's car park.

» Turn right after a mile, signposted 'Minchinhampton only'.

» The route goes straight through the village (for the sweetshop and tea room, turn right at the crossroads, on to High Street, and pedal along to the war memorial – the shop is on the right) for a mile, until you reach Minchinhampton Common.

» Turn right at the junction, then first left, and immediately right – on to Brimscombe Hill (signposted Brimscombe).

» Turn left opposite the red telephone box, ¼ mile down.

» Follow this road for 2 miles to Winstones ice cream shop.

» Carry on up to the main road, and then turn left, and take the next right on to Bear Hill. Follow the road downhill – do not take the lane signed Houndscroft St Chloe.

» At the bottom is a main road. Turn right towards Stroud, then take the first left, on to Paul's Rise; 100 metres up this road, turn left on to the cycle path and continue for 2 miles to Nailsworth.

» The cycle track ends in a car park, near Egypt Mill restaurant. Carry on around right, until you reach the main road.

» Turn left. On reaching the mini roundabout, you'll see William's Food Hall ahead.

» Turn left at the roundabout to climb up to Minchinhampton Common.

» The Halfway House is at the top of the hill, on your right.

» From the pub, carry back along the main road for 2 miles until you come to the staggered crossroads with Brimscombe Hill diagonally opposite.

» Turn right, signposted Cirencester, and keep going for 2 miles to the Ragged Cot, on your right.

STOP AND SEE

EN ROUTE

M&B Stores *5–7 West End, Minchinhampton, Gloucestershire, GL6 9JA; 01453 883265*
Located by the war memorial in the marketplace, M&B Stores is an olde worlde sweetshop where you can stock up on sherbet strips and cola bottles.

Winstones *Greenacres, Bownham, Stroud, Gloucestershire, GL5 5BX; 01453 873270; www.winstonesicecream.co.uk*
The Winstone family has been serving up exquisite white vanilla for over 80 years. Order a little tub with butterscotch sauce and head to the conveniently located bench nearby, to soak up the sun and stare out over the valley.

OFF ROUTE

Painswick *Stroud, Gloucestershire*
Perched on a hillside surrounded by woodland, this is regarded by many to be one of Britain's most beautiful villages. And I'm inclined to agree.

Tetbury *Gloucestershire*
The main streets of this gorgeous Cotswolds town have hardly changed since the Middle Ages. Everywhere you look there are crooked old shop fronts with weathered oak beams, inviting you in for a nose.

The Woolpack Inn *Slad Road, Slad, Gloucestershire, GL6 7QA; 01452 813429; www.thewoolpackinn-slad.com*
This traditional Cotswold pub was Laurie Lee's local – he of *Cider with Rosie* fame. You'll find good ales at the bar and inspiring views from the garden. Maybe you'll be tempted to write something over a glass of Scrumpy?

EAT, DRINK, SLEEP

The Ragged Cot *Cirencester Road, Minchinhampton, Gloucestershire, GL6 8PE; 01453 884643; www.theraggedcot.co.uk*
Smart, friendly pub with delicious ales and a regularly changing local menu featuring dishes like belly of Old Spot pork. There's a sun-soaked conservatory to eat in, and in summer you can sit outside and watch horses from the nearby stables trot by. Cosy rooms with flat-screen TVs are available upstairs.
Doubles from £75 per night.

Forwood Farm *Well Hill, Minchinhampton, Gloucestershire, GL6 9AB; 01453 731620; www.forwoodfarm.com*
This restored 17th-century country house on the edge of Minchinhampton has two bright bedrooms with wood beams, antique beds, and en suite bathrooms with heated stone floors.
Doubles from £60 per night.

Hazelwood *Church Street, Nailsworth, Gloucestershire, GL6 0BP; 01453 839304; www.hazelwood.me.uk*
A Victorian house just a few minutes' walk from the centre of Nailsworth, where you'll find independent shops and cafés, and access to some great rides and walks. There are two rooms to choose from – both en suite – with original fireplaces and big, sturdy beds. The owners, Karen and Alan, will happily lend maps and leaflets with local information.
Doubles from £65 per night.

RENT

Noah's Ark *Bourne Mills, Brimscombe, Stroud, GL5 2TA; 01453 884738; www.noahsark.co.uk*
At the bottom of nearby Hyde Hill, Noah's Ark rents a variety of bikes for all shapes and sizes. Adult's bike costs £15 a day.

HELPFUL HINT

Go for a mountain bike if you can – you'll need lots of gears for that hill.

12

GUITING POWER TO BROADWAY

Cotswold hills, a quirky country house, and fields full of lavender…

THE NORTH COTSWOLDS are renowned for being drop-dead gorgeous – tiny lanes and villages full of honey-coloured cottages. But with most folk heading to all the same places, there are one or two crowd-free corners left to explore.

Heading out of Guiting Guest House you free-wheel downhill and bank left on to a treelined lane. Around you, the Cotswold Hills undulate off into the distance, and the sounds of bleating sheep and clucking grouse reverberate off the nearby woods.

After cruising through the blink-and-you'll-miss-them villages of Kineton and Temple Guiting, you thread your way through fields where blackberry bushes do battle with drystone walls, and on through Taddington. Black chickens peck away optimistically at the earth outside the weathered stone cottages as you whizz past to Pauline's Veg – a small barrow selling fresh rhubarb, chutneys, and jams straight from the farm. Don't expect to see the eponymous owner, though; it works on an honesty basis.

Before long you're peeling off left into Snowshill, coasting down into the *Miss Marple*-like quaint village – a hotchpotch of tiny cottages around the church. If you turn right here a short, steep climb takes you up to Lavender Farm, where the fields flood with purple every July.

It's just a smooth downhill run to Broadway; by the time you reach its tea shop your eyes will be watering and you'll be ready for a stodgy cake.

From Broadway you head south-west, up a small climb into Stanton, where buttermilk-coloured cottages line the main street. It's like entering a time warp – a horse-drawn carriage clip-clopping towards you wouldn't look out of place as you pedal up the high street to the Mount Inn, with its views all the way to Wales on a clear day.

When you eventually manage to tear yourself away, cruise to Stanway, passing a lane lined with aged oaks that stand like pillars in an ancient Roman city. Here, too, there's a temptation to stop and stretch out on Stanway Manor's immaculately groomed lawns before you push on, to Hailes, past a fruit farm perfect for a strawberry-picking stop; save them to eat on top of the next hill (it's a big'un, but the view from the top will take your mind off those aching limbs). If it's late afternoon you'll see the sun bathing the nearby valley in a golden glow; it's enough to make you feel all warm about the world. More so when you realise you're three miles from Guiting.

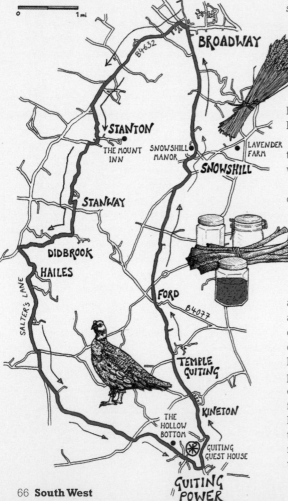

THE ROUTE

DISTANCE 22 MILES
DIFFICULTY ⬡⬡⬡⬡⬡
START **Guiting Guest House**
Post Office Lane, Guiting Power, GL54 5TZ

» Left out of Guiting Guest House down to a small grass triangle, ¼ mile away, opposite the gates of a big house: turn left.

» Follow this lane through Kineton and Temple Guiting until you reach the junction at Ford: go straight over the main road.

» Continue between the fields for 2½ miles, passing through Taddington, then reaching a junction: turn left for Snowshill.

» Go through the village (past Snowshill Manor) before dropping downhill for just over 2 miles, to arrive in Broadway.

» Turn left at the junction by the green.

» Turn left again after ¼ mile, on to the B4632, signposted Winchcombe.

» Follow this road for just over 2 miles, then turn left for Stanton.

» Go through Stanton, then left for Stanway.

» Continue through Stanway, and past the manor, until you reach a crossroads: go straight over, towards Didbrook.

» After just over a mile, at the junction with the B4632: turn left and immediately left.

» Pass through Hailes, climbing up the steep hill along Salter's Lane.

» At the top of Salter's Lane, turn left.

» Then turn right, signposted Guiting Power.

» Bear left at the fork after ¼ mile, towards Guiting Power.

» Follow the road for just under 3 miles, arriving back in Guiting Power.

STOP AND SEE

EN ROUTE

Snowshill Lavender Farm *Snowshill, Broadway, Worcestershire, WR12 7JY; 01386 854821; www.snowshill-lavender.co.uk*
Finding this place is easy. Just head right from the church in Snowshill village and look for the purple fields. The smell is incredible, and there's a rather nice café here, too, serving home-made cakes – made with lavender, of course.

Snowshill Manor *Snowshill, Broadway, Gloucestershire, WR12 7JU; 01386 852410; see www.nationaltrust.org.uk*
Beautiful 17th-century manor, housing a collection by eccentric former owner, Charles Wade. There are 22,000 fascinating items – from Samurai armour to old bicycles. Wonderful vistas from the gardens, too.

The Mount Inn *Stanton, nr Broadway, Worcestershire, WR12 7NE; 01386 584316; www.themountinn.co.uk*
Probably the best pub-garden view in England – looking out over cottage rooftops below, and all the way across to the Welsh Black Mountains.

OFF ROUTE

Lower Slaughter *Gloucestershire*
Yet another obscenely beautiful village; one in which traffic makes way for ducks crossing the road. The Old Mill is definitely worth nipping into for a home-made ice cream (butter crunch is a personal fave).

Sudeley Castle *Winchcombe, Gloucestershire, GL54 5JD; 01242 604244; www.sudeleycastle.co.uk*
Former residence of Henry VIII's surviving wife, Katherine Parr, this stately home has a history stretching back over a thousand years. Tour the house and view the amazing contemporary art collection in the gardens.

EAT, DRINK, SLEEP

Guiting Guest House *Post Office Lane, Guiting Power, Gloucestershire, GL54 5TZ; 01451 850470; www.guitingguesthouse.com*
This 16th-century former farmhouse has six rooms, and owners Barbara and Rob know the area inside out. They'll even make you a packed lunch for the ride.
Doubles from £70 per night.

The Cow Byre *Temple Guiting Manor, Temple Guiting, Gloucestershire, GL54 5RP; 01451 851862*
Beautifully restored barn in the grounds of a manor house, with one double bedroom. Heated stone floors and a private garden ensure luxury and seclusion after your ride. To make things super-easy, a parcel of eggs, butter, milk, and bread awaits you. £250 for two nights.

Mill Hay Country House *Snowshill Road, Broadway, Worcestershire, WR12 7JS; 01386 852498; www.millhay.co.uk*
Magnificent country house tucked away between Snowshill and Broadway, with three rooms. Roaring fires, an ancient rose garden, and a lake in the grounds. Bliss. Rooms from £129; adults only.

The Hollow Bottom *Guiting Power, Cheltenham, Gloucestershire, GL54 5UX; 01451 850392; www.hollowbottom.com*
Wood beams, open fires, and ruddy-cheeked punters from the racing scene form the backdrop here. Equestrian memorabilia adorns the walls, and the food is prepared by an ex-Claridges chef.

RENT

Cotswold Cycles *Longlands Farm Cottage, Chipping Campden, Gloucestershire, GL55 6LJ; 01386 438706; www.cotswoldcountrycycles.com*
This place stocks Dawes bikes – mountain bikes and hybrids with 24 gears. Locks, pumps, and toolkits included, for £15 a day.

SOUTH EAST

13

EAST END TO EAST BOLDRE

A weekend of Dire Straits and East Enders…

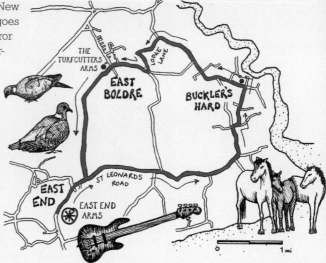

DESPITE ITS MISLEADING NAME, the New Forest is actually pretty ancient. In fact, it goes back to 1079, when William the Conqueror ring-fenced the area as his own private deer-hunting ground. Good thing he did, really, as it protected this vast stretch of England from future development – leaving intact a natural wonderland that's perfect for cycling.

Setting off from the East End Arms, the country pub owned by Dire Straits' bassist, John Illsley, you head right – down the narrow lane towards the hamlet of East End – emerging on to the village green. Forget your archetypal, manicured, cricket wicket-type green, however, and picture a patch of untamed heathland that thumbs its nose at the neatness of the surrounding cottages.

Making a right here, you will find yourself surrounded on both sides by head-high ferns, which quickly drop away to reveal ripe yellow wheat fields petering off into the distance. There are so few cars along here that the birds just hang out at the roadside, skittering around and chattering away to one another – sparrows, pigeons, and blackbirds – all busy doing nothing…

Pedalling further down the lane, you pass the ruins of a big old tithe barn on the edge of St Leonards Grange, which was run by Cistercian monks in the Middle Ages. Back then the barn was the biggest of its kind in England, and it still has a presence about it even now – its grey-stone walls weathered from centuries of wind, rain, and sun.

Swinging right, just along the road, you end up at another place that oozes history – this one with a maritime twist. Tucked away in a rabbit warren of lanes, Buckler's Hard is where many of the ships for Admiral Nelson's fleet were built in the early 1800s. And while it might seem, at first glance, like a rather random location for a boatyard, if you lock up the bikes and take a look around, you'll see that it's handily placed next to the River Beaulieu

(pronounced 'byu-ley'), which heads straight out into the English Channel.

Over the centuries, this peaceful waterway carried many warships off to battle – including landing craft for the D-Day invasion in the Second World War. Today, though, it's an open-air museum-cum-village, and you'll be glad you stopped by. Especially if you stay long enough to take a scenic boat ride along the river.

When you've had your fill of naval heritage, why not call in at the handily placed hotel along the lane – the Master Builder's house – where you can grab some lunch before getting back in the saddle.

Making your way slowly back towards East End, you come across gangs of horses lazing about on the verges, sunbathing – but no sign of the deer that William the Conqueror was so keen to pursue.

From here the route passes through East Boldre – where the Turfcutters Arms has a rather tempting garden if you feel like resting for a swift half; then it's on back to East End, in time for supper.

On the menu? Venison of course.

THE ROUTE

DISTANCE 9 MILES

DIFFICULTY ◐◐

START East End Arms *Lymington Road, East End, Hampshire, SO41 5SY*

» Head right, from the East End Arms, into East End, then take the first right – on to St Leonards Road.

» Follow this road for 2½ miles, passing St Leonards Grange, on your left, before taking the next right, for Buckler's Hard.

» After 200 metres, the road bends sharply left; keep following it until you see a turning on your right for Buckler's Hard.

» Continue, past the Buckler's Hard turning, for another 1½ miles, then take the second left, on to Lodge Lane, for East Boldre.

» The road bends left, around the graveyard; take the first turning right on to Cripple Gate Lane, signposted East Boldre.

» At the next junction, in East Boldre, turn left and follow the sign for East End (turn right if you want the Turfcutters Arms).

» Continue along this road for 2 miles, before reaching East End and retracing your route to the pub.

STOP AND SEE

EN ROUTE

Buckler's Hard *Beaulieu, Brockenhurst, Hampshire, SO42 7XB; 01590 616203; www.bucklershard.co.uk*

Aside from playing an important role in maritime history, this isolated village is also rather lovely to look at – two rows of red-brick cottages staring at each other across the village green. Once you've explored the museum itself (and the displays inside the cottages), why not take a stroll – or boat ride – along the river?

OFF ROUTE

Beaulieu Palace House *Brockenhurst, Hampshire, SO42 7ZN; 01590 612345; www.beaulieu.co.uk*

History buffs, petrolheads, and garden

geeks of all ages will love it here. The house dates back to the 13th century and is packed with furniture, paintings, and artefacts from many ages. There are interactive tours for youngsters, relaxing grounds – and a gleaming collection of cars in the National Motor Museum.

EAT, DRINK, SLEEP

East End Arms *Lymington Road, East End, Hampshire, SO41 5SY; 01590 626223; www.eastendarms.co.uk*

A proper country pub with a touch of rock 'n' roll. The only clues that this place is owned by a member of rock band, Dire Straits, are the black-and-white photos of fellow muso legends like John Lennon, Keith Wood, and Jimi Hendrix. The food is top notch (as is the service), and the five upstairs rooms feature flat-screen TVs and all the trimmings. Book room three for a great view of the sunset.
Doubles from £95 per night.

The Master Builder's *Buckler's Hard, Beaulieu Estate, Hampshire, SO42 7XB; 08448 153399; www.themasterbuilders.co.uk*

Nine individually styled rooms in the former home of shipbuilder Henry Adams

feature colourful spreads, rugs from Rajasthan, deep-red walls, and heavy wooden furniture. The restaurant below serves delicious dishes like slow-roasted Gressingham duck with bacon, peas, and fondant potato.
Doubles from £105 per night (two-night minimum bookings at weekends).

The Turfcutters Arms *Main Road, East Boldre, Hampshire, SO42 7WL; 01590 612331; www.theturfcutters.co.uk*

There are three self-contained apartments to choose from in the recently renovated barn, each with personal patio areas where you can sit back with a glass of vino and toast the remains of the day. If you're feeling peckish, try the pub's famous game bangers and mash.
Doubles from £70 per night.

RENT

Cyclexperience *2 Brookley Road, Brockenhurst, Hampshire, SO42 7RR; 01590 623407; www.cyclex.co.uk*

These guys stock bikes to suit all ages, abilities, and species – even dogs. They'll pick up and deliver, with bikes costing £14 per day, tandems £29.

PAGHAM HARBOUR TO WEST WITTERING

White-sand beaches and windsurfing in West Sussex...

STANDING ON THE BEACH at West Wittering, you have to keep reminding yourself that this is England. Pristine sand the texture of talcum powder stretches along the shore in both directions, and the blue-green sea delivers a constant supply of waves to keep the assembled wind- and kite-surfers happy. It's the kind of scenery you get in Florida's Gulf Islands or – more exotic still – Barbados (seriously).

Of course, the temperatures aren't quite as tropical in West Sussex, but the lifestyle is definitely as relaxed. The Witterings – both East and West – are renowned for having their own microclimate, creating a warm bubble of calm where you can escape the rest of the world for a while.

Getting to West Wittering from the Crab & Lobster pub in Pagham Harbour involves a five-mile jaunt through narrow back lanes, before you hang a left by the Old House at Home pub and take the ruler-straight road that leads to the beach.

Dudes and dudettes with windswept hair shuffle around in flip-flops, carrying various kinds of boards, while excited dogs wait for their owners to get within stroking range before shaking themselves free of sea water.

If you're feeling really energetic, why not book a paddle-boarding lesson with the guys at X-Train? Or you could just flop out on the sand and soak up some rays (as I did).

If you stay here too long, though, you'll miss out on some smooth-cruising lanes. Heading back out to the Old House at Home, you rejoin the route and pass the Beach House café (which does a mouth-watering crayfish and strawberry salad), before starting a long loop that eventually takes you back towards Pagham Harbour.

A few miles after leaving West Wittering you'll reach Itchenor, where the Ship Inn has tables outside that catch the afternoon sun. Walk to the harbour and the landscape opens out, giving you a cracking view over the Chichester Channel, with a flotilla of small sailing boats lying dead-still in the glassy water. They weren't exaggerating when they designated this place an Area of Outstanding Natural Beauty.

With the sun's shadows beginning to lengthen, you retrace your steps back out of Itchenor and on to quiet lanes once more. Thick, lush hedgerows on either side shelter you from the breeze, and a mile or so later you close the circle – rejoining the road you took from Pagham Harbour to Wittering a few sun-drenched hours ago.

Back at the Crab & Lobster, there's no question that you're back in good old Blighty; they don't serve fish and chips like this in Barbados.

THE SHIP INN · ITCHENOR · BIRDHAM · SHIPTON GREEN · B2179 · WEST WITTERING · HIGHLEIGH · ALMODINGTON · THE CRAB & LOBSTER · PAGHAM HARBOUR · THE BEACH! · EAST WITTERING · EARNLEY

0   1 mi

THE ROUTE

DISTANCE 18½ MILES

DIFFICULTY ○○○

START The Crab & Lobster

Mill Lane, Sidlesham, West Sussex, PO20 7NB

» Left out of the Crab & Lobster car park, then follow Mill Lane for ½ mile and turn right, towards Chichester, at the junction.

» Take the first left, signposted Highleigh.

» After less than a mile, take the third left (just after the school), for Earnley.

» Stay on this road for 1½ miles (still following Earnley signs) to a junction: turn left towards the Witterings.

» After ¾ mile, at Earnley, turn right at the grass triangle – towards the Witterings.

» After ½ mile, turn left at the junction, towards Wittering. Take the next right, on to Stocks Lane (after Middleton Close).

» Continue along Stocks Lane (left on to Cakeham Road if you want lunch at East Wittering), then Northern Crescent, then Oakenham Road into West Wittering.

» For the beach, turn left after the Old House at Home pub; the ride carries on round to the right, along Rookwood Road and on to the B2179 for the next 1½ miles.

» Turn left on to Itchenor Road at the crossroads, leaving the B2179.

» Bear left at the next junction, for Itchenor. Continue, to the waterfront, a mile away.

» From Itchenor, go back to the last junction; but don't fork right (back on to Itchenor Road), but follow the sign for Chichester and stay on the road as it sweeps left.

» After ¼ mile, at a junction with the B2179 again; bear left, signposted Chichester.

» At the roundabout, take the first exit.

» After almost a mile, turn right, towards Almodington and the Wild Bird Hospital.

» Take the next left, signposted Highleigh.

» Take the next right – towards Highleigh and Ham – past Sidlesham Primary School.

» Now simply retrace your route to the junction with the B2145, turn right towards Selsey, then left back to Pagham Harbour.

STOP AND SEE

EN ROUTE

West Wittering Beach

www.westwitteringbeach.co.uk

Whatever you fancy from your day at the beach – windsurfing, kite-surfing, or plain old paddling – this huge expanse of sand has everything you need (including a café within walking distance). It's renowned for visiting birdlife, too, so bring the binoculars.

The Ship Inn *The Street, Itchenor, Chichester, West Sussex, PO20 7AH; 01243 512284; www.theshipinnitchenor.co.uk*

A friendly pub serving a selection of local ales, including Ballard's Best Bitter and regular guest tipples. As you'd expect, with the estuary just five minutes' walk away, the seafood is as fresh as it gets – changing regularly depending on the day's catch.

OFF ROUTE

Salterns Way *see www.conservancy.co.uk (Click on 'Out & About' then 'Cycling'.)*

If you feel like getting back in the saddle, why not check out this 11-mile route that runs from East Head up to the centre of Chichester? It takes you along a mixture of quiet roads and cycle paths through protected countryside.

Chichester Harbour *01243 670504; www.chichesterharbourwatertours.co.uk*

Take to the water on the passenger boat *Wingate III*, for a 1½-hour cruise from Itchenor, which will give you a chance to explore the nooks and crannies of the natural harbour – all with a chirpy commentary, of course.

EAT, DRINK, SLEEP

The Crab & Lobster *Mill Lane, Sidlesham, West Sussex, PO20 7NB; 01243 641233; www.crab-lobster.co.uk*

Perched on the banks of Pagham Nature Reserve, this 350-year-old pub serves up delicious fresh-fish dishes like poached fillet of sea trout with lobster ravioli. Walk it off on one of the quiet paths that criss-cross the surrounding wetland, before heading back to your room for a soak.

Doubles from £140 per night.

The Beach House *Rookwood Road, West Wittering, Chichester, West Sussex, PO20 8LT; 01243 514800; www.beachhse.co.uk*

This family-run guest house, just a short cycle from the beach, has a 'holiday' vibe, with the front doors opening on to a small terrace with tables. The rooms are simple, smart, and fresh; the restaurant serves local seafood and other home-cooked dishes.

Doubles from £85 per night.

Landseer House *Cow Lane, Sidlesham, Chichester, West Sussex, PO20 7LN; 01243 641525; www.landseerhouse.co.uk*

You'll feel instantly relaxed as you take breakfast in the bright white conservatory overlooking the garden. Landseer is well-placed for country strolls (Pagham Harbour is walkable from here). Or opt for one of the self-contained cottages opposite...

Doubles from £90 per night.

RENT

Bike-Master *Unit 13, Polthooks Ind. Estate, Clay Lane, Chichester, West Sussex, PO18 8AH; 07944 302974; www.bike-master.co.uk*

There's a range of adult hybrids available for £18 per day; on request they'll deliver and collect them, too.

15

DITCHLING TO WIVELSFIELD GREEN

Off the beaten track in the shadow of Ditchling Beacon...

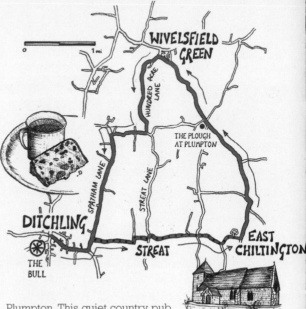

WHEREVER YOU GO around Ditchling, you're always under the watchful gaze of its eponymous Beacon. Rising up out of the surrounding flatland, this huge grassy mound makes it very difficult to get lost – even when you're ducking and diving along the network of narrow dirt tracks that whisk you away from the crowds.

Having left Ditchling village a couple of miles earlier and taken a swift left and right, you'll reach a dirt road, where cars dare not follow. Out here the bicycle is king, and as you glide effortlessly along the track, ears of golden corn growing in the fields on either side dip in a sweeping bow of regal acknowledgement.

Look to your right and you'll see the Beacon again, spotlit by the sun for your viewing pleasure. The track you're following extends for the next few miles, passing through the tiny hamlet of Streat and skirting along the edge of Plumpton Racecourse. Keep an ear out for the telltale thunder of hooves as you pass – if you need some encouragement to up the pace, the sound of a dozen racehorses pounding towards you generally does the trick...

Continue on to East Chiltington, where an old, weathered church signals your arrival back on to tarmac. Heading left, through the hamlet, you emerge out on to a wide, smooth lane that takes you all the way to Wivelsfield.

If you're wondering where the Beacon is, it's still there – on your left now as you reach the Plough at Plumpton. This quiet country pub comes just in the nick of time – a chunk of home-made cottage pie just the job for filling up those empty legs.

From here it's largely flat all the way to Wivelsfield Green, where you loop left and start the gentle downhill run back towards Ditchling. Poking above the trees in the distance you'll see the Beacon again; conveniently placed to guide you back to the village. In fact, it's hardly been out of your sight all day.

THE ROUTE

DISTANCE 15 MILES

DIFFICULTY ○○○

START The Bull

High Street, Ditchling, East Sussex, BN6 8TA

» Turn left out of the Bull car park, down Lewes Road, towards Ditchling Beacon, and take the second 'proper' (not dirt) track left, on to Spatham Lane (½ mile from Ditchling).

» After less than ¼ mile, take the right-hand fork on to the dirt road.

» Follow this track for a mile – bearing left at the first farm, then immediately right – continuing on (effectively straight) to Streat.

» At Streat you pass a church on your left, where the track sweeps left – momentarily on to tarmac; you then veer immediately right, rejoining the dirt road – even though it's signposted 'private road', there is public access (don't veer left up Streat Lane).

» After ½ mile, the edge of Plumpton Racecourse is to your left, and the track becomes tarmac. Shortly after, you reach a junction: turn right, then immediately left (effectively straight on).

» You follow this track for ½ mile, until it stops at a junction next to a church. Turn left and follow the lane to the next junction, with the red telephone box – about ¼ mile away.

» Turn left and follow the lane for 3 miles (passing the Plough), until you reach a mini roundabout at Wivelsfield Green. Take the first exit, on to Hundred Acre Lane.

» After 1¼ miles, you reach a junction: turn right – towards Ditchling.

» After ½ mile, turn left on to Spatham Lane – signposted Mid Sussex Golf Club.

» Stay on this road for nearly 2 miles (passing the track you took to Streat, on your left), until reaching the junction with the B2116. Turn right, back to Ditchling.

STOP AND SEE

EN ROUTE

The Plough at Plumpton *Plumpton Green, Lewes, East Sussex, BN7 3DF; 01273 890311;*

www.theploughatplumpton.co.uk

The original Plough pub was an old airfield hut located at the end of the runway at nearby RAF Chailey. But there's nothing like a Spitfire attempting to land just above your roof to spoil a good pint, so it was moved to this spot in 1943. The hut has been replaced by something more pub-like on the outside, but the beer's just as good.

Ditchling Tea Rooms *6–8 West Street, Ditchling, East Sussex, BN6 8TS; 01273 842708; www.ditchlingtearooms.co.uk*

While you could come here for breakfast or lunch, the cream teas are what I love about this place. Go for the Ditchling De-Luxe – besides the requisite scone you also get to choose a cream cake…

OFF ROUTE

Lewes *East Sussex*

Fancy a bit of history before lunch? Start at the castle (01273 486290), which dates back to around 1066, nip over to Anne of Cleves House (built in the 15th century, it formed part of Anne's divorce settlement from Henry VIII; see www.sussexpast.co.uk), and top it all off with a look around the ruins of Lewes Priory (www.lewespriory.org.uk). If you're here on the first Saturday of the month, there's a farmers' market selling local treats.

Glynde Place *Glynde, East Sussex, BN8 6SX; 01273 858224; see www.glynde.co.uk*

Not to be confused with Glyndebourne – home of the eponymous opera festival just along the road – this splendid country house dates back over 400 years. As you'd expect, it's packed with treasures, and the view from the gardens looks out over Sussex. Enjoy the peace, quiet, and great cups of tea, too.

EAT, DRINK, SLEEP

The Bull *High Street, Ditchling, East Sussex, BN6 8TA; 01273 843147;*

www.thebullditchling.com

Slap bang in the heart of Ditchling village, this stylish pub, with its four smart rooms, is the ideal base for a weekend of cycling and eating. The restaurant menu changes daily; cross your fingers that the chicken and ham-hock pie is on – it's dee-lish. Doubles from £80 per night.

Tovey Lodge *Underhill Lane, Ditchling, East Sussex, BN6 8XE; 08456 120544; www.sussexcountryholidays.co.uk*

To go for a swim, relax in the sauna, or jump into the hot-tub? This will be the tricky decision you'll face when you return from your ride. Tovey Lodge has five rooms to choose from (three suites and two doubles), and a sumptuous lounge to chill out in, too. Doubles from £70 per night.

The White Horse *16 West Street, Ditchling, East Sussex, BN6 8TS; 01273 842006; whitehorseditchling.com*

This place has a rather dubious history… Dating back to the 12th century, it houses a network of tunnels in the cellar that's thought to have been used by smugglers. Thankfully it's all above board nowadays – you won't find any contraband stashed away – and, if you're booking into one of the seven rooms, it's extremely comfy, too. En suite doubles from £85 per night.

RENT

Hassocks Community Cycle Hire *The Hassocks, Station Approach East, Hassocks, East Sussex, BN6 8HN; 07521 961909; www.visithassocks.co.uk*

This locally run cycle-hire scheme is based handily (for those arriving by train) in the grounds of the pub right next to Hassocks station. There are childrens' and adults' bikes available – the latter costing from £25 a day – all come with helmets included. Phoning ahead is recommended; closed Monday and Tuesday.

16

STAPLECROSS TO BODIAM CASTLE

Magnificent views and stately castles...

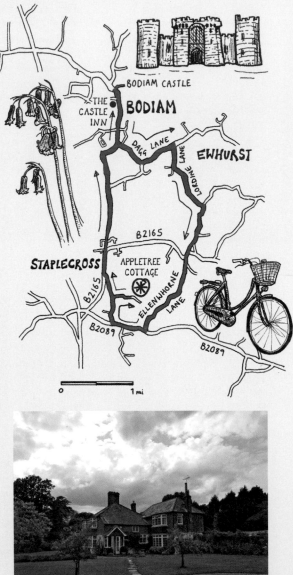

FROM THE FRONT BEDROOMS at Appletree Cottage you can see for miles across the East Sussex countryside. Sunshine pours into the rooms all afternoon, but by that time you'll probably be sunbathing in the grounds of nearby Bodiam Castle...

Head along the track from the cottage and join Beacon Lane, where a high hedge and bluebell-speckled verge sets the scenic tone for the day. The road takes you down to Staplecross, where you leave it to pass chalk-white cottages en route to Bodiam.

Squeezing between steep, rocky banks on either side, the road eventually drops down to reveal the castle up ahead, its turrets and battlements still in immaculate condition and begging for exploration.

As you cross the drawbridge you'll see ducks bobbing about in the moat beneath. From the tops of the four towers, the views are a match for those at Appletree Cottage – swathes of woodland and hills stretching out before you. After soaking up the views and atmosphere inside the courtyard, imagining what medieval life must have been like here, it's time to whip out the picnic blanket and work your way through the papers for a few hours, as the little ones run around on the immaculately groomed lawns.

And, when you feel like getting up, you can take a boat trip along to nearby Newenden – or jump back on the bike and head back the way you came for half a mile, before swinging left and climbing gently up into Ewhurst. Soon you're gliding effortlessly down Lordine Lane, where fields on your right fall away into a small valley, reappearing almost a mile away with the trees on the ridgeline silhouetted against the late-afternoon sun. Keep your camera handy over the next few miles; the jaw-dropping views just keep coming. Following a fairly straight course, you pass through copses and alongside little paddocks, emerging on to the main (not particularly busy) road back to the turning for Beacon Lane. Breeze up the hill and spend the rest of the day doing your best impression of a starfish on the enormous lawn at Appletree Cottage.

THE ROUTE

DISTANCE   9½ MILES
DIFFICULTY   ○○○
START   Appletree Cottage

Beacon Lane, Staplecross, TN32 5QP

» Turn right out of Appletree Cottage and head down the track to the road.

» Turn right and pedal to the junction ¼ mile away: join the B2165 and continue straight on, into Staplecross village.

» After ¼ mile, fork left, for Bodiam Castle.

» After 2 miles, descend to Bodiam Castle.

» Turn left out of Bodiam Castle's grounds and retrace your route back to Dagg Lane. Turn left on to Dagg Lane.

» Climb gently for less than a mile, turning left at the junction, towards Ewhurst Green.

» Enter the village around ¼ mile later, and turn right on to Lordine Lane.

» Just under a mile later, turn right on to Sempstead Lane.

» At the junction, after ½ mile, briefly join the B2165 again, then take the first left on to Ellenwhorne Lane.

» After a mile you reach a junction with the B2089. Turn right and pedal for less than ½ mile, then go right, on to Beacon Lane.

» Ride uphill until you reach the entrance to the dirt track leading to Appletree Cottage.

STOP AND SEE

EN ROUTE

Bodiam Castle *Bodiam, East Sussex, TN32 5UA; 01580 830196; see www.nationaltrust.org.uk*
This place is like something straight out of *Dungeons & Dragons*. Built in 1385, it has survived the years with grace. Admire the towers, moat, and long-distance views of the countryside before picnicking on the grass outside and boating on the river.

The Castle Inn *Bodiam, East Sussex, TN32 5UB; 01580 830330; www.thecastleinnbodiam.com*
Red-brick pub in Bodiam village, across the road from the castle. There's a great beer garden out the back, or why not sit outside, next to the village green, with a pint of Spitfire or Thatchers Gold cider, and watch the chickens strutting around on the grass?

Kent and East Sussex Railway *01580 765155; www.kesr.org.uk*
You don't have to be an anorak to love these big old locomotives. There's a huge range of trains here – from steam-powered beasts to more modern engines. And you can get a ticket to ride on over 10 miles of track.

OFF ROUTE

Sissinghurst Castle Garden *Biddenden Road, nr Cranbrook, Kent, TN17 2AB; 01580 710701; see www.nationaltrust.org.uk*
Romantic, peaceful garden that's ablaze with colour all year long. Built around an Elizabethan mansion, it offers tons of nooks and crannies where you can tuck yourself away with a picnic and forget the world.

EAT, DRINK, SLEEP

Appletree Cottage *Beacon Lane, Staplecross, East Sussex, TN32 5QP; 01580 831724; www.appletreecottagestaplex.com*
Warm, sunny rooms, gorgeous views, and an enormous back garden... Originally two farmers' cottages built in around 1820, they were subsequently knocked into one. An incredibly peaceful spot.
Doubles for £80 per night.

Woodside *Junction Road, Staplecross, Robertsbridge, East Sussex, TN32 5SG; 01580 830903; www.woodsidebandb.com*
Choose between two quirky but well-kitted-out rooms. The Gothic Suite features a seven-foot waterbed, en suite bathroom with free-standing slipper bath, and goodies including chocolates, flowers, and fluffy bathrobes. Meanwhile, the Cream Room has a king-sized double bed and ornately decorated bathroom. There's a home cinema, and in-house massage options. Doubles from £90 per night.

Slides Farm *Silverhill, Robertsbridge, East Sussex, TN32 5PA; 01580 880106; www.slidesfarm.com*
Two spacious, contemporary rooms in a self-contained wing, with a west-facing terrace that's ideal for a post-ride tea in the afternoon sun. They do their own cider here, too, and after a day of fresh air you get to curl up in Egyptian cotton sheets. Divine. Doubles from £80 per night.

The Curlew Restaurant *Junction Road, Bodiam, East Sussex, TN32 5UY; 01580 861394; www.thecurlewrestaurant.co.uk*
Smart eatery run by Mark and Sara Colley, with dishes like Barbary duck breast with rhubarb, fennel, and goats' cheese on the menu; a wonderful wine list; and good beers.

The Station House *Station Road, Northiam, Rye, East Sussex, TN31 6QT; 01797 252116; www.stationhousenorthiam.co.uk*
Friendly village pub less than four miles from Appletree Cottage, serving locally sourced beers and food. Try the slow-cooked New Romney lamb.

RENT

Rye Hire *1 Cyprus Place, Rye, East Sussex, TN31 7DR; 01797 223033; see www.ryesussex.co.uk*
A good selection of all-terrain bikes and equipment. An adult's bike costs £12 a day.

HELPFUL HINT

Bring a picnic blanket so you can stretch out on the grass at Bodiam Castle.

17

OLD WIVES LEES TO FAVERSHAM

An enchanted wood, a hidden pub, and a quick stop at a cider farm…

THERE'S A LOT MORE to this part of Kent than meets the eye, as you'll discover when you walk through the door of Pond Cottage. Beyond its archetypal rustic red-brick veneer you'll find a sumptuously decorated spacious room – inspired by owner Jude Adams' travels in India. With its lavish turquoise bedspreads and luxury drapes, it feels like you've entered an exotic boudoir – even more so when you spy the hot tub in the terraced garden.

The surrounding countryside has some surprises in store, too. Head left out of the drive and it's not long before you reach a striking Tudor house – all white wattle and daub walls and black beams – where you veer off and find yourself in an enchanting wood.

Cruising through the labyrinth of trees, it feels like you're entering a Lewis Carroll story. Blackbirds scratch about in the leaf litter, squirrels leap across the road ahead, and all you can hear are birds twittering about in the branches overhead. And, as a final idyllic flourish, the floor is awash with bluebells.

With all this magical scenery around, you might think the ride has already peaked, but then you emerge from the woods and bank left to reach a pub. At the Rose & Crown, Tim Robinson serves up a range of real ales – from Adnams Bitter to Harvey's Sussex Best. The beer garden is bordered by woodland and, if you fancy ditching the bikes and heading off on foot for a while, Tim (or wife Vanessa) can recommend some great walks.

Back in the saddle, you carry on from the pub and out into open fields – the lane winding its way towards the village of Sheldwich and beyond. Come summer, everything around here is coated in colour; yellow rape-flower fields, bordered by lush green verges, while the sky is populated by fluffy clouds, blown straight in from the sea.

Crossing the main road after Sheldwich, you cruise past a couple of farms and drop down through woodland, before a steepish climb takes you up into Painters Forstal. A refreshing drink awaits at the Alma pub, so grab a table in the little garden and smell the fresh air – tinged with the scent of freshly cut grass.

Cider-heads might prefer to keep going and stop for a drop at Pawley Farm, where owner Derek Macey will give you a quick tour and tasting session (if you ask nicely). There are 50 acres of orchards, which burst into white and pink blossom every spring; in September you can watch the apples being pressed.

You're now only a couple of miles from Faversham, where the medieval marketplace is lined with tea shops, restaurants, and pubs. Try the pork-pie ploughman's at Purple Peach – it's immense.

On the return leg, a conveyor belt of hop gardens and apple orchards scrolls by on either side, before you arrive back outside the Tudor house. It's now a countdown to hot-tub time at magical Pond Cottage.

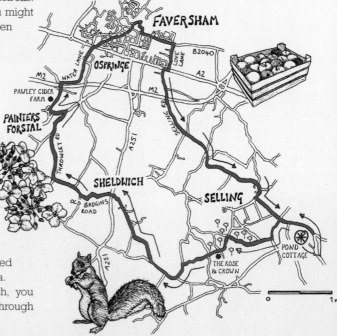

THE ROUTE

DISTANCE	16½ MILES
DIFFICULTY	○○○
START	Pond Cottage

Selling Road, Old Wives Lees, Kent, CT4 8BD

» Turn left out of Pond Cottage and follow the lane for ½ mile to a crossroads (Tudor house on your left): turn left, for Selling.

» After ¼ mile, turn right (farmhouse on your left) and enter the woods.

» Turn left at the crossroads after ½ mile, just after the visitors' car park on your right.

» Pass the Rose & Crown and drop downhill to a staggered crossroads: go straight over (signposted Badlesmere).

» After ½ mile you reach a fork: turn right for Badlesmere and Sheldwich.

» Continue downhill and as the road swings right make sure you follow it – don't veer off straight. Traversing a little valley, you climb up into Sheldwich after 1½ miles.

» Cross over the junction with the A251 at the end of the village, into Old Badgins Road.

» Carry on for ¼ mile to the next junction: turn right on to Wilgate Green Road.

» After ¼ mile, descend a steep hill to a junction: turn right on to Throwley Road.

» Just over a mile later (at the second fork in the road) turn left – doubling back on yourself – uphill into Painters Forstal.

» Go through the village, past the Alma pub, and Pawley Farm on your left.

» Cross the motorway and at Water Lane turn right and head downhill.

» Continue through Ospringe. Less than a mile later you reach a junction with the A2: turn right, then first left (into Ospringe Road).

» Ospringe Road soon becomes South Road; follow the one-way system, past the brewery, as it takes you around 180 degrees, via Conduit Street and Quay Lane, to a junction: turn right, into Court Street.

» Passing the marketplace (ahead of you as the road bends left), you reach a crossroads with traffic lights: turn left, on to East Street.

» Follow this road (as it becomes Whitstable Road) for just over ½ mile, to a mini roundabout: turn right, on to Love Lane (following signs for Canterbury/Whitstable).

» After ¼ mile turn right at the junction with the A2. Then first left – on to Selling Road.

» Continue for 2½ miles, through Gushmere.

» As the road bends round right, take the second left, signposted Chartham/Chilham.

» After ½ mile you'll pass the Tudor house; then carry on for ¼ mile to Pond Cottage.

STOP AND SEE

EN ROUTE

The Rose & Crown *Perry Wood, Selling, nr Faversham, Kent, ME13 9RY; 01227 752214; www.roseandcrownperrywood.co.uk*
Hidden away in a secretive wood ringed by narrow country lanes, the Rose & Crown has some tasty ales, a beautiful garden, and does a mean steak and ale pie.

The Alma *Painters Forstal, Kent, ME13 0DU; 01795 533835; www.shepherd-neame.co.uk*
Dating back to 1837, this white, wooden-walled pub is the perfect place to stop for a pint or a bite. Brewery-owned it might be, but it's rich in character and serves delicious beer (try the Early Bird ale) that goes down a treat in the pretty garden.

Pawley Farm *Painters Forstal, Kent, ME13 0EN; 01795 532043*
An old farm on the outskirts of the village, where Derek Macey and his family have been making traditional cider and apple juice for decades. Stop for a tour or a tasting session (best to ring ahead).

Shepherd Neame Brewery *17 Court Street, Faversham, Kent, ME13 7AX; 01795 542016; www.shepherd-neame.co.uk*
Beer has been produced here for over 850 years, and on this fascinating (and thirst-quenching) tour, you'll begin in a beautifully restored medieval hall before heading into the brewery's inner sanctum.

OFF ROUTE

Canterbury *Kent*
Explore the iconic cathedral, cobbled roads, and medieval houses of this historic city.

EAT, DRINK, SLEEP

Pond Cottage *Selling Road, Old Wives Lees, Kent, CT4 8BD;* 07795 424070; *www.pondstays.com*
Original features blend with modern touches (including the garden hot-tub), and the breakfasts are superb – ask Jude to whip up a smoothie.
Doubles from £170 for two nights (min. stay).

Selgrove *Porters Lane, Sheldwich, Faversham, Kent, ME13 0DP; 01795 591081; www.favershambandb.co.uk*
Red-brick family home in pretty Sheldwich. Two smart en suite rooms to choose from with tranquil views over fields and gardens. Doubles from £75 per night.

Church Oast *Hernhill, Faversham, Kent, ME13 9JW; 01227 750974; www.churchoast.co.uk*
Run by Jill and Brian Geliot, this cute B&B lies on Hernhill's village green. It was originally an oast house for drying hops that made local beer. Three rooms to choose from with views over the village or the gardens. A tad twee.
Doubles from £80.

Purple Peach *1 Market Place, Faversham, Kent ME13 7AG; 01795 537927*
Colourful corner café in the centre of Faversham serving cream teas, delicious home-made pies, and sandwiches.

RENT

Downland Cycles *The Malthouse, St Stephens Road, Canterbury, Kent, CT2 7JA; 01227 479643; www.downlandcycles.co.uk*
A good range of bikes available. An adult bike costs £15 a day. Book in advance.

18

DEAL TO RINGWOULD

Sea views, seafood, and sea air…

SMART ROOMS, GOURMET BREAKFASTS, and the seafront less than a minute's walk away: these are just some of the aspects you'll love about Number One. In addition there are flat-screen TVs, gadget-tastic coffee machines, and a clutch of great bars and restaurants on the doorstep. My favourite thing about staying here, however, is that it puts you in pole position for a great cycle ride that starts at the end of the street.

Pedal to the waterfront and head right along the cycle path, past a collection of weathered old fishing boats beached on the gravel. Shortly after setting off you'll pass Henry VIII's impressive artillery fort, Deal Castle, perched right by the waterfront and ready to defend the country against any invaders. Save a visit until later; for now the path takes you out of the town, past pastel-coloured beach houses lined up opposite the shore. Glance left and you'll see ferries on the horizon – chugging their way across the Channel to France.

The cycle path ends after a mile or so, but before you disappear into the lanes there are a couple of pubs worth poking your nose into. Scruffy exterior aside, the Zetland Arms serves a mean pint of Speckled Hen and boasts uninterrupted sea views from the benches outside. The nearby Rising Sun can also be filed under 'no frills', but stocks good beers and has cute clapboard walls.

Heading inland you join the little road that leads up through the village of Kingsdown and out on to open fields – which are ablaze with yellow rape flowers each spring. Dropping down to the main road, you go straight over a staggered crossroads and cruise into Ringwould, passing idyllic white cottages before emerging on to open farmland once more – a strip of sea just visible on the horizon ahead.

Making a right after the village, you skirt between fields and cross a level crossing. You're back on the fringes of Deal; a mile or so from now you'll emerge into town – conveniently just opposite the castle.

THE ROUTE

DISTANCE 7 MILES

DIFFICULTY ◐◐

START Number One B&B

1 Ranelagh Road, Deal, Kent, CT14 7BG

» From Number One, head down to the waterfront and, with the sea in front of you, take a right.

» Follow the cycle path along the seafront to the end (about 1½ miles), where you have to turn right on to Cecil Road.

» At its end, turn left on to Kingsdown Road.

» Follow this past the Rising Sun pub, round to the right and uphill into Kingsdown.

» Continue through the village and round to the right, to a junction with the A258.

» Cross the main road (going left and immediately right) and on into Ringwould.

» Follow Church Lane as it bends left, right, and left – then go right, on to Sutton Street.

» After leaving the village, take the first right, back towards Deal.

» After ¼ mile, go straight over the crossroads, towards Deal.

» Keep going for another ¼ mile until reaching a level crossing: go straight on.

» After ¼ mile, go over the crossroads on to Cross Road.

» After another ¼ mile, go straight over the staggered crossroads on to Mill Hill.

» Mill Hill turns into Mill Road. Shortly after, the road bends round to the right – but you keep straight on, along Mill Road.

» At the end of Mill Road turn right – on to Park Avenue.

» Park Avenue becomes Gilford Road, and brings you back to Deal – by the castle.

STOP AND SEE

EN ROUTE

Zetland Arms *Wellington Parade, Kingsdown, Kent, CT14 8AF; 01304 364888*
Located conveniently at the end of the seafront cycle path, the Zetland is a little scruffy on the outside but serves a good pint – and even better sea views.

Deal Castle *Marine Road, Deal, Kent, CT14 7BA; 01304 372762; see www.english-heritage.org.uk*
A coastal Tudor artillery fort built by Henry VIII for defending England against invasions. Take a look around and see how cramped conditions were for the soldiers inside – and how fabulous the sea views are from the battlements.

Walmer Castle *Kingsdown Road, Deal, Kent, CT14 7LJ; 01304 364288; see www.english-heritage.org.uk*
Another Tudor castle; this one is surrounded by gorgeous gardens.

OFF ROUTE

South Foreland Lighthouse *The Front, St Margaret's Bay, Dover, Kent, CT15 6HP; 01304 852463; see www.nationaltrust.org.uk*
A couple of miles' stroll along the cliff-top path near the Zetland Arms brings you to this lovely old lighthouse – with stunning vistas out over the Channel. They don't make 'em like this any more.

EAT, DRINK, SLEEP

Number One B&B *1 Ranelagh Road, Deal, Kent, CT14 7BG; 01304 364459; www.numberonebandb.co.uk*
Four smart, funky rooms with flat-screen TVs, Nespresso coffee machines, and iPod docks. Near the seafront. Bike storage, too.
Doubles from £75 per night.

Beaches *34 The Strand, Walmer, Kent, CT14 7DX; 01304 369692; www.beaches.uk.com*
Two fresh white rooms that blend period character with classy modern touches and amazing views.
Doubles from £80 per night.

The Royal Hotel *Beach Street, Deal, Kent, CT14 6JD; 01304 375555; www.theroyalhotel.com*
A throwback to the grand old days of travelling, the peach-coloured Royal Hotel has kept a watchful eye over the seafront since the early 1700s. Book 'Wellington', with its roll-top bath in the room.
Doubles from £100 per night.

The Bohemian *47 Beach Street, Deal, Kent, CT14 6HY; 01304 374843; www.bohemianbythesea.com*
Soak up the sun in the back garden with a pint of Aspall Cyder or Gadds' local ale.

81 Beach Street *81 Beach Street, Deal, Kent, CT14 6JB; 01304 368136; 81beachstreet.co.uk*
Delicious food and tons of character. The menu changes all the time, but there's always great fish – most of it local.

RENT

V's Emporium *30 Mill Hill, Deal, Kent, CT14 9EW; 01304 366080*
Bikes to suit all sizes and styles here. Adult's bike for £15 a day. They'll deliver, too.

AROUND LONDON

19

DORKING TO COLDHARBOUR

Tasty tipples among the Surrey Hills…

FLOURISHING VINEYARDS less than an hour from London? Yeah, right. This was my initial reaction on discovering Denbies Wine Estate, but as you pedal off from the farmhouse B&B tucked away in its grounds, it's only a matter of seconds before you catch your first glimpse of the vines – laden with juicy red and white grapes.

Bouncing along the dirt track, the air humming to the tune of grasshoppers, you reach a gate at the end and follow the small section of bridleway to the edge of Dorking. Here, a quick wiggle right and left has you freewheeling down to a junction at the edge of the high street. Go left if you fancy nipping into town for a cuppa at the Courtyard Café; or continue right – towards the scenic stuff.

A mile and a half later you're in the pretty village of Westcott – home to fabled shop, Nirvana Cycles. This place really lives up to its name, so you might find it a struggle to drag yourself (nose and palms pressed against the windows) away, and up the sloping Logmore Lane. Beyond the church the road gets narrower and blackberry bushes move in on either side, dangling their wares in a tempting bid for you to stop and sample. On your right, wooded hills fall away into the distance, but before long trees enfold you and it feels like you're entering a secret world – far away from nine-to-five stress.

After a couple of miles of intermittent climbs and let-it-all-go descents, you turn right towards Coldharbour, pedalling up between steeply sculpted rocky banks on either side; spindly silver birch trees standing out against the rust-brown leaf litter. At the outskirts of Coldharbour you can't help but stop to fantasise about which of the little cottages you'd like to live in: the red-brick, the clapboard, or the whitewashed stone – it's hard to choose. Especially with their bird's-eye view down through the wooded valley to the hills you passed on your way up to Westcott.

After a well-earned lunch stop at Coldharbour's Plough Inn, where they brew their own – bizarrely named – beer (Tallywacker or Crooked Furrow, anyone?), you re-enter the woods. Tall, thick trees with rusty-red trunks surround you and tower overhead – you could almost be among sequoias in the deep forests of North America, but for glimpses of Sussex unfolding through the gaps.

There's a gentle climb before you duck right and follow the sign for Broadmoor. This is where the fun starts: over the next mile the road drops downhill, giving you an awesome build up of speed as you zip between the trees and high hedgerows.

If you're feeling parched you could always call in at the Wotton Hatch pub (on your left at the junction) before turning right for Westcott. But once you reach the village, getting back to Denbies is a cinch; just go back the way you came and before long you'll be stretching out in the garden at the B&B, watching the sun go down over those vines.

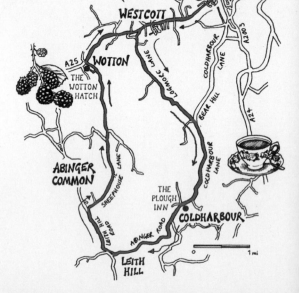

THE ROUTE

DISTANCE	16 MILES
DIFFICULTY	○○○○
START	Denbies Wine Estate

London Road, Dorking, Surrey, RH5 6AA
» Head right out of Denbies Farmhouse and take the first left along the track.
» When this bends right, ¼ mile along, carry straight on, along the grass to the gate.
» Go through the gate and keep going straight along the bridleway, until you emerge on to Yew Tree Road.
» Turn right at the next junction, then left immediately on to Chalkpit Lane. This drops downhill and becomes Station Road; at the end turn right, on to Westcott Road (A25).
» At the traffic lights go straight on, to Westcott village (stick to the path if you don't fancy the road).
» Just past the village green, take the third left, on to Westcott Heath, which quickly becomes Logmore Lane.
» Follow this for just over 1½ miles, then turn right at the junction, on to Coldharbour Lane and into Coldharbour after 1½ miles.
» From here you follow the road out of the village and take the first fork right, signposted Leith Hill car parks.
» Keep right at the next fork, following the signs for Abinger Common and Wotton.
» After ¼ mile, turn right for Broadmoor.
» At the next fork (¼ mile later), keep right – following the sign for Wotton.
» Continue, climbing up to the junction with the A25, next to the Wotton Hatch pub.
» Turn right, and follow this road through Westcott and on to Dorking. (Use the path on your left if you feel more comfortable.)
» At the traffic lights at Dorking, turn left and retrace your steps back to Denbies.

STOP AND SEE

EN ROUTE
Nirvana Cycles *5 The Green, Guildford Road, Westcott, Surrey, RH4 3NR; 01306 740300; www.nirvanacycles.com*

This place stocks some serious mountain bikes. Since it opened in 1995, Nirvana has gained near legendary status as an essential stop-off for cyclists from all over Britain. Even if you're not in line for a new steed, staff will happily point you in the direction of some gnarly local trails.

The Plough Inn *Coldharbour, Surrey, RH5 6HD; 01306 711793; www.ploughinn.com*
Located on the edge of the woods, this diminutive village boozer serves up a range of beers brewed on site, as well as Biddenden cider. The food's not bad, either.

OFF ROUTE
Leith Hill Tower *nr Coldharbour, Surrey; 01306 712711; see www.nationaltrust.org.uk*
This turreted Gothic tower, built between 1764 and 1765, made Leith Hill the highest point in south-east England (depending on who you talk to). Trivia aside, the view is worth the stroll up through the woods: on a clear day you can see all the way to the English Channel. And that's indisputable.

EAT, DRINK, SLEEP
Denbies Wine Estate *London Road, Dorking, Surrey, RH5 6AA; 01306 876616; www.denbies.co.uk*
There was a time when English wine drew sniggers from ruddy-nosed wine snobs.

Not any more. This tranquil 265-acre site produces wines that have rivalled famous French fizzes, and if you book a room at the onsite B&B, you could spend the weekend finding out what makes it so quaffable. There are seven rooms to choose from (number three has the best view), and a fine dining restaurant round the corner. Doubles from £95 per night.

The Brow *Fulvens, Peaslake, Surrey, GU5 9PG; 01306 730434; see www.bedandbreakfast-directory.co.uk*
This basic but sunny en suite bedroom, above a clapboard house in the beautiful village of Peaslake, is within walking distance of a pub (the Hurtwood Inn) and the prettiest (probably) village shop in England. There are some superb walks through the surrounding woods, and you're only a short ride away from our cycle route. From £60 per night.

RENT
Nirvana Cycles *(See 'Stop and See' for contact details.)*
There's a fleet of Giant Terrago mountain bikes available for £25 a day, which will give you the choice of staying on the road or trying out some of the North Downs' famous trails. Each bike comes with a pump, inner tube, and puncture repair kit.

20

ALDBURY TO FRITHSDEN

Canal boats, a castle, and a hidden vineyard…

IT'S A MIDWEEK AFTERNOON at the Alford Arms in Frithsden, and the tables outside are drenched in sunshine. For the lucky punters sat soaking it up, life doesn't get much better.

This quiet Victorian pub is one of those watering holes that you tend to find by accident. Tucked away in a shallow, tree-covered valley near Berkhamsted, it's the kind of place where people give you a friendly, knowing look when you arrive – as if welcoming you in on their little secret. At least that's how it felt when I coasted to a halt, after the five-mile ride from Aldbury.

Having left the Greyhound Inn just after lunch – another pub in an obscenely picturesque location – a bit of huffing and puffing had taken me up Toms Hill Road and out on to the top, where I'd eventually

peeled off right, into the Ashridge Estate. This leafy 5,000-acre park fills you with gratitude for the National Trust. Located only 20 miles from the sprawling chaos of London, it could so easily have been swallowed up by hungry developers. Thanks to the Trust, though, that hasn't happened, so as you cruise through the estate it's good to pause for a grateful second and tune in to the sounds of birdsong filling the canopy overhead.

Pedalling on past the house itself, which dates back to 1813 – all neo-Gothic crenellated walls and steeply arched windows – you leave the estate and drop downhill through the trees. At the bottom you bank left and ride along the valley, pulling up at the Alford Arms for a leisurely thirst-quencher. If you're hankering after a glass of vino, try the Solaris – a cool, crisp zero-wine-miles white produced by the bijou vineyard just behind the pub.

Recharged and refreshed, you'll find the climb up out of Frithsden a doddle; it's then a flat run to the edge of Berkhamsted, where you swoop downhill to the canal. Just before you reach this you could peel off right for a quick look at the castle. All that remain are its evocative ruins but, trust me, this place has some serious history. The building was commissioned by William the Conqueror in 1066, but in the 12th century Thomas Becket called the place home – as did Geoffrey Chaucer, 200 years later.

There's plenty of time to ponder what they would have thought of 21st-century 'Berko' while you're pootling along the canal, its towpath leading you back into greenery. Inland waterways inspire relaxation – partly because narrowboats have a top speed akin to a baby's crawl. But it's about the stillness of the water, too, and the simplicity of the lifestyle. By the time you peel off it and back to Aldbury, there's no question: life doesn't get much better than this.

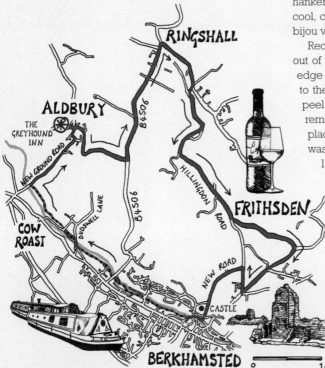

THE ROUTE

DISTANCE 15 MILES

DIFFICULTY ⭘⭘⭘

START The Greyhound Inn

Stocks Road, Aldbury, Hertfordshire, HP23 5RT

» Turn right out of the Greyhound Inn and head to the junction (keeping the pond on your right): now turn left, on to Toms Hill Road to leave Aldbury.

» Follow the hill up to the junction at the top: turn left towards Dagnall.

» Stay on this road for nearly 2 miles, until you see a turning on your right, signposted Ashridge College. Turn right here.

» About a mile later, take another right-hand turning for Ashridge College (by the memorial).

» Continue on the road through the Ashridge Estate, passing the college and dropping downhill, until you see a turning signposted Frithsden: swing left here.

» After almost a mile you'll pass the Alford Arms and arrive at a junction shortly after: turn right, towards Berkhamsted.

» You'll reach a crossroads after a mile: turn right, towards Berkhamsted.

» Take the next left, for Berkhamsted.

» This is New Road; follow it downhill, into Berkhamsted, under the railway bridge then right on the other side, on to Lower Kings Road. (If you want to visit the castle, turn right just before the bridge.)

» Shortly after, cross the bridge over the canal on your left and turn right, down the ramp and on to the towpath.

» Follow the towpath – with the canal on your right – for the next 3 miles.

» At Dudswell Lane – after 2 miles – you cross over the bridge and continue along on the towpath on the right of the canal.

» At the second bridge (about a mile later), you bear right to leave the towpath – and turn right at the road.

» This road takes you back to Aldbury – a mile away – past the Valiant Trooper pub.

STOP AND SEE

EN ROUTE

The Ashridge Estate *On the Hertfordshire/ Buckinghamshire border, between Aylesbury and Hemel Hempstead; see www.nationaltrust.org.uk*

There's much more to this peaceful estate than just trees. Why not take a stroll along the woodland trails, keeping an eye out for the resident fallow deer, then climb the Bridgewater Monument, where you can look out over the Chilterns?

The Alford Arms *Frithsden, nr Hemel Hempstead, Hertfordshire, HP1 3DD; 01442 864480; www.alfordarmsfrithsden.co.uk*

This sun-kissed 19th-century pub has an extensive wine list – including a couple of varieties from the vineyard next door. The food's good too, try the slow-roast garlic and rosemary lamb.

Frithsden Vineyard *Frithsden, Hemel Hempstead, Hertfordshire, HP1 3DD; 01442 878723; www.frithsdenvineyard.co.uk*

Tucked away up the lane behind the Alford Arms, this diminutive vineyard has about 5,000 vines. If you're here on a weekend, it's worth calling in and asking the owners – Simon and Natalie – for a tasting. There are a couple of whites and a rosé to try.

Berkhamsted Castle *Berkhamsted, Hertfordshire; see www.english-heritage.org.uk*

It's hard to believe that this is the place where William the Conqueror received word of the English surrender after the Battle of Hastings. As you wander round the ruined walls, you'll be following in some seriously important footsteps…

EAT, DRINK, SLEEP

The Greyhound Inn *Stocks Road, Aldbury, Tring, Hertfordshire, HP23 5RT; 01442 851228; www.greyhoundaldbury.co.uk*

Ensconced in the centre of Aldbury, just up from the village pond, this cosy pub has eight rooms to choose from, and a fabulous menu including pea and mint risotto. Doubles from £75 per night.

The Brownlow *Ivinghoe, Leighton Buzzard, Bedfordshire, LU7 9DY; 01296 668787; www.thebrownlow.com*

Originally built as a pub to serve the Grand Union Canal, which passes right by, the Brownlow has been a private home since the 1960s. The converted stables house five smart en suite rooms, and there are cycle rides starting from the towpath at the end of the drive. Doubles from £75 per night.

Berko's Bed & Breakfast *305 High Street, Berkhamsted, Hertfordshire, HP4 1AJ; 01442 384136; www.berkosbandb.co.uk*

A basic but comfy family-run guest house on Berkhamsted High Street. Puts you within walking distance of the canalside pubs and restaurants, and minutes away from some blissful cycling. Doubles from £39 per night.

RENT

Mountain Mania Cycles *4–10 Miswell Lane, Tring, Hertfordshire, HP23 4BX; 01442 822458; www.mountainmaniacycles.co.uk*

These guys really know their bikes. The hire fleet features adult-only Trek 4300s with suspension forks, for £40. Helmets and repair kits are available separately.

21

AYOT ST LAWRENCE TO 'OLD' WELWYN

Introducing the hidden lanes of Hertfordshire...

THE BROCKET ARMS is one of those pubs in which you immediately feel like a local. Instead of walking through the door to be confronted by questioning looks from the assembled regulars, you'll find smiley barmaid Izzy ready with the kind of easy banter you'd expect from an old friend.

On your right, as you walk in, is a restaurant area with ceilings so low that *everyone* needs to duck beneath the overhanging beams. And in the bar an inglenook fireplace – blackened by centuries of wood smoke – holds centre stage.

Once you've dropped your bags in the room upstairs, grab your bike and bear right on to the lane outside, pedalling past smart cottages with neatly trimmed hedges before the quiet, narrow road swings left through a dense cluster of trees.

After another mile or so, and a couple of twists and turns, you're travelling between honey-coloured fields. Look out for the beautiful red-brick church on your right; with its sharp steeple and white-patterned stonework it would look more at home in an Italian hill town than the country lanes of Hertfordshire.

A right turn takes you in a loop that brings you out on the village green at Ayot St Peter. This is where you'll find your first pub of the day, the historic Waggoners – which now has a French twist, courtesy of owners Laurent and Aude.

A thirst-quenching pint of London Pride later, you ride back to the green and bear right for the town of Welwyn (or 'Old' Welwyn, as the locals call it). The road weaves its way between thick hedgerows full of singing choirbirds, then descends to reveal Welwyn below. It's a great stretch for letting go of the brakes, taking your feet off the pedals and just *gliding* downhill towards the junction. Eventually you arrive at the High Street – rosy cheeked and watery eyed – ready for a glass of something sweet and fizzy. There's a good choice of pubs here: the White Hart, at the

top of the high street as you arrive in town, or the Wellington, which is further down.

Continuing on, you make a left and cruise along to the end of the street, ducking left again on to Fulling Mill Lane, which looks more like the entrance to a cycle path. Now it all gets narrow and intimate again, the road winding between more golden fields before it reaches a crossroads. Ahead lie enormous pillows of corn interspersed with dark green hedges, as far as the eye can see.

Nipping over the crossroads, you take a left and encounter the first real uphill part of the ride, but it's nothing too taxing. Just shift to a low gear and you can spin your way to the top and still have enough energy to chat along the way. Over to your left there's plenty to keep your mind off the climb: watch the warm breeze create a Mexican wave across the carpet of corn as it blows gently towards you.

Near the top, the brambles close in on either side, letting you know that you're almost back in Ayot St Lawrence. All that remains is a right turn at the junction, and you'll be back at the Brocket Arms very soon. In fact, if you give Izzy a yell from here she'll probably have a pint ready and waiting.

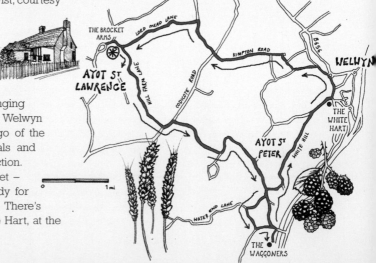

THE ROUTE

DISTANCE   8½ MILES
DIFFICULTY   ○○○
START   The Brocket Arms

Ayot St Lawrence, Hertfordshire, AL6 9BT

» From the Brocket Arms, turn right and follow the lane on to Hill Farm Lane.

» Continue for just under a mile before taking the first left, on to Codicote Road.

» Take the first right, on to Ayot St Peter Road (towards Ayot St Peter).

» Just over a mile later, after passing Ayot St Peter's church, turn right – on to Ayot Little Green Lane (signposted Little Green).

» At the end of this road (after ¼ mile) you reach a fork: bear left, on to Water End Lane.

» This takes you on to Ayot Green, then to the village centre: at the next junction bear right then turn right into Brickwall Close for the Waggoners pub.

» After the pub, retrace your steps back along the village green, past the junction you emerged from, following the sign for Ayot St Peter and Ayot St Lawrence.

» Less than ½ mile later, turn right, on to Homerswood Lane.

» Follow this, as it becomes White Hill.

» This drops downhill to a junction on the edge of Welwyn: turn right, on to School Lane.

» At the end of this road, turn left, on to High Street (for the White Hart pub, turn right).

» This becomes Codicote Road at the church; carry on to a roundabout, then take the first left – on to Fulling Mill Lane.

» Follow this, as it becomes Kimpton Road.

» After a mile or so you reach a crossroads: continue straight over.

» Take the next left, on to Lord Mead Lane.

» At the top of the hill turn right, on to Hill Farm Lane, and ride on, to the Brocket Arms.

STOP AND SEE

EN ROUTE

The Waggoners *Brickwall Close, Ayot Green, Hertfordshire, AL6 9AA; 01707 324241; www.thewaggoners.co.uk*

This 400-year-old coaching inn was once a major stop-off for thirsty travellers heading north. These days it's owned by a French couple, and serves up delicious beer and a creative Gallic-inspired menu.

The White Hart *2 Prospect Place, Welwyn, Hertfordshire, AL6 9EN; 01438 715353; www.thewhitehartel.net*
Located just off the top of Welwyn High Street, this family-run hotel and bar combines traditional pub touches like the old fireplace, with petrol-blue walls and funky picture frames housing patterned fabrics.

OFF ROUTE

Shaw's Corner *Ayot St Lawrence, Hertfordshire, AL6 9BX; 01438 829221; see www.nationaltrust.org.uk*
Just along the lane from the Brocket Arms, this red-brick Arts and Crafts-style house was once home to the famous playwright, George Bernard Shaw. Inside, it feels as if he might return at any minute – his desk chair pulled aside as though he's just popped out for a stroll around the peaceful garden, which is well worth a look.

Knebworth House *Knebworth, Hertfordshire, SG3 6PY; 01438 812661; www.knebworthhouse.com*
Probably more famous for its rock concerts than anything else, this place was once home to the writer Edward Bulwer Lytton – who coined the phrase 'the pen is mightier than the sword'. You could spend days just

admiring the weathered turrets, towers, and gargoyles, but step inside and you'll find room after room of fine old furniture.

EAT, DRINK, SLEEP

The Brocket Arms *Ayot St Lawrence, Hertfordshire, AL6 9BT; 01438 820250; www.brocketarms.com*
Friendly staff, good food, and six comfy rooms (opt for room 3) make this place the perfect escape destination – especially if you live in London. Built in the 14th century, it has everything you want from an old country pub. Inglenook fireplace: tick. Sagging ceilings: tick. Real-ale selection: tick.
Doubles from £85 per night.

The White Hart *See 'Stop and See' for contact details*
This independent hotel has 13 smart rooms to choose from, each with its own character. All are en suite, with Jacuzzi baths and stylish wallpapers, and downstairs the restaurant serves dishes like Barnsley lamb chop with buttered new potatoes.
Doubles from £110 per night.

The Wellington *1 High Street, Welwyn, Hertfordshire, AL6 9LZ; 01438 714036; www.wellingtonatwelwyn.co.uk*
Six recently renovated, uniquely styled rooms with wooden floors, exposed red bricks, and posh gadgets including iPod docks, flat-screen TVs, and Nespresso coffee machines. Downstairs there's a bright-and-breezy restaurant serving seared scallops with pea purée, pea shoots, crispy pancetta and wasabi, along with other tasty dishes.
Doubles from £80 per night.

RENT

There are no nearby cycle hire facilities, so you'll either need to book one at home before you leave or bring your own.

22

FINCHINGFIELD TO GREAT BARDFIELD

Thatched roofs, puddle ducks, and village greens…

STANDING IN THE CENTRE of Finchingfield, you'd never guess you're less than an hour from London. With ducks waddling along the street beside the local pond and thatched, half-timber houses huddled around the village green, it's as far away from the hassle and bustle as you could ever wish.

Setting off from the Fox Inn at the heart of the village, you pedal uphill past the Red Lion and make a right at the top, descending into serious tranquillity… Entering an avenue of leafy trees and peering out on either side, you get glimpses of the gorgeous Essex countryside – a sea of oatmeal-coloured fields spilling into the distance.

You're unlikely to encounter any other vehicles along here – the road is barely wide enough to fit a car – and as you drop down (following signs for Walthams Cross) it's so quiet that you can hear the soft whirring of your tyres as they roll over the tarmac.

Soon you'll see signs for Great Bardfield, before finally emerging on the edge of the village. If you turn left here you'll come to the Great Lodge – a beautiful historical house, gardens, and adjacent vineyard – where the owner, Alan, conducts tours. To continue the ride though, you go right, up into Great Bardfield, where there are a couple of nice pubs if you're feeling thirsty.

Heading towards Great Sampford from the village, you cruise past some cottages and the view suddenly opens out ahead of you – enormous shafts of sunlight piercing the pregnant clouds to spotlight the cornfields below.

Meanwhile, the road undulates its way along through Hawkspur Green, the birds in the trees

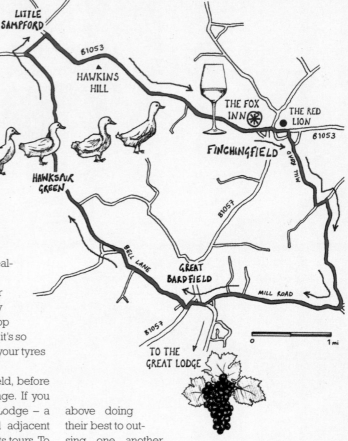

above doing their best to out-sing one another. Keeping an eye out for signs to Finchingfield, you hang a right at Little Sampford and drop downhill past the pretty little church, to the main road.

Making a right, you climb Hawkins Hill (short, but a bit of a thigh-burner), where more expansive views greet you at the crest. If you're in need of some encouragement to get you over this final hump, just think: in about 20 minutes' time you'll be sipping the froth off your pint back in Finchingfield.

THE ROUTE

DISTANCE   9 MILES

DIFFICULTY   ⭕⭕⭕

START   The Fox Inn

The Green, Finchingfield, Essex, CM7 4JX

» From the centre of the village, pedal up the short hill past the Red Lion.

» At the top, turn right on to Vicarage Lane (just before the Three Tuns pub).

» Turn right again after a mile, signposted Walthams Cross.

» After 1½ miles go right at the junction, for Great Bardfield.

» After another mile you pass a white windmill on your right and drop downhill into Great Bardfield, reaching a junction at Mill Lane (if you want to visit the Great Lodge, turn left here).

» Turn right and head up a small hill into Great Bardfield.

» Bear left at the fork at the top of the hill, on to the village's High Street.

» Turn right on to Bell Lane (just before the Bell pub), signposted Little Bardfield.

» After a mile fork right, for Great Sampford.

» Pass through Hawkspur Green.

» A mile later, take the right fork at the grass triangle into Little Sampford – signposted Great Sampford and Finchingfield.

» Drop down past the church (on your right), reaching a junction with the main road (B1053): turn right towards Finchingfield.

» Cruise along here for 1½ miles (climbing Hawkins Hill en route) to Finchingfield.

STOP AND SEE

EN ROUTE

The Great Lodge *Great Bardfield, Braintree, Essex, CM7 4QD; 01371 810776; www.thegreatlodgeexperience.com*
Beautiful, red-brick farmhouse and 16th-century Grade I-listed barn. It was originally built by Henry VIII for Anne of Cleves. Book a tour of the grounds, which includes a free wine-tasting at the vineyard with owner Alan Jordan.

The Vine *Vine Street, Great Bardfield, Braintree, Essex, CM7 4SR; 01371 810355*
Lovely old pub in the centre of the village, offering a wide choice of ales, and delicious fish (from Billingsgate Market) and chips.

OFF ROUTE

Hedingham Castle *Bayley Street, Castle Hedingham, Essex, CO9 3DJ; 01787 460261; www.hedinghamcastle.co.uk*
Allegedly Britain's best-kept Norman keep, this incredible old building dates back to 1140. Whether you're a history junkie or not, you'll love this place; explore the castle, chill out by the lake, look out for wildlife in the woods, or grab a cuppa in the café (the cakes are superb).

Cassidy's Deli *9 High Street, Dunmow, Essex, CM6 1AB, 01371 878060; cassidysdeli.co.uk*
This is a foodie's dream come true: pastries, pies, cooked meats, delicious chocolates, and tons of other mouth-watering treats.

EAT, DRINK, SLEEP

The Fox Inn *The Green, Finchingfield, Essex, CM7 4JX; 01371 810151; www.thefoxinnfinchingfield.co.uk*
Slap bang in the centre of the village, this pub boasts original timber beams and (on chilly days) a roaring fire in the hearth. Sit outside in summer and watch the ducks paddling in the pond, opposite. Landlord Keith also owns Cassidy's Deli in nearby Dunmow, so you can be sure that the food here hits the spot.

Brook Farm *Wethersfield, Braintree, Essex, CM7 4BX; 01371 850284; www.brookfarmwethersfield.co.uk*
Pretty pink farmhouse with three rooms, three miles from Finchingfield. Parts of the house date back to the 13th century; the rooms are cosy and comfy, with wood

beams and period furniture. Landlady Anne is really friendly – and a whizz at cooked breakfasts.
Doubles from £70 per night.

The Red Lion *6 Church Hill, Finchingfield, Essex, CM7 4NN; 01371 810400; www.theredlionfinchingfield.com*
This whitewashed 15th-century coaching inn is about 20 seconds' walk from the village duck pond. Landlords David and Iain serve delicious steaks – supplied by a local butcher's – along with a fine selection of real ales. There are four refurbished rooms upstairs, which blend funky throws, black chandeliers, silver chests of drawers, and other modern twists with original wood beams and wonky old walls.
Doubles from £110 per night.

RENT

TrailNet *Great Notley Country Park, Braintree, Essex, CM77 7FS; 01376 345643; www.trailnet.org.uk*
TrailNet has a range of bikes for all shapes and sizes – including tricycles, trailers, and tandems. Open Tuesday, Wednesday, Saturday, and Sunday – and every day during school holidays – with adult's bikes for £10 a day, they'll even deliver, too.

HELPFUL HINT

If you decide to stop at the Great Lodge's vineyard, leave room in your backpack for a couple of bottles to take away.

23

TILLINGHAM TO BRADWELL WATERSIDE

Stunning views, great pubs, gorgeous villages, and ancient history...

IT ALL BEGINS at the Cap and Feathers in the titchy village of Tillingham. The pub dates back to the 15th century and once doubled as an undertaker's. Look out for the wooden beam that's been smoothed away into an arch at one end; this was created to allow the coffin bearers' top hats to pass cleanly underneath. They used to lay the coffins on the tables here, too – just ask Rob, the landlord.

Grab your bike and head left from the pub, passing the village green to cruise out along the smooth road towards Bradwell Waterside. A right turn has you passing clapboard cottages then open fields, before you rock up outside the Green Man pub (all timber beams and white walls) after a few flat miles. Why not treat yourself to a quick drink before carrying on to the waterfront – the view will be just as splendid in a couple of pints' time (maybe more so, actually).

Peering across the Blackwater Estuary, you can see all the way across to Mersea Island (see ride 24, p118) on the opposite bank, about four miles away. Meanwhile, somewhere in between, the white, blue, and pink sails of yachts are billowing in the warm summer breeze.

Ducking right, up on to the grassy bank, you'll see the eerie outline of the power station ahead of you. It's surprising that even this uber-industrial landmark has a beauty of its own, perched close to the waterfront. The local birdlife has taken quite a shine to it, too – keep your eyes peeled for the peregrine falcons that nest here. In fact this whole area is a haven for birdlife – with cuckoos, turtle doves, and an assortment of marine birds making their homes here.

Continuing along the grassy path (which is actually the sea wall), you wind your way around the water's edge; various little shingle beaches appear on your left at low tide, ideal if you fancy a quick stop.

Butterflies bob about clumsily around the bushes at the side of the path, missing your front wheels more by luck than judgement and, as the green-grass path becomes black shingle, you emerge into a small field with an old weathered chapel – St Peter's – just up ahead.

In fact 'old' is not the word; this place dates back a whopping 1,400 years and was built on the site of a Roman fort. Come here in May and you'll see it surrounded by bright yellow rapeseed fields; the air so thick with fragrance you can almost see it.

A track from the chapel leads you between the fields to Bradwell-on-Sea (not to be confused with Bradwell Waterside from earlier), where you can now see the power station on your right. White timber houses mark your arrival back to modern civilisation as the dirt track becomes tarmac and brings you out – conveniently – opposite the Kings Head pub.

Why not stop for a thirst-quencher or duck into the church opposite for a quick peek? There's plenty of time. For the last leg of the journey you simply head right out of the pub and cruise towards Southminster, rejoining the loop to bring you back to Tillingham.

THE ROUTE

DISTANCE	11 MILES
DIFFICULTY	○○
START	The Cap and Feathers

8 South Street, Tillingham, Essex, CM0 7TH

» From the Cap and Feathers pub head left along the main road out of the village (towards Bradwell Waterside).

» After 1½ miles turn right, signposted Bradwell Waterside.

» Once you're in the village, go past the Green Man pub and on to the waterfront.

» Here, turn right on to the grassy bank. Follow the path, towards the power station.

» Continue along the path for around 3 miles, until you reach St Peter's Chapel.

» Take the dirt track in front of the chapel, following it to Bradwell village.

» You'll reach the village after 1½ miles. At the junction facing the King's Head, turn left.

» Follow this road for 1½ miles to the next junction. Turn left for Southminster.

» Around ¼ mile later, turn left again and pedal the 1½ miles back to Tillingham.

STOP AND SEE

EN ROUTE

The Green Man *Waterside, Bradwell-on-Sea, Essex, CM0 7QX; 01621 776226, www.greenmanbradwellonsea.co.uk*
Family-friendly pub serving Green King IPA, Adnams Bitter, and other ales, along with pub faves like peppered lemon chicken supreme, or poached salmon if you're feeling healthy.

St Peter's Chapel *www.bradwellchapel.org*
Surrounded by fields on one side and wonderful views across the water on the other, this beautiful little chapel is all red roof-tiles and weathered-stone walls. Peek inside and soak up the peace and quiet.

OFF ROUTE

Springstep Dairy Farm *Mundon Hall, Vicarage Lane, Mundon, Maldon, Essex,* CM9 6PA; 01621 740357; *www.springstep-dairy.co.uk*
Meet the goats (there are 450 of them), alpacas, and cows at this gorgeous little farm about half-an-hour's drive from Tillingham. A great place for youngsters.

Burnham-on-Crouch *Essex*
This lovely little town on the waterfront has a traditional sweetshop (As You Like It), white clapboard ice cream shop (the Cabin Dairy Tea Rooms), and lots of good pubs – all just half-an-hour's drive from Tillingham.

EAT, DRINK, SLEEP

The Cap and Feathers *8 South Street, Tillingham, Southminster, Essex, CM0 7TH;* 01621 779212
An atmospheric olde worlde pub with plenty of wooden timbers, wonky old walls, and an original red-brick fireplace. Drink Wibbler's Dengie Best and other delicious ales here. Upstairs are a few renovated B&B rooms that won't break the bank. Doubles from £30 per night (really).

The Oyster Smack Inn *112 Station Road, Burnham-on-Crouch, Essex, CM0 8HR;* 01621 782141; *www.theoystersmack.co.uk*
Bright modern pub with really friendly young staff, a restaurant, and four smart B&B rooms upstairs (five more out back). Local ales include Maldon Gold and Woodforde's Wherry.
Doubles from £65 per night.

Mangapp Manor *Southminster Road, Burnham-on-Crouch, Essex, CM0 8QC; 07769 676735; www.mangappmanor.co.uk*
You'll find this beautiful 12th-century farmhouse tucked away in 12 acres of gardens and paddocks, just outside Burnham. Inside are three sumptuously styled rooms with period furniture, and there's a sun-kissed lake in the grounds. Double rooms from £75 per night.

RENT

Unfortunately, the nearest cycle hire places are 20 miles away, so you'll need to bring a bike with you.

HELPFUL HINT

The path from Bradwell waterfront to St Peter's Chapel is quite bumpy, so you'll need a mountain bike or hybrid.

24

WEST MERSEA TO CUDMORE GROVE

Seafood, birdlife, and shabby-chic eateries...

MERSEA ISLAND, off the Essex coastline, is many things to many people. In the space of just a few miles you'll find traditional-style holiday camps that would have photographer Martin Parr reaching for his camera, and shabby-chic eateries serving some of the freshest seafood that England has to offer.

In the midst of all of this is beautiful Oysterbed Cottage, an old mariner's home dating back to 1890, that's been lovingly restored by Emily and Stuart Turnbull. They've brought the cottage stylishly up to date without losing any of its original character. Today its walls are awash with the tranquil shades of pastel greens, oatmeals, and antique whites but, most excitingly, it's less than a five-minutes cycle to the beach.

Swing by the Mersea Delicatessen just along the street, stuff your backpack with cured meats, cheese, olives, and other goodies, and you're all set for a day of sun, sand, and fresh, salty air.

A couple of turns see you on to the waterfront, with the Blackwater Estuary stretched out ahead. All you do now is turn left and just pedal – for about four miles. As long as you've got the sea on your right, you can't go wrong (right?). The first section takes you across a stretch of grass and sand along the edge of the beach, where you might want to get off and push. But what does that matter? It gives you an opportunity to gaze out over the water; sailboats glide hither and thither, and Bradwell Power Station rises up from the Dengie Peninsula on the opposite shore (see ride 23, p112).

Further along, on Victoria Esplanade, you pass a row of ice cream-coloured beach huts lined up for inspection, and continue on up the beach while seagulls squawk encouragement and the breeze carries wafts of sizzling sausages from nearby BBQs.

Now head back inland, taking a left into the campsite at Fen Farm and following the footpath up to the road – the smooth tarmac feels a lot easier after a morning spent plodding across the sand and grass.

When you reach the car park at Cudmore Grove, there's a whole area of grass waiting for you. Time to stretch out, soak up the estuary view, and get stuck into that picnic, before leisurely heading back...

THE ROUTE

DISTANCE   10 MILES
DIFFICULTY   ○○
START   **Oysterbed Cottage**

High Street, West Mersea, Essex, CO5 8JE

» Left from Oysterbed Cottage, down the High Street, then left on to Yorrick Road.

» At the end, turn right on to Kingsland Road and continue to the waterfront.

» Turn left and cycle along the beach until you see a gap in the hedge on your left; go through this and carry on along the grass to emerge on Victoria Esplanade.

» Continue along Victoria Esplanade until you reach Seaview Holiday Park.

» Go past the beach huts on your right, and through the tunnel of trees ahead – emerging on to a grassy area.

» The path follows the coast through Waldegraves Holiday Park, along the edge of a cornfield, and back to the beach.

» Shortly after, you arrive at Coopers Beach Caravan Park. Carry on along the sea wall, down the steps, and on, to Fen Farm.

» Look for the footpath sign, which takes you left, around the edge of the site – past reception and out to the road.

» Turn right at the road and after ¼ mile go straight on into Broman's Lane.

» Another ¼ mile brings you to Cudmore Grove car park.

» To get back to Oysterbed Cottage retrace your steps along the coast.

STOP AND SEE

EN ROUTE

Two Sugars *31 Victoria Esplanade, West Mersea, Essex, CO5 8BH; 01206 383426*
As the name suggests, this white café (on the right as you head towards Cudmore Grove) serves up a sweet brew. Don't expect any frills, though; it's a proper seaside caf – albeit one that used to be a gun emplacement during the Second World War. Sit, sip, and look out over the Blackwater Estuary.

Cudmore Grove *Broman's Lane, East Mersea, Essex, CO5 8UE; 01206 383868; see www.visitparks.co.uk*
Spend the afternoon with a book, catching rays on the sand, or take a walk along the sea wall. Besides offering a gorgeous view, this country park is a haven for wildlife, including migrating birds, badgers, and adders. Rangers run guided walks and family-oriented activity days.

OFF ROUTE

Mersea Island Vineyard *Rewsalls Lane, East Mersea, Essex, CO5 8SX; 01206 385900; www.merseawine.com*
Essex wine may seem like a strange concept, but rumour has it that even the Romans grew grapes here. Take a quick tour and tasting if you're here from April to September or, if beer is more your thing, there's a microbrewery on site, too.

Coastal Walk to the Strood
Set off on foot from the West Mersea marina and head along the waterfront. A sandy path takes you past oyster beds and marshy creeks to the ruler-straight Roman road leading off the island. On the way back you'll be in time for lunch at the Company Shed.

EAT, DRINK, SLEEP

Oysterbed Cottage *High Street, West Mersea, Essex, CO5 8JE; 07949 166354; www.oysterbedcottage.com*
Original fireplaces, crisp cotton sheets, DVD player, and a kitchen filled with mod cons. Out the back there's a lockable shed for bring-your-own bikes.
Weekend from £290; sleeps up to five.

Victory Inn *92 Coast Road, West Mersea, Essex, CO5 8LS; 01206 382907; www.victoryatmersea.com*
This friendly waterfront pub has seven rooms to choose from – each individually styled. Go for one of the sea-view rooms

overlooking the tops of swaying boat masts, all the way across to the Dengie Peninsula. If you're feeling lazy you can eat downstairs, where dishes like home-roasted ham, egg, and chips provide an alternative to the ubiquitous seafood.
Doubles from £55 per night.

Broman's Farm *Broman's Lane, East Mersea, Essex, CO5 8UE; 01206 383235; www.bromansfarm.co.uk*
A restored 14th-century farmhouse on a quiet lane, complete with a garden and pond. There are two rooms (a double and a twin), both achieving countryside cosy without straying into chintz-a-rama. There's a nature reserve just along the road.
Sea-view double from £70 per night.

West Mersea Oyster Bar *Coast Road, West Mersea, Essex, CO5 8LT; 01206 381600; www.westmerseaoysterbar.co.uk*
Opposite the Victory Inn, this is one of the most popular eateries on the island. The formula is simple: brown clapboard shed plus wooden tables and delicious seafood (try the pan-fried skate wing with new potatoes) equals foodie pleasure.

The Company Shed *129 Coast Road, West Mersea, Essex, CO5 8PA; 01206 382700*
Forget waiters, wine lists, and all that snazzy stuff, we're talking about a fishmonger's with tables and a little cutlery. Oysters, crabs, lobsters, scallops, and cockles are just some of the delicacies fresh out of the surrounding waters. You can't book, so expect to queue, but it's worth it. Just don't forget to bring your own bread and wine.

RENT

R&A Cycles *16 Barfield Road, West Mersea, Essex, CO5 8QT; 01206 384013*
A range of mountain bikes available from £10 a day (£25 cash deposit). The fleet changes depending on stock, so ring ahead.

EAST ANGLIA

25

BUTLEY TO ORFORD

Castles, cottages, and a night in a monastery…

GAZING UP at the grand Gothic windows of Butley Priory, you half expect an East-Anglian Rapunzel to appear at one of them and unfurl her golden locks. With its ornately carved stonework – all coats of arms, elegant archways, and gargoyles – this place is a fairy tale that begins in the breakfast room…

Enormous French doors are thrown open on to the garden, silhouetting the grand piano against the blue sky, and the scents of lavender and rose waft in as you help yourself to another steaming pot of tea.

The ride to Orford begins on a smooth, deserted road bordered by pines, the sunlight strobing through the branches as you pedal effortlessly along past the Oyster Inn and make a right turn.

You're on Mill Lane now, where the verges are awash with red poppies every July; cornfields and wild meadows slipping by on either side as you join a couple of B-roads that take you all the way into Orford.

This is home to one of my favourite restaurants – the Butley Orford Oysterage – where the tables have paper for cloths, and the seafood served is caught just a few hundred metres away in the estuary. Aromas of smoking fish drift up from the nearby alleyway, mingling with the omnipresent salty sea breeze.

The Oysterage overlooks Orford's market square, where the red-brick cottages huddle together like friends doing the hokey-cokey, and at the castle, 100 metres away, you can see land and water colliding in the distance.

If it's picnic weather, why not grab a bottle of local apple juice and some fresh rolls from the village shop and stroll along to the harbour, where fishermen beaver about with weathered old boats?

Pedalling out of Orford you'll pass gardens ablaze with orange and yellow flowers, and handwritten signs announcing 'courgettes for sale – 10p each'.

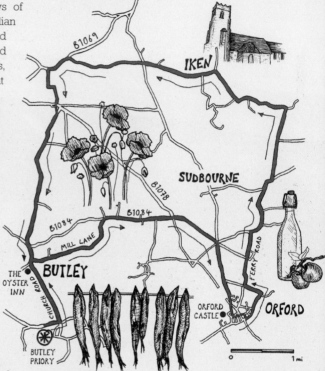

Continue towards Iken, passing fields where the cereal crops stand on end like fur, gently ruffled by the wind's unseen hand.

There's a tiny thatched church tucked away at the end of the lane here, its graveyard overlooking the River Alde, and at low tide you can walk across the marshes from Iken to the shops and eateries of Snape Maltings.

The remaining five miles back to Butley take you past Tunstall Forest, which is laced with good walks, and you arrive at the Priory just as the sun is casting long shadows on the lawn. This time of day is often referred to as the 'magic hour' which, in this fairy tale-like place, seems especially appropriate.

THE ROUTE

DISTANCE 18½ MILES
DIFFICULTY ○○○
START Butley Priory

nr Woodbridge, Suffolk, IP12 3NR

» Turn right out of Butley Priory's drive and then left at the next junction.

» Carry on for 1½ miles, until you reach the junction by the Oyster Inn. Bear right then take the first right, on to Mill Lane.

» Just over a mile later you reach a junction with the B1084: turn right.

» Two miles later you reach another junction: turn right and continue to the marketplace in Orford.

» Turn left into the marketplace and follow the road past the church, round to the right, taking the second left on to Daphne Road.

» This becomes Raydon Lane and brings you to a junction after less than a mile (at the second grass triangle): turn left on to Bullockshed Lane.

» At the next junction, turn right on to Ferry Road.

» Turn right at the next 'proper' junction – signposted Iken.

» Stay on this road for the next 4½ miles, until you reach a crossroads: go straight across, towards Woodbridge.

» Just over a mile later, turn left on to the B1069, towards Woodbridge.

» Take the next left, on to Walk Farm Road.

» Carry on to the crossroads with the B1078: go straight over, into Mill Lane.

» At the next junction, turn right.

» At the next junction, 2 miles on, go right.

» When you reach the Oyster Inn, turn left.

» Take the first right, after 1 mile, to arrive back at Butley Priory.

STOP AND SEE

EN ROUTE

Orford Castle *Orford, Woodbridge, Suffolk, IP12 2ND; 01394 450472; see www.english-heritage.org.uk*
It's hard to believe that this place is over 800 years old. Built by Henry II in the 12th century, the keep's biscuit-brown stonework looks as solid as ever. From the battlements above, the views over the Suffolk countryside are particularly stirring; is that the wind causing your eyes to water?

Orford River Trip *Orford Marine Services, Orford Quay, Orford, Woodbridge, Suffolk, IP12 2NU; 01394 450169; www.orfordrivertrips.co.uk*
If the sun's shining, why not take a boat trip on the estuary? You'll get cracking views of the castle and nature reserve at Havergate Island, plus a free history lesson… all in the space of seven sun-kissed miles.

OFF ROUTE

Snape Maltings *nr Aldeburgh, Suffolk, IP17 1SR; 01728 687171; www.snapemaltings.co.uk*
Shop, eat, browse, or stroll. You can do it all at these converted 19th-century buildings perched on the banks of the River Ore – just 20 minutes' drive from Butley.

EAT, DRINK, SLEEP

Butley Priory *nr Woodbridge, Suffolk, IP12 3NR; 01394 450046; www.butleypriory.co.uk*
Intricate stonework, sumptuous beds, and dramatic high ceilings form a theatrical contrast with the peace and quiet outside. Go for a stroll beyond the garden and you'll find the ruins of an old archway – all that remain of the monastery that once stood here. Ask landlady Frances for the full story. Doubles from £90 per night.

The Drift *Sandy Lane, Iken, Suffolk, IP12 2HE; 01728 688801; www.thedriftiken.co.uk*
Spacious, self-contained accommodation in the grounds of a thatched cottage. The upstairs bedroom looks out over surrounding fields. If you're still feeling energetic after the ride, there's a lovely local walk to Iken Church and the River Ore. From £70 per night.

The Crown and Castle *Orford, Woodbridge, Suffolk, IP12 2LJ; 01394 450205; www.crownandcastle.co.uk*
This place is tucked away just off the market square and, when you walk in, the first thing you notice is the calm. There are 19 stylish yet simply decorated rooms spread between the house and the garden, and a delicious menu of lobster, sea bass, and other locally caught treats. Doubles from £125 per night.

RENT

Friends Garage *Front Street, Orford, Suffolk, IP12 2LP; 01394 450239*
There are mountain bikes for adults and kids, along with a range of 'sit-up-and-beg' styles if you're after something more comfy. From £6 a day.

26

WESTLETON TO WALBERSWICK

The ride that has everything – except hills…

ICE CREAM, BEER, OR BEACH? This is the dilemma you'll face when you arrive in Dunwich, having cycled the two-and-a-half miles from the Westleton Crown. The quiet road here is bordered by heathers, which blend into one continuous purple and green blur as you whizz past in the midsummer sun, before pulling up by a side road that leads to the shore. I'm not usually a fan of shingle beaches, but this one is so peaceful that you can't help but slip instantly into holiday mode.

Glance right, along the coast, and you'll see the huge golf ball reactor at Sizewell B power station – teed up on the edge of the sea, waiting for some giant to ping it across to Holland. Look left and there's Southwold Lighthouse, away down the coast.

Hard though it is to believe, Dunwich was a thriving international port back in the 11th century, with 3,000 inhabitants, eight churches, and a buzzing waterfront. The North Sea eroded away the lot, though, and today the only remnants of its glory days are the ruins of All Saints Church on the nearby cliffs. All is not lost, however, as a beachside café and a rather nice pub, the Ship, have sprung up in the intervening years.

From here the road climbs gently out of the village, passing under an archway of trees before bringing you out at the main road to Walberswick (if you're asking for directions here, it's easier to do it with a mouthful of boiled sweets). Not that you'll need to; all it takes is a couple of right turns to bring you into the village, after cruising across stretches of unkempt countryside dominated by prehistoric-looking ferns.

If you're feeling the need for more beach, you're in luck. This one is sandy – and famous for crabbing – so grab yourself a line and some bait and see how many you can catch.

In the nearby harbour, brown clapboard fishermen's sheds line the waterfront and there's a chain ferry that will take you across to Southwold on the other side, if you're up for adding some more miles to your journey.

After a day of sea air, though, it's tempting to just sit on the dock listening to the gulls before grabbing a cuppa at the Potter's Wheel tea shop on the village green. The route back to Westleton sees you fork left as you leave Walberswick, bouncing along a sandy track with dense greenery on either side.

The scenery along here is more akin to the African bush than anything you'd expect to find by the English seaside, especially with the odd deer rustling about in the undergrowth. After a couple of miles you emerge back on the road that led you out of Dunwich a few hours earlier – and now it's a straight run back to Westleton, for an early evening ale.

THE ROUTE

DISTANCE   15½ MILES

DIFFICULTY   ○○○

START   **The Westleton Crown** *The Street, Westleton, Southwold, Suffolk, IP17 3AD*

» Head right from the Crown and leave the village, taking the first right (Dunwich Road).

» After 2 miles you'll reach Dunwich. Stay on this road and it will lead you out the other side, bringing you to a crossroads.

» Turn right (to Walberswick), then right again, taking the road into Walberswick.

» To get back to Westleton from Walberswick, retrace your steps to the edge of the village, but turn left on to Lodge Road. You'll immediately pass Stocks Lane, before carrying on to reach a dirt track.

» After ½ mile, you reach a fork on the dirt track; carry straight on (not right).

» The track brings you out at the junction you reached after leaving Dunwich earlier. Turn right to rejoin the road, and you'll immediately be at the crossroads.

» Turn left, signposted Westleton, and follow the road back to the Crown.

STOP AND SEE

EN ROUTE

Dunwich *Suffolk*

Take a stroll along this magnificent stretch of shingle, extending as far as the eye can see. Away from the beach there are some great walks through protected heathland, where you might spot nightjars and warblers.

Walberswick *Suffolk*

Say it out loud and it sounds slightly ridiculous – a baddie from a Dickens novel. But with a beautiful beach, ramshackle arrangement of shops beside the green, and an impossibly cute harbour, it's one of those places that will instantly win you over.

OFF ROUTE

Minsmere Nature Reserve *nr Saxmundham, Suffolk; 01728 648281; see www.rspb.org.uk*

Four square miles of wetland, woodland, beach, and heath ensure a melting pot of resident wildlife at this reserve. Guided walks mean you don't miss a trick, and it's an easy cycle from Westleton – you'll see signs on the way to Dunwich.

Southwold *Suffolk*

A highlight of this seaside town is the line of brightly coloured huts along the shore, resembling an assortment of boiled sweets. It's also home to the Adnams Brewery (go on a tour; 01502 727200; www.adnams.co. uk) and Mark's Fish Shop (delicious; 01502 723585), all easily accessible by the chain ferry from Walberswick.

EAT, DRINK, SLEEP

The Westleton Crown *The Street, Westleton, Southwold, Suffolk, IP17 3AD; 01728 648777; www.westletoncrown.co.uk*

There are 34 upmarket rooms to choose from – my favourites being Birren and Tree Creeper, each with roll-top baths in the room. You can eat in the pub's red-brick restaurant, glass-walled Garden Room, or bar – depending on your mood. It's the same delicious menu wherever you go. Doubles from £90 per night.

The Ship *Dunwich, Saxmundham, Suffolk, IP17 3DT; 01728 648219; www.shipatdunwich.co.uk*
Once the haunt of local smugglers, the meanest thing this weathered red-brick boozer serves nowadays is a roast. Surrounded by nature reserves and with the beach just a five-minute walk away, it's the perfect base for a weekend of fresh air and food. Choose from 10 smartly decorated rooms.
Doubles from £95 per night.

The Anchor *The Street, Walberswick, Suffolk, IP18 6UA; 01502 722112; www.anchoratwalberswick.com*
Expect stone-coloured walls, wooden floors, and a menu including braised pork belly with noodles and ginger broth. Meanwhile, in the huge garden, you'll find six spacious, simple rooms (two more in the main building) with underfloor heating, and the beach is just 200 metres away. Doubles from £110 per night.

RENT

Heritage Cycles *Blackshore, Southwold, Suffolk, IP18 6TA; 01502 723683; www.heritagecycles.co.uk*
Forget hybrids, mountain bikes, and all that modern rubbish. Here you can help yourself to all sorts of bicycle exotica including a Pashley Princess Sovereign (for the lady), which comes complete with bell, wicker basket, and skirt guard. Or how about a Pashley Guv'nor for the gent? From £20 a day.

27

HONINGHAM TO LYNG

Old airfields, daredevil rabbits, and a white fox…

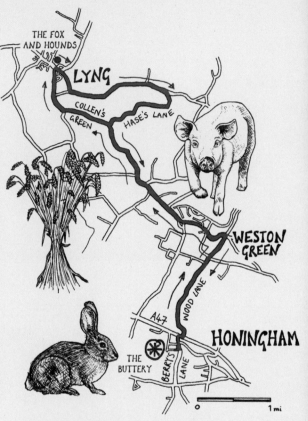

PEDALLING THROUGH THE LANES towards the village of Lyng, you might think you're being watched. Not by humans – it's mostly just fields and farms around here – but by the smaller, furrier locals that live in the hedgerows. Every few minutes a kamikaze bunny darts out from the sidelines, as if racing you to the next gate – its white backside going like the clappers.

Located about 20 minutes north of Norwich, this area is generally overlooked by the crowds that habitually flock to the Norfolk coast every time it's sunny. Out here you'll be (un)lucky if you see another car for the entire five miles it takes to get to the Fox and Hounds at Lyng.

The ride begins at the Buttery in Honingham – a quirky, octagonal cottage surrounded by woodland on the Berry Estate – where you bear left and cross the main road, immediately entering an avenue of overhanging trees.

Although nowadays the landscape here is dominated by vast carpets of golden corn, during the Second World War it was awash with airfields that formed Britain's first line of defence against Hitler's advancing army.

Swinging left after a couple of miles, you pass one of these bases – RAF Attlebridge – where bombers once lined up on the runway like lumbering metal birds. Today it's a poultry farm, the hangars now home to chickens and turkeys (as evinced by the telltale whiff).

A short while later you will pass fields full of pigs rooting around in the dust – their corrugated shelters are laid out over the land in militarily precise rows. Meanwhile, the road plunges through a tunnel of greenery, eventually emerging into Lyng, where you'll spot the white walls of the Fox and Hounds – gleaming like a welcome banner that shouts 'get your beer here!'

The ceilings of this old pub are impossibly low: even average-sized punters struggle to stand upright. But the welcome is warm – from owners Dean and Clio – and the steak sandwich just the ticket for restoring wobbly legs.

Leaving the village, you pass the road that brought you here and carry on, forking right after a quarter of a mile and climbing a few hundred metres back into the lanes. Cereal fields as far as you can see are interrupted only by a peppering of copses.

Pedalling along with the tailwind rustling through the grass verges, you reach the turning that took you to Lyng just few hours earlier – completing a loop that brings you back home to the Buttery. Just watch out for those bunnies…

VILLAGE HALL

HALL DRIVE
NR9 5AR

HOCKERING 3 | ELSING
PEASELAND GREEN

THE ROUTE

DISTANCE 16 MILES
DIFFICULTY ○○○
START **The Buttery** *Berry Hall, Honingham, Norwich, Norfolk, NR9 5AX*

» Turn left out of the Berry Estate, and ride along Berry's Lane to the A47.

» Cross over the staggered crossroads at the A47, on to Wood Lane, which becomes Paddy's Lane.

» At the hamlet of Weston Green, turn left on to Weston Green Road.

» Follow this to the next junction: bear right.

» As the road sweeps right, take the second left on to Collen's Green.

» Follow this road for 1½ miles and take the second left, signposted Lyng.

» Stay on this road all the way into Lyng.

» At the next junction, in Lyng, the Fox and Hounds pub is ahead on your left. The route turns right – to leave the village.

» Take the first right, on to Rectory Road. After ½ mile, this bends left (by a red-brick house) to become Easthaugh Road.

» In 1½ miles, take a right, on to Hase's Lane.

» This becomes Collen's Green. Now retrace your steps back along here – on to Weston Green Road again – and to the Buttery via Paddy's Lane and Wood Lane.

STOP AND SEE

EN ROUTE

The Fox and Hounds *The Street, Lyng, Norfolk, NR9 5AL; 01603 872316; www.thefoxandhoundslyng.co.uk*
Woodforde's Wherry, Abbot, and other ales await in this white-walled local. Take a seat outside and thumb through the papers.

OFF ROUTE

River Wensum Canoe Trip
08454 969177; www.thecanoeman.com
Glide along the backwaters of the Norfolk Broads in a canoe, drifting past fields and country pubs – where you can stop and sip whenever you fancy. A lovely, lazy day out.

City of Norwich Aviation Museum *Old Norwich Road, Horsham St Faith, Norwich, Norfolk, NR10 3JF; 01603 893080; www.cnam.co.uk*
Whet your appetite for Norwich's aviation heritage with a trip to this family-friendly museum, close to the airport. There are around 15 aircraft in various states of repair, including Jaguars, a Harrier, and an enormous Vulcan bomber.

EAT, DRINK, SLEEP

The Buttery *Berry Hall, Honingham, Norwich, Norfolk, NR9 5AX; 01603 880541; www.thebuttery.biz*
Fresh bread and a fridge full of other breakfast goodies mark the start of a peaceful weekend in this thatched cottage. Upstairs there's a spa bath and cosy bedroom; downstairs a lounge containing maps of woodland walks around the estate. Sleeps two; £95/£85/£80 per night, for a 1/2/3-night stay.

Carrick's at Castle Farm *Castle Farm, Swanton Morley, Dereham, Norfolk, NR20 4JT; 01362 638302; www.carricksatcastlefarm.co.uk*
This red-brick, family-run farm sits on the banks of the River Wensum, with strategically placed benches that are just the ticket for a post-ride read. There are four luxurious rooms to choose from and some great cycle rides nearby. Doubles from £90 per night.

Maple Barns *24 Greengate, Swanton Morley, Dereham, Norfolk, NR20 4AD; 01362 637260; www.maplebarns.co.uk*
Two lovely converted barns in the courtyard of a Victorian coach house, both with oak floors, wood-burning stove, and a garden looking out across the fields. Each has room for one couple; cycle hire available on request.
Barn from £175 per weekend.

The Ugly Bug *High House Farm Lane, Colton, Norwich, Norfolk, NR9 5DG; 01603 880794; uglybuginn.co.uk*
Good food, a gorgeous lake, and rambling gardens... These are just three reasons to come to this friendly local, a few miles down the road from the Buttery.

RENT

Broadland Cycle Hire *BeWILDerwood, Horning Road, Hoveton, Norwich, Norfolk, NR12 8JW; 07887 480331; www.norfolkbroadscycling.co.uk*
Here you'll find a full range of bikes available for adults and children, plus tandems, tag-alongs, baby seats, helmets, and other equipment. For £14 a day; cheaper if hiring more than one.

28

FOULSHAM TO HEYDON

Narrow lanes, old English architecture, and England's prettiest village...

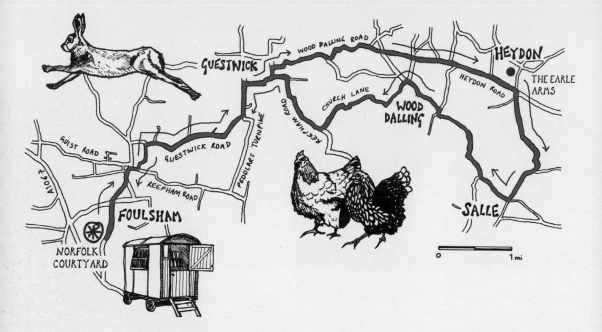

THE SHEPHERD'S HUT AT Norfolk Courtyard B&B is as rudimentary as it gets with a roof over your head. There's (just) enough space for two, a fold-out table, and a tiny wooden shelf-bed with a small crate underneath – the latter formerly a sleeping cot for orphaned lambs, which is conveniently sized for a holdall.

Simon and Catherine Davis restored this Victorian wooden cabin on wheels, painstakingly ensuring that everything in it is authentic – from the lanterns that light the place, to the tin plates you eat from. Agricultural antiques are Simon's lifelong passion, and across the field from the hut there's a treasure trove of goodies from Britain's rural past. Goose crooks (for rounding up stroppy birds), poachers' traps, shepherds' smocks, and other odds and sods are crammed in to the rafters, which makes for an interesting afternoon's rummaging. Unless, that is,

you'd prefer to take to the surrounding country lanes for a spot of cycling.

Heading left out of the driveway, you cruise to Foulsham, swing right through the village and glide down Guestwick Road. At times there's barely any border between road and field here; it's as if a roll of tarmac has simply been laid on top of the grass.

Pedalling even deeper into this oh-so-quiet countryside, you pass a 12th-century stone church in the hamlet of Guestwick, where rabbits bop about between the gravestones. As you roll past a red-brick farmhouse you'll spy chickens, and keep an eye out for hares as you pass the open fields – Norfolk has more of them than anywhere else in the UK.

Eventually you will reach the village of Heydon, where a clutch of red-brick cottages gathers around the green. The Gothic water pump on the grass is in pristine nick and you'll struggle to see any cables

or other modern trappings. It's as though someone stopped the clock here sometime in the 1700s. Pause at the Earle Arms pub for lunch (or elevenses in the chintzy tea room), before pushing on towards Salle.

There are no hills to worry about around here, so you can relax and enjoy the scenery as you reach the gates to Salle Park Estate. Phone ahead and you can book a private tour of the ornate walled gardens, or simply turn right at the old gatekeeper's cottage and cruise along to the hamlet itself. Look out for the village hall with its stepped, Dutch gable ends; the lord of the manor must have banned ugly buildings.

From Salle, it's on to Wood Dalling, where the architectural wonders just keep on coming. There's yet another lovely church – this one with a pond outside; if you've kept any crumbs from your tea and cake stops, the resident ducks will happily take them off your hands.

Making a left here, you weave your way along between enormous open fields before arriving in Guestwick again. From here you simply follow your wheel-tracks back to Foulsham for a well-earned brew outside the – perhaps architecturally less inspiring, but nonetheless lovely – shepherd's hut.

THE ROUTE

DISTANCE   12 MILES
DIFFICULTY ◐◐
START   Norfolk Courtyard

Westfield Farm, Foxley Road, Foulsham, Norfolk, NR20 5RH

» Head left out of Norfolk Courtyard and follow the road to Foulsham.

» Pedal along the High Street and take the right fork at Bank House, before the church, on to Reepham Road.

» Take the first left, on to Guestwick Road.

» This becomes Foulsham Road before banking left and becoming Station Road.

» Shortly after, the road turns hard right – becoming Old School Road. This takes you into Guestwick.

» Leave the village and the road bends sharply right, becoming Wood Dalling Road (for Wood Dalling and Cawston).

» Stay on this lane as it becomes Guestwick Road (again) and then Heydon Road, following the sign for Heydon.

» On Heydon Road take the fourth turning left (dead-end sign) to Heydon village; next, head back the way you came and go straight over the crossroads.

» Follow this lane for a mile as it gradually bends right and at the gatekeeper's cottage opposite the Salle Park Estate: turn right.

» Pass through the village, and then take the first right.

» Stay on this road to Wood Dalling. At the church turn left on to Church Lane and follow it along to the end.

» Bear right on to Guestwick Lane (which becomes Reepham Road), and follow it to Guestwick church.

» Now turn left (signposted Foulsham) and simply retrace your steps back: Old School Road, Station Road, Foulsham Road, and Guestwick Road, to arrive at the junction with Reepham Road.

» Turn right, and follow the road around left, on to Foulsham High Street and head on back to Norfolk Courtyard.

STOP AND SEE

EN ROUTE

Heydon Hall *Heydon, Norfolk, NR11 6RE*
All faded bricks and orderly Elizabethan chimney stacks, this breathtaking manor has been in the Bulwer family since 1756. Take a stroll in the grounds.

Village Tea Shop *The Street, Heydon, Norfolk, NR11 6AD; 01263 587211; www.heydonvillageteashop.co.uk*
Lacy tablecloths, Victoria sponges, and a window looking out on to the village green: a recipe for a good old-fashioned tea shop.

Salle Park Estate Gardens *Salle Park, Norfolk, NR10 4SF; 01603 870499; www.salleparkestate.co.uk*
Book an appointment with the head gardener and you can explore the formal lawns, topiary, and rose gardens that surround this magnificent red-brick Georgian manor house.

OFF ROUTE

Pensthorpe Nature Reserve *Fakenham Road, Fakenham, Norfolk, NR21 0LN; 01328 851465; www.pensthorpe.com*
Red squirrels, cranes, and otters are just some of the rare creatures you're likely to see at this 500-acre haven of wetlands, wild meadows, and gardens. There's a café serving home-cooked food and a gift shop selling candles and quirky children's toys.

EAT, DRINK, SLEEP

Norfolk Courtyard *Westfield Farm, Foxley Road, Foulsham, Norfolk, NR20 5RH; 01362 683333; www.norfolkcourtyard.co.uk*
If the shepherd's hut is a tad light on creature comforts for you, why not book one of the four luxurious rooms here? Country antiques sit beside contemporary patterned fabrics, and there's underfloor heating to keep your toes warm. Doubles from £75 per night.

Stable Cottage *Heydon Hall, Heydon, Norfolk, NR11 6RE; 01263 587343; www.heydon-bb.co.uk*
Escape the outside world in one of two rooms with roll-top baths, fresh flowers, and windows that open on to parkland. There's a resident barn owl to keep you company, and Heydon is a three-minute stroll away. Doubles from £80 per night.

Ivy House *Market Hill, Foulsham, Norfolk, NR20 5RU; 01362 683372; www.ivyhousefoulsham.co.uk*
There are two rooms to choose from (one double, one single) in this Georgian house in the centre of Foulsham. It may not be as smart as Norfolk Courtyard or Stable Cottage, but has half an acre of grounds for you to relax in after your ride. Plus it's conveniently close to a good pub. Double from £56 per night.

The Queens Head *2 High Street, Foulsham, Norfolk, NR20 5AD; 01362 683339; www.thequeenshead-foulsham.co.uk*
It might not be the swankiest pub you'll ever go to, but its owners, Jenny and Alan, serve good home-cooked food (including fresh fish, their own pork and free-range chickens), and a selection of ales.

The Earle Arms *The Green, Heydon, Norfolk, NR11 6AD; 01263 587376*
Strategically placed opposite the village green, this pub has hops hanging from beams inside and a menu featuring home-cooked lamb's liver and bacon with mash. You might find it difficult to leave.

RENT

MPG Leisure *Norwich Road, Fakenham, Norfolk, NR21 8AU; 01328 853861; www.mpgleisure.com*
A good selection of adult bikes, trailers, and tandems, from as little as £11 a day. And delivery is free of charge.

WELLS—NEXT—THE—SEA TO WIGHTON

A sandy beach, a stately home, and a surprisingly smart pub…

WHILE THE REST OF THE WORLD rushes about on deadlines, timetables, and crammed commuter trains, here in this quiet corner of Norfolk people are stretched out on the village green, shoes off, chatting.

Wells-next-the-Sea has a lot to offer for such a small place; a minute's ride from its grass hub, the narrow streets open out on to a quayside where the masts of multiple boats bob about drunkenly. And as you pootle along the cycle path by the harbour you hear the water rhythmically slapping against the sea wall and mast pulleys clanking in the breeze. Off to your right there's an uninterrupted view out to sea; distant rain clouds hover over the horizon like UFOs, extending pencil grey legs down to the water.

Where the sea wall ends, you join a path that hugs the coast to Holkham. Take a right fork, a few metres along, and you'll end up at the beach – where a parade of brightly coloured huts is lined up, shipshape and ready for inspection. Stick to the coast path, though, where the scenery alternates between tall grasses and wild orchids growing in patches of wetland. A dense strip of arrow-straight pine trees shelters you from the sea wind soughing through the branches overhead.

Soon you peel off left and pass through the gates of Holkham Hall Estate, where deer tiptoe about on the immaculately trimmed grass. The parkland here is enormous (as is the house, itself worth a visit), and the driveway stretches on for two miles – briefly parting right and left as you pass an ostentatious obelisk and finally make it to the exit gates.

Heading left on to a quiet lane you pop over a couple of crossroads before it's mostly downhill to Wighton. On your left, expansive golden fields lead to the sea – a thin navy strip on the horizon a few miles away, sparkling under the sun.

If this doesn't make you feel that all's right with the world, the fact that you're less than five minutes from a great pub probably will. In Wighton, a few quick turns see you arriving outside the Carpenters Arms, which is a lot more stylish than your average country boozer – with its smart grey walls and dark wooden tables. Friendly landlady Rose has put together a simple but tasty menu with dishes like crayfish tails and crusty bread (which tastes even better when washed down with a crisp glass of white).

Getting back to Wells from here is a cinch. Just follow your wheel-tracks back out of the village and head right. Then it's just a smooth lane and a couple of junctions before you're grabbing a drink from the Crown and heading outside to kick off those shoes…

THE ROUTE

DISTANCE 14½ MILES

DIFFICULTY ○○○

START **The Crown** *The Buttlands,*
Wells-next-the-Sea, Norfolk, NR23 1EX

» Head away from the Crown pub with the village green on your left.

» Turn right at the end of the road, then left, on to Staithe Street.

» At the end of Staithe Street turn left, then first right, through the quayside car park and on to the path alongside the sea wall.

» At its end, head left through another car park, on to the coastal path; follow the National Cycle Network (NCN 1) sign.

» Continue for 1½ miles before turning into the car park on your left; head through this and down Lady Ann's Road, which brings you out opposite Holkham Hall.

» Enter the estate, go past the hall and continue out to the gates at the other end.

» Turn left out of the gates, and go straight over the crossroads just along the lane.

» A mile later, go straight over another set of crossroads.

» Follow this road until you reach Wighton. For the Carpenters Arms, turn right at the junction, then immediately left. Keep following this road past the church; it bends left to bring you to the pub.

» From the pub, retrace your steps back out of the village and turn right – signposted Wells-next-the-Sea.

» After 1½ miles bear left at the junction – following the sign for the town centre.

» Take the first right, on to Polka Road. Then turn left on to Station Road.

» Take the second left, on to the Buttlands, to arrive outside the Crown.

STOP AND SEE

EN ROUTE

Wells-next-the-Sea Beach

This enormous stretch of sand the colour of milky coffee is famous for its bright beach huts that stand on stilts. Strong tides

can make swimming tricky, but it's the perfect place to spend the afternoon building sandcastles or exploring the wind-sculpted dunes.

Holkham Hall *Wells-next-the-Sea, Norfolk, NR23 1AB; 01328 710227; www.holkham.co.uk*
Holkham is one of the UK's grandest stately homes, with 3,000 acres of grounds, a lake, and a herd of 800 fallow deer. You could easily spend a whole day here.

The Carpenters Arms *55–57 High Street, Wighton, Norfolk, NR23 1PF; 01328 820752; www.carpentersarmswighton.co.uk*
A smart gastropub with Rose at its helm. The menu features dishes like venison steak on a red onion-and-summer-berry compote, and warm treacle tart for afters.

OFF ROUTE

Boat Trip to Blakeney Point *Between Sheringham and Wells-next-the-Sea, Norfolk; 01263 740241; see www.nationaltrust.org.uk*
Leave the bike behind and jump on a boat for a glimpse of the grey seals that lounge about on Blakeney Point. Owned by the National Trust, it's an important breeding area for seabirds, too.

EAT, DRINK, SLEEP

The Crown *The Buttlands, Wells-next-the-Sea, Norfolk, NR23 1EX; 01328 710209; www.thecrownhotelwells.co.uk*
Tucked away in a corner at the end of the village green, the Crown has 12 stylish

rooms with Roberts radios, flat-screen TVs, and solid wooden sleigh beds. Downstairs in the sunny dining room, tasty sirloin steaks and local seafood are served alongside Adnams ales.
Doubles from £90 per night.

The Globe Inn *The Buttlands, Wells-next-the-Sea, Norfolk, NR23 1EU; 01328 710206; www.holkham.co.uk/globe*
There are seven sunlit rooms to choose from, with wooden floors, original fireplaces and metal-framed beds. In the restaurant downstairs they serve refreshing dishes like chicken and chorizo salad with spinach, pine nuts, and chilli oil; alternatively, just take a pint outside to sup on the green.
Doubles from £105 per night.

Meadow View Guest House
53 High Street, Wighton, Norfolk, NR23 1PF; 01328 821527; www.meadow-view.net
Run by Rose from the Carpenters Arms, this luxurious guest house has five swish en suite rooms with large beds, bath robes, and more cushions than you know what to do with.
Doubles from £80 per night.

The Albatros *Wells-next-the-Sea, Norfolk*
This Dutch barge, moored in the harbour, has seen some action in its time. Once used for carrying soybeans from Europe, it now serves up tasty Dutch pancakes (try the apple, cinnamon, and syrup one).

RENT

On Yer Bike *The Laurels, Nutwood Farm, Wighton, Norfolk, NR23 1NX; 01328 820719; www.norfolkcyclehire.co.uk*
You'll find mountain bikes, trailers, child seats, and tag-alongs that all come with locks, pumps, repair kits, and route maps at this place. A day's rental costs £13 per adult. And you can request delivery (for an extra charge).

30

SEDGEFORD TO SNETTISHAM

Just you, the cornfields, and a few startled doves...

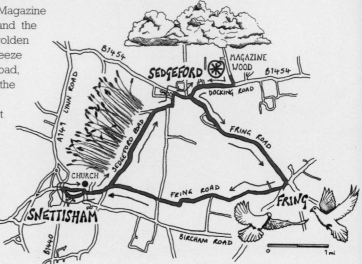

STANDING IN THE GARDEN at Magazine Wood, all that lie between you and the coast are fields upon fields of golden corn. Meanwhile, overhead, the sea breeze blows powder-puffs of cloud in from abroad, and around you, Maggie and Marmite – the resident dogs – run riot around the lawn.

Leaving them to their races, you set off down the treelined track and hang a right towards Sedgeford.

Before you reach the village, duck off left and drop down Fring Road – a narrow lane that threads between the flat, open fields for which Norfolk is famous. On the way to Fring, the only interruptions to these chalky-brown expanses are clusters of trees and the occasional red-brick cottage.

A couple of right turns later and you're pedalling down a lane that's little more than a cycle track. Surprised doves crack and flap their wings as they beat a hasty escape, announcing your presence to dozens of small animals ferreting in the bushes.

As you climb now, ever so gently, the general pancake-like nature of the East-Anglian landscape allows you to see for miles. In the distance there's a farmer steadily loading a trailer full of straw bales, no doubt hoping to get them safely to the barn before the approaching shower dishes out a soaking.

The subtle clicking of chain on cogs is the loudest sound you'll hear before you arrive at the edge of Snettisham. Ahead of you is St Mary's church spire, piercing the sky with its sharp Gothic spikes, and when you reach the village centre a quick right turn has you rolling up outside the Old Bank Coffee Shop – which cooks up a terrifically filling 'Bank burger' with all the trimmings.

Nip round the back and pass by the Rose and Crown pub to start the loop's last leg. On sunny days the pub's whitewashed walls and red-tiled roof stand out crisply against the blue sky.

Just along the lane you end up outside St Mary's church again (pop inside and check out the stained glass windows – you'll need to grab the key from the village shop), before swinging left and making your way back to Sedgeford. Glance left, across the pillows of golden corn, and you'll see the sea glinting in the sunlight on the horizon as you spin the pedals. It's shaping up for a cracking sunset back at Magazine Wood – where Marmite and Maggie are still going mad outside on the lawn...

THE ROUTE

DISTANCE   9½ MILES

DIFFICULTY   ✿✿

START   **Magazine Wood**

Peddars Way, Sedgeford, Norfolk, PE36 5LW

» Head right out of Magazine Wood and follow the track to the main road.

» Turn right to Sedgeford; take the first left, on to Fring Road.

» Follow this lane to Fring. Then turn right and right again, continuing until you reach a junction with Sedgeford Road: turn left.

» Stay on this road, passing St Mary's church on your right, before you reach the junction with the B1440.

» Turn right and you'll see the Old Bank Coffee Shop ahead. Just before this, take the right fork on to Hall Road.

» At the end, turn right again – on to Old Church Road.

» Follow this along past the church and round to the right; turn left at the junction.

» Follow this road all the way to Sedgeford.

» At the junction with the B1454, turn right to cycle back to Magazine Wood.

STOP AND SEE

EN ROUTE

The Old Bank Coffee Shop *10 Lynn Road, Snettisham, Norfolk, PE31 7LP; 01485 544080* Bright bistro serving great coffee. Sit outside in the sunshine or come back in the evening for home-made fishcakes and other tasty dishes (bring your own wine).

OFF ROUTE

RSPB Snettisham *Hunstanton, Norfolk; 01485 542689; see www.rspb.org.uk* Put simply, this is one of Europe's most important estuaries for wading birds and wildfowl. When the water engulfs its mudflats on big tides, tens of thousands take to the air at once, filling the sky with their flapping wings.

Holme-next-the-Sea Beach *www.holme-next-the-sea.co.uk* This huge stretch of golden sand is the

perfect place for a lazy stroll. Stretch out and feel the cool sand between your toes, or brace yourself and nip in for a dip.

EAT, DRINK, SLEEP

Magazine Wood *Peddars Way, Sedgeford, Norfolk, PE36 5LW; 01485 570422; www.magazinewood.co.uk*
Walk through the private entrance and you'll find yourself in a luxurious suite with a king-sized bed, plasma TV, iPod dock, and a spacious bathroom that comes with a walk-in shower. Ask nicely and Pip (the owner) will bring you one of her delicious breakfasts to eat in your room.
From £90 per night.

Sedgeford Hall *The Sedgeford Hall Estate, Sedgeford, Norfolk, PE36 5LT; 01485 572855; www.sedgefordhallestate.co.uk*
This Grade II-listed house with 1,200 acres of woods and parkland has three rooms with all the elegant trimmings anyone could possibly need to feel pampered. Opt for the four-poster room with a queen-sized bed and separate dressing room.
Doubles from £80 per night.

The Rose and Crown *Old Church Road, Snettisham, Norfolk, PE31 7LX; 01485 541382; www.roseandcrownsnettisham.co.uk*
Take your pick from 16 stylish rooms with crisp white sheets, power showers, fluffy towels, and Molton Brown toiletries. Awaiting you downstairs in the stone-floored traditional pub are local ales and a menu of filling meals such as beer-battered fish, hand-cut chips, and mushy peas.
Doubles from £95 per night.

RENT

AE Wallis *34–40 High Street, Heacham, Norfolk, PE31 7EP; 01485 571683; www.aewallis.co.uk*
Handily located about three miles from Sedgeford, AE Wallis offers a selection of bikes available for adults (£12 per day) and kids. They will deliver, too, for a small fee.

MIDLANDS

31

OXHILL TO BRAILES

Hidden villages, fine food, and stunning views…

THIS AREA IS ONE of England's best-kept secrets. Not only will you find breathtaking views galore, but almost every little hill you climb reveals yet another idyllic village, safely tucked away from mainstream crowds.

Head off down the lane from Oxbourne House B&B, pedal past the red-brick village hall, and on to the weather-worn church. Whoever says sparrows are endangered should see this place: there are hordes of them, all trying to out-tweet one another on the roofs of cottages lining the main street.

Leaving Oxhill, you emerge on to a ruler-straight road bordered by softly undulating fields, which leads directly to Middle Tysoe – where you encounter the first climb of the day. Don't worry, it's not get-off-and-push steep, and the view from the top is one of my favourites: 360 degrees of gentle hills and ancient woods.

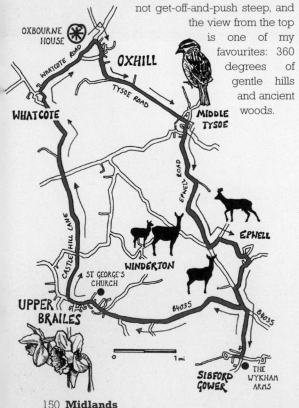

Half a mile later, you're freewheeling down to Epwell. Entering this tiny village feels like stumbling across a *Lord of the Rings* film set; at any second Frodo Baggins could emerge from one of the mustard-coloured cottages opposite the church, on his way for a pint at the Chandlers Arms – with its Hobbit-sized doorway and wood-burning stove. Karen, the landlady, whips up delicious home-made sandwiches here, including hot pear and Stilton – and a bacon, banana, and cheese combo.

Meanwhile, there's a wonderful lunch menu waiting at nearby Sibford's Wykham Arms, whose interior mixes ancient wooden beams and worn stone with modern touches like pistachio-green walls. If the weather's good, head to the sheltered patio outside, which becomes a suntrap from midday.

Architecture junkies will love the 17th-century house opposite: renovated in 1915 by Frank William Thomas Charles Lascelles (actor, sculptor, and all-round creative chap), it's an incredible hotchpotch of stained glass, square turrets, and thatched roof.

After working your way through the menu you'll be ready to tackle the climb back up to the main road before cruising to nearby Brailes. You're right on the border between England's South and Midlands here, and a green and brown collage of small fields unfolds for miles on either side. Visit in spring and the verges are bursting with colour; cream and yellow daffs blurring with splodges of cerise and purple as you hurtle on down to arrive in the village.

The first you see of it is the church tower, disproportionately large for a community so small. There's a great pub here, too (the George Hotel), as well as a French *pâtisserie* (La Tradition) run by an actual Frenchman, Regis.

Saddlebags laden with his delicious croissants, you're ready for the last leisurely leg. A smooth road takes you along to Whatcote and the Royal Oak – if you've any room left, the sausage and mash here is deelish. Or hold out till Oxbourne House, where owner Posy makes a mean cream tea…

OXFORDSHIRE BLUE PLAQUES BOARD

Frank William Thomas Charles
LASCELLES
1875 - 1934

Pageant Master,
writer, painter, sculptor
The man who staged the Empire

Built and lived here

SIBFORD GOWER PARISH COUNCIL

THE ROUTE

DISTANCE 16 MILES

DIFFICULTY ⚪⚪⚪⚪

START Oxbourne House

Oxhill, Warwickshire, CV35 0RA

» Head left from Oxbourne House and take the first right, into Oxhill village.

» Keep going, past the church and out into the lanes, until you reach a junction at Middle Tysoe: turn right.

» The road bends round to the right as you enter the village – but you go straight on, signposted Epwell.

» Climb the hill and carry on for a mile or so, then turn left, towards Epwell, at the fork just past White Home Farm.

» Cruise downhill for ¼ mile, then first right.

» Go through the village, past the church, bearing right, to a junction: turn right.

» Leave the village, then left at the junction.

» At the fork 300 metres later, bear left.

» Take the first right for Sibford Gower and the Wykham Arms.

» After lunch, retrace your steps to the B4035 at the top of the hill: turn left at the junction, and follow the B4035 to Brailes.

» Keep going through Brailes, past the George Hotel and La Tradition, and take the first right, signposted Whatcote.

» At the strange junction set-up (at the top of the climb): the road you're on banks right – but you go straight on, following the sign for Whatcote and Oxhill. Don't turn left!

» Keep following this road until you reach Whatcote, about 3 miles away.

» At Whatcote, turn right at the junction opposite the Royal Oak, towards Oxhill. You're now a mile from Oxbourne House.

STOP AND SEE

EN ROUTE

The Chandlers Arms *Epwell, Banbury, Oxfordshire, OX15 6LH; 01295 780747; see www.hooky-pubs.co.uk*

A cosy country pub with a rustic interior of exposed beams and a wood-burning stove.

Don't anticipate any gastro fanciness, though: this is the real (ale) deal, and home-made sandwiches are the order of the day.

The Wykham Arms *Sibford Gower, Oxfordshire, OX15 5RX; 01295 788808; www.wykhamarms.co.uk*

This sunny gastropub is off-the-beaten-track enough to avoid the crowds. Relaxed owners Damian and Debbie are trained chefs, hence the mouth-watering seasonal menu. Try the seared Malaysian-style chicken satay.

St George's Church *Brailes, Oxfordshire*

Quiet little Brailes was once one of the most prosperous towns in England – the clue's in the church spire. Dating back to 1450, it's far larger than you'd expect for such a small village. But in the Middle Ages, Brailes was a meeting point for drovers from all over England, who'd graze their sheep here before taking them on to Banbury market. In medieval architecture, a big spire meant *loadsamoney*. The fact sheets inside will give you the fascinating lowdown.

OFF ROUTE

Hook Norton Brewery *Brewery Lane, Hook Norton, Oxfordshire, OX15 5NY; 01608 737210; www.hooknortonbrewery.co.uk*

They've been brewing tasty Hooky ales here since 1850, and it's still all refreshingly low-key. Take a guided tour and see the original steam engine that still powers the place, meet the shire-horses that deliver to local pubs, and – of course – sample a few pints of Oxfordshire's favourite tipple.

EAT, DRINK, SLEEP

Oxbourne House *Oxhill, Warwickshire, CV35 0RA; 01295 688202; www.oxbournehouse.com*

A large modern home on the edge of the village, with an enormous back garden and tennis court looking out across fields. There are two rooms (go for the family room, which

has a spacious bathroom and living area), and self-catering annexes. Super-friendly owners Posy and Graeme have lots of ideas about hidden local treasures to explore. Doubles from £75 per night.

Buttslade House *Colony Road, Sibford Gower, Oxfordshire, OX15 5RX; 01295 788818; www.buttsladehouse.co.uk*

Your own private hideaway. The en suite double is tucked away in a cottage on the grounds of 17th-century Buttslade House. Smart and peaceful, it's the perfect place to unwind after a mellow ride through the lanes. The Wykham Arms is a minute's walk. Doubles from £75 per night.

Mine Hill House *Holloway Lane, Lower Brailes, Oxfordshire, OX15 5BJ; 01608 685594; www.minehillhouse.co.uk*

Big old farmhouse dating back to 1733, with a lovely garden overlooking the rolling fields of Warwickshire, Gloucestershire, and Oxfordshire. There's one room (cosy and rustic) with a quirky annex that's accessed via the bathroom – ideal for the kids. If you're feeling really lazy, Hester will cook a three-course meal in the evening. Double room from £90 per night; dinner £30 per head (pre-booking essential).

The Peacock *Main Street, Oxhill, Warwickshire, CV35 0QU; 01295 688060; www.thepeacockoxhill.co.uk*

Although owners Pam and Yvonne call this place a pub, it's really more of a restaurant – albeit one that has a relaxed, olde worlde atmosphere. It's won an *Observer* award for best Sunday roast, and the shepherd's pie is out of this world. The beer's great, too.

RENT

Stratford Bike Hire *(see p155 for contact)*

Family-run op with a range of bikes. Adult's bike £13 per day (with pump, lock, helmet, and tools). They'll deliver – phone for prices.

32

CLIFFORD CHAMBERS TO HIDCOTE GARDENS

Rolling meadows and tranquil gardens in the land of Shakespeare...

STRATFORD-UPON-AVON may be famous for its Shakespearean connection, but the nearby hamlet of Clifford Chambers is allegedly the Bard's *true* birthplace.

Cycling along its one street, you pass rows of red-brick cottages with immaculately trimmed topiary, while the only sounds around are the intermittent crowing from a nearby cockerel and hum of a distant lawn-mower. At the end of the village you leave it all behind, and peel off on to a bridleway.

Bouncing along through an avenue of trees, you emerge back on to tarmac at Atherstone-on-Stour, which is where the scenery starts to get *really* interesting. Meadows sweep away on either side as you climb slightly uphill, gaps in the hedgerows revealing groups of sheep chewing their way methodically through grassy lunches.

Freewheeling down into tiny Preston-on-Stour, you pass a wobbly-looking wood-timbered cottage that puts the Leaning Tower of Pisa to shame. Rest assured, though, there's little danger of it falling over; according to Will Spencer, who owns the farm next door, it's been here for over 500 years.

If you're feeling peckish, there's a village shop just along the road, where Nina serves up a mean beef and horseradish sandwich. And as you sit in the sun-soaked garden, washing it down with a cuppa, you probably won't see a single car drive past the whole time.

From here you press on towards Quinton, with the views getting more stunning all the time: birds of prey silhouetted against the sky, the village's church spire appearing on the skyline ahead, sheep dotted around distant pastures like mini balls of cotton wool.

After climbing up over a hill (come on, there's usually one), your reward is a relaxing afternoon pottering around Hidcote Gardens. It's worth nipping down the lane to the hamlet, too, where a gathering of thatched cottages encircles a small pond, and white puddle-ducks snooze on the green. During the summer you can pick your own strawberries

from the farm here – ideal accompaniments if you bought some snacks at Nina's, earlier.

From here you head along to the tiny village of Hidcote Boyce, with the view on your right stretching for over five miles and the air punctuated with the bleating of lambs.

There's a bit of a climb out of the village, but it's not long before you're freewheeling down into Ilmington, where a pint of Old Hooky awaits at the Howard Arms. Inside there's an open fire going (even in summer) and, if you're hungry, the fish and chips here is rather superb. Refuelled and raring to go, you cruise back through Preston-on-Stour and on to Clifford Chambers. Not a Bard day at all (sorry, I couldn't resist it)...

THE ROUTE

DISTANCE   17 MILES
DIFFICULTY   ○○○○
START   Cross o' th' Hill Farm

Clifford Road, Stratford-upon-Avon, CV37 8HP

» From Cross o' th' Hill Farm, head to the main road and turn right. Follow this for a mile then turn left for Clifford Chambers.

» Go down the street to the gates of the big house, ahead: turn right, on to the bridleway.

» Follow this along the edge of the fields (left, left, right), emerging on to tarmac at Atherstone-on-Stour. Turn right.

» Follow the road to Preston-on-Stour. Go through the village, passing the Village Shop, and reaching a crossroads: turn right.

» After 2 miles there's a junction: turn right.

» Take the next left.

» Follow this road for 2½ miles, to the entrance to Kiftsgate Court Gardens; take the next left – for Hidcote Gardens. To reach Hidcote and also Top Farm (for PYO fruit), follow the lane to the end and turn right.

» From Hidcote, retrace your route back to the junction opposite Kiftsgate Court Gardens and turn left – for Hidcote Boyce.

» Follow the road downhill and take the next left, into Hidcote Boyce – signed Ilmington.

» Continue on to Ilmington; keep going, past the Red Lion, and you'll see the Howard Arms on your left by the green.

» Exit the village, follow signs for Stratford.

» After passing the entry sign for Wimpstone, you'll reach a crossroads: turn left, signposted Preston-on-Stour.

» After a mile or so, you'll reach a junction: go straight over, into Preston.

» Retrace your route back through the village, over to Atherstone-on-Stour and across the bridleway to Clifford Chambers and Cross o' th' Hill Farm.

STOP AND SEE

EN ROUTE

The Village Shop *Preston Lane, Preston-on-Stour, Warwickshire,*
CV37 8NG; 01789 450938
Traditional store selling home-made cakes and sandwiches. There's a sweet little tea garden, too, and if you ask nicely, owner Nina will make up a packed lunch for the ride.

Kiftsgate Court Gardens *Chipping Campden, Gloucestershire, GL55 6LN; 01386 438777; www.kiftsgate.co.uk*
Series of beautiful interconnecting gardens planted by three generations of the same family. Take a peaceful stroll along the terraces, through bluebell-carpeted woods, and round the contemporary water garden. Stress will seem like an alien concept.

Hidcote Gardens *Hidcote Bartrim, nr Chipping Campden, Gloucestershire, GL55 6LR; 01386 438333; www.nationaltrust.org.uk*
Just along the lane from Kiftsgate, Hidcote is another spot where tranquillity rules. Step into the gardens and you'll immediately be greeted by the scent of flowers. There are tons of nooks and crannies where you can get wonderfully lost – all rather romantic.

OFF ROUTE

Stratford-upon-Avon *Warwickshire*
It would be daft to be this close to all the history, culture, and coffee shops that Stratford offers, and not to take a peek. You can walk here from Cross o' th' Hill Farm (maps available) in 15 minutes. Treat yourself to a bit of Shakespeare with a play at the Courtyard Theatre, take a boat trip on the river, or simply stroll the streets and stare at the unbelievably old buildings.

EAT, DRINK, SLEEP

Cross o' th' Hill Farm *Clifford Road, Stratford-upon-Avon, Warwickshire, CV37 8HP; 01789 204738; www.cross-o-th-hill-farm.com*
Three beautiful rooms in a large, homely farmhouse B&B. Decima and David make you feel instantly welcome, with enthusiastic suggestions about what to see and do. The rooms are spacious, with lovely views. Doubles from £94 per night.

The Howard Arms *Lower Green, Ilmington, Warwickshire, CV36 4LT; 01608 682226; www.howardarms.com*
This 400-year-old Cotswold-stone inn has bags of character. There are eight rooms altogether: three above the pub, with solid, period-style furniture and smart styling, and five swanky new rooms out back (modern and spacious). The pub has an open fire, excellent service, and a stream that runs through the middle when it rains. Yes, really. Doubles from £135 per night.

White Sails *85 Evesham Road, Stratford-upon-Avon, Warwickshire, CV37 9BE; 01789 264321; www.white-sails.co.uk*
Chic, boutique guest house with a large garden on the edge of town. Four sumptuous rooms each with a big bed and indulgent bathroom ensure you totally chill. Doubles from £95 per night.

Lambs *12 Sheep Street, Stratford-upon-Avon, Warwickshire, CV37 6EF; 01789 292554; www.lambsrestaurant.co.uk*
On the outside this place is all timber beams and wonky walls, but step inside and it's been jazzed up. Wooden floors and original features sit alongside funky high-backed leather chairs – and the menu's rather delicious, too.

RENT

Stratford Bike Hire *Seven Meadows Road, Stratford-upon-Avon, Warwickshire, CV37 6GR; 07711 776340; www.stratfordbikehire.com*
See p153 for details.

HELPFUL HINT

You'll need a mountain bike for the bridle path from Clifford Chambers to Atherstone.

33

ASHFORD BOWDLER TO PIPE ASTON

A medieval church, a magnificent castle, and old cobbled streets…

THE FIRST THING you notice about Orchard House is the calm. Having slipped away from work early and escaped to the countryside, you can run the roll-top bath, chuck in some bubbles, and wash away a week's worth of stress. Although it feels quite modern inside, the house dates back 300 years – the exposed beams in the bedroom walls are a clue to its antiquity.

The village itself is even more ancient, with the church allegedly dating back to 1211. Nowadays it clings precariously to the banks of the River Teme, but if you pop your head in you'll see two blocked-up Norman doorways at each end. According to locals, the main road used to pass through here and the doors were used by pilgrims looking for an en route blessing (like a spiritual 'drive-through').

You'll feel pretty blessed yourself, as you head out into the rather splendid Shropshire countryside. After a quick right and left to cross the main road, you'll be cruising along a narrow lane where the hedgerows on either side reach way up over your head. Somewhere in the background you can hear sheep calling to each other across the fields, and if you peek through the gaps in the hedges on your left you'll catch a glimpse of the Shropshire Hills.

A single-track lane leads to a small 12th-century church set back from the road. It's worth stopping off for a rest here; there's a weathered old bench in the churchyard where you can sit and contemplate the green and gold tiling of the fields below.

From here you drop down sharply and traverse the hillside – a plateau of farmland stretching all the way to Herefordshire. Two miles later, and still hugging the hill, you cruise up between leafy trees – where blackbirds bounce about in the leaf litter looking for titbits, their excitable chatter amplified by the tightly spaced trunks. Emerging from the woods on to unkempt meadows, you'll see the pinks of foxgloves and raspberries rebelling against the extensive greenery.

There's a bit of a climb between here and the next junction, but soon you're on the way to Ludlow via the pretty hamlet of Pipe Aston, where the gardens of white cottages are ablaze with oranges, reds, and purples erupting from immaculate flowerbeds.

As you reach the outskirts of Ludlow, you see the town laid out below in all its glory – notably the weathered castle walls which, from up here, are the colour of elephants' skin. Dating back 1,000 years, this former military outpost was originally built by the Normans (them again) to fend off the marauding Welsh chieftains, before becoming a royal palace for a few centuries. But this is just skimming the surface of the rich history contained within these walls, and a visit here is a fascinating way to round off the day.

After all the ride's ups, downs, and historical intrigue, you deserve some serious calories. Ludlow is famous for its foodie shops and eateries, so why not pay a visit to Deli on the Square for some cakes and elderflower pressé to take back to Orchard House? It's only a couple of miles before you're back to all that wonderful relaxation.

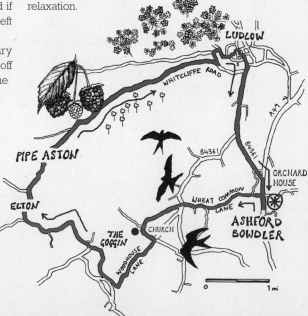

THE ROUTE

DISTANCE 13½ MILES
DIFFICULTY ◐◐◐○
START Orchard House

Ashford Bowdler, Shropshire, SY8 4DJ

» If you'd like to check out the church first, head right out of Orchard House's drive and pedal along to the village.

» Retrace your steps back past Orchard House, to the main road.

» Turn right on to the A49 for about 150 metres, taking the first left on to Wheat Common Lane.

» Continue for 1½ miles to the crossroads with the B4361; go straight over, towards Richard's Castle.

» Stay on this road for 1½ miles, passing the medieval church at Richard's Castle, then down to a crossroads: turn right on to Woodhouse Lane.

» Keep following this road as it hugs the hill, signposted The Goggin and Elton.

» At the end of the lane turn right, for Ludlow.

» Over the next 3 miles you'll pass through Elton and Pipe Aston before arriving above Ludlow. Just before you reach Whitcliffe Common take the turning left and descend into Ludlow. Cross Dinham Bridge and pedal past the castle, into the town square.

» From the square, head right, down Silk Mill Lane and over the bridge, on to Overton Road (the B4361).

» Follow this for a mile to the junction with the A49. Turn right and it's then just ½ mile back to Orchard House, which you'll find on your left.

STOP AND SEE

EN ROUTE

St Bartholomew Church *Richard's Castle, Herefordshire*
Stop and savour the tranquillity outside this 12th-century church. No longer used for regular services, it makes a great place for a snack. Look out for the swallows darting in and out of the eaves.

Ludlow Castle *Castle Square, Ludlow, Shropshire, SY8 1AY; 01584 873355; www.ludlowcastle.com*
Stop for a cup of tea and a wander around the magnificent ruins of this medieval castle. For centuries this stronghold formed the frontier between England and its unconquerable neighbour, Wales.

OFF ROUTE

Mortimer Forest *Between Pipe Aston and Ludlow; 01584 813826; see www.forestry.gov.uk*
Originally the hunting ground of Saxon kings, this dense woodland is littered with walking- and cycling-trails.

EAT, DRINK, SLEEP

Orchard House *Ashford Bowdler, Shropshire, SY8 4DJ; 01584 831270; www.orchard-barn.co.uk*
This renovated clapboard barn has three cosy rooms with exposed wooden beams (book the Byre if you want the roll-top bath). Breakfast is in a sunny dining room looking out on to the spacious garden – an ideal place to relax after your ride.
Doubles from £80 per night.

Abbots Lodge *Wigmore, Herefordshire, HR6 9UD; 01568 770036; www.abbotslodgebandb.co.uk*
A stylish, spacious room with a sheepskin rug, wood-burning stove, solid wooden bed, and your own private terrace. Shut yourself away and let the owner, Janet, cook up something fancy for dinner.
From £90 per night.

Ludlow Castle *See 'Stop and See' for contact details.*
Free-standing baths, flat-screen TVs, and complimentary passes to the castle. If all this isn't incentive enough to book one of these luxurious self-catering apartments in the grounds of the castle, how about the

hamper they'll have waiting for you on your arrival? It's packed with goodies from an award-winning deli nearby.
Three-night stay for four people from £480.

La Bécasse *17 Corve Street, Ludlow, Shropshire, SY8 1DA; 01584 872325; www.labecasse.co.uk*
Treat yourself to a meal by Michelin-starred head chef, Will Holland. While you soak up the atmosphere among the oak-panelled walls, he'll put together treats like new-season lamb in a herb crumb with pea purée, fennel jam, and liquorice sauce. It's not as expensive as you might think, either, with two courses available for under £50.

The Church Inn *The Buttercross, Ludlow, Shropshire, SY8 1AW; 01584 872174; www.thechurchinn.com*
If you're after a cosy real ale pub, this is it. There are eight tipples on at any one time, from Twisted Spire to Boiling Well – produced locally by the Ludlow Brewing Company. The puddings are good, too – try the Church Inn mess.

RENT

Wheely Wonderful Cycling *Petchfield Farm, Elton, Shropshire, SY8 2HJ; 01568 770755; www.wheelywonderfulcycling.co.uk*
Located conveniently close to this cycle route, they've got a fleet of hybrids, lightweight mountain bikes, tandems, and trailer bikes – ideal if you're bringing little ones. Adult bikes cost £18–£24 per day.

34

SHOTTLE TO CARSINGTON WATER

Look down on a miniature Midlands world…

FROM THE SWING CHAIR in the garden at Dannah Farm, all you can see are the humped green backs of fields meeting the bright blue sky. And with the sun blazing down and bees busy at work in the flowerbeds, you'd be forgiven for not moving a muscle. If you do venture out, however, you'll be richly rewarded.

Cruise along the narrow lane from the farm, with fields cascading down into the Ecclesbourne Valley on your left, and you'll be tempted to whip out the camera immediately. But there are even better views to be had up ahead, at Alport Height. Standing on the viewing point it feels like you're on top of the world, with vistas stretching for 60 miles on a clear day – all the way to Worcestershire's Malvern Hills.

The fabulous panoramas continue as you carry on along the vale, past small birds that fling themselves in front of your wheels then flutter off in the nick of time. Peer down to the left for a glimpse of Wirksworth in the valley below; from your lofty vantage point it looks like handfuls of model houses have been sprinkled into the valley from above.

Head downhill to join the cycle path at Black Rocks Country Park. In the mid 1800s this was the High Peak railway line that shunted stone, cotton, and other raw materials around the country; now it's part of a system of tranquil trails threading through the Derbyshire countryside.

If you're hungry when you reach Brassington, call in at Ye Olde Gate Inn for a slice of fidget pie – a lively combination of ham, cheese, and potato – just what you need to refuel empty legs. Not that you'll require much energy for the next part, as you can freewheel practically all the way down to Carsington Water – which you'll soon see spread out before you, glimmering. Coast along the mellow waterfront cycle path that leads you towards Wirksworth. After a morning spent looking down on the world, you now get to admire it all from below – the fields above dotted with distant sheep.

Before long you're up high again, having ascended the other side of the valley, where you can look across at the lanes you rode along this morning. There's just one more climb to get you back over to Dannah Farm, and you may want to walk it. The good news, though, is that once you're there you can spend the rest of the day in the spa cabin – the views are pretty good from the hot-tub, too.

THE ROUTE

DISTANCE   20½ MILES

DIFFICULTY   ○○○○○

START   **Dannah Farm** *Bowmans Lane, Shottle, Belper, Derbyshire, DE56 2DR*

» Head right out of the farm, along Chequer Lane. This becomes Sprout Lane, then Alport Lane, taking you past Alport Height.

» Continue for another mile (as it becomes Hey Lane), then take the right fork (it's the fifth right) on to Breamfield Lane.

» Follow this to the end, turn left on to Belper Lane, and drop downhill to a junction: go straight on to the B5035.

» As the B5035 bends left at the Malt Shovel Inn, you bear right (effectively straight) on to Oakerthorpe Road.

» Reaching Bolehill, Oakerthorpe Road bears sharp left and you'll see Brickfields Close on your right; turn right, down the unmarked road immediately after Brickfields Close.

» Quarter of a mile later, turn right on to the High Peaks Trail at Black Rocks.

» Bear right on to this trail, cross the railway bridge and carry on for 3 miles; after passing the quarry and Harborough Rocks,

you'll reach the B5056.

» Take the track left (instead of joining the main road); skirt along the edge of the fields, then turn left on to the lane.

» Continue to Brassington, passing under a railway bridge.

» Continuing straight through Brassington, along Dale End and Town Street, you reach the junction with the B5035.

» Turn right then take the first left, signposted Carsington Water.

» Take the first left, into Carsington Water.

» Turn left at the next junction and follow the road to the car park, where you bear left to join the cycle path.

» Follow the cycle path for a mile or so before veering off left at Sheepwash car park, to arrive at a junction with the B5035.

» Turn left then immediately right, following the sign for Carsington (and also the blue cycle sign (54A)).

» Continue through Carsington and on to Hopton, reaching a junction with the B5035.

» Bear left on to the B5035 then take the first right, on to Stainsborough Lane.

» Follow this lane for over a mile, taking the third left, on to Topshill Lane.

» Less than ¼ mile later go straight over the staggered crossroads, on to Tinkerley Lane, signposted Idridgehay.

» At the end bear left on to Wood Lane.

» At the bottom of the hill you reach a junction with the B5023: turn right then immediately left, on to Jebb's Lane.

» Follow Jebb's Lane to the top of the hill then turn left, on to Top Lane.

» At the end of Top Lane, turn left on to Palace Lane, towards Alport.

» At the next junction, turn right, on to Chequer Lane (towards Shottle), arriving at Dannah Farm ¼ mile later.

STOP AND SEE

EN ROUTE

Alport Height *Alport Lane, nr Wirksworth, Derbyshire*

Just along the lane from Dannah Farm, this 300-metre peak gives you almost 360 degrees of countryside views. Stop for a snack and look out all the way across Shropshire and into Worcestershire.

Ye Olde Gate Inn *Well Street, Brassington, Derbyshire, DE4 4HJ; 01629 540448*

Dating back to 1616, this lively village tavern serves a mixed menu of pub classics and modern additions, such as monkfish kebabs, without compromising on the traditional atmosphere. Check out the wooden beams, which were salvaged from ships sunk during the Spanish Armada's attempted invasion.

Carsington Water *Ashbourne, Derbyshire, DE6 1ST; 01629 540478; www.carsingtonwater.com*
Sail, kayak, windsurf, climb… or simply sit back with a coffee and admire the green hills of the Peaks rising up on all sides. When was the last time you got to do that?

OFF ROUTE

Haddon Hall *Bakewell, Derbyshire, DE45 1LA; 01629 812855; www.haddonhall.co.uk*
Probably the most pristine example of a fortified medieval manor house you'll ever see. Since the 12th century it has somehow managed to survive the Revolution, fire, and changing tastes of capricious aristocrats, to remain intact. Take a tour around the house and stroll in the peaceful terraced gardens.

EAT, DRINK, SLEEP

Dannah Farm *Bowmans Lane, Shottle, Belper, Derbyshire, DE56 2DR; 01773 550273; www.dannah.co.uk*
Joan, the owner, brings you tea and cake the moment you arrive – setting the tone for an indulgent weekend. There are 10 uniquely designed suites to choose from – many with spa baths or hot-tubs; all with flat-screen TVs, iPod docks, and other goodies. And then there's the spa cabin… Doubles from £140 per night.

Number 37 *37 Coldwell Street, Wirksworth, Derbyshire, DE4 4FB; 01629 824258; www.number37wirksworth.co.uk*
This former 'gentleman's residence', on a quiet Wirksworth street, has two stylish rooms (one twin; one double) with great views. Owners Chris and Denise also offer vegetarian, vegan, or meat evening meals – just let them know what you fancy. Rooms from £60 per night.

Breach Farm *Carsington, Derbyshire, DE4 4DD; 01629 540265; www.breachfarm.co.uk*
If Dannah Farm is a tad pricey, try this grey-stone farmhouse set in 14 acres: located just along the road from Carsington Water, with wide-open views and resident chickens wandering around. Take your pick from two en suite rooms (a double and a single). Double from £70 per night.

Le Mistral *23 Market Place, Wirksworth, Derbyshire, DE4 4ET; 01629 824840*
This red-fronted French bistro serves tasty Toulouse sausages and mash with onion gravy, plus a range of specials. Sit upstairs and look out over the street, or book a table in the arched cellar for more intimacy.

RENT

Carsington Sports & Leisure Cycle Hire *Carsington Water, Ashbourne, Derbyshire, DE6 1ST; 01629 540478; see www.carsingtonwater.com*
Mountain bikes, tag-alongs, child seats, and buggies are all available, with adult bikes costing £15 per day, including helmet.

HELPFUL HINT

Bring a bike with lots of gears – there are a few demanding hills.

35

BONSALL TO WINSTER

See over the hills and far away...

TUCK YOURSELF AWAY IN some corner of Cascades Gardens, with nothing more than birds, butterflies, and a good book for company, and no one need ever find you. The house may only be a minute's walk away, but here, among the four acres of flowerbeds and walks that burrow into cliffs, you enter another world – one in which the only disturbance is an occasional bumblebee lumbering about in the flowers.

Built in 1823 by the owner of the mill that once stood here, the house and gardens lie on the edge of Bonsall, surrounded by excellent cycling country that takes you across hilltops and down into green valleys. Climbing gently into the village, past the pub, and on up between rows of cottages, you emerge on to a lush lane that looks out across grassy meadows.

A mile or so later you fork right and it's not long before Matlock is slowly unveiled by the sloping, downhill landscape. From way up here it's difficult to make out individual houses, with the mass of grey stone buildings looking like a flow of lava was poured into the green valley and left to set long ago.

Although you probably won't see any cars, the lane down to town is steep and narrow, so keep an eye out. At the bottom it sweeps left and you cruise along to Snitterton, passing verges speckled with pinky-purple flowers.

Carrying on through Oker, you climb gently out of the village, up through Wensley, and on to Winster

– accompanied the whole way by wide, open views of the Peaks in every imaginable shade of green.

You'll probably be ready for a cuppa by the time you reach Winster; the village shop sells good coffee and home-made cake or – if you're after something more substantial – the Old Bowling Green pub offers a range of ever-changing chef's specials.

Once you're suitably refuelled, the climb up East Bank quickly brings your legs back to life. At the top there's a 180-degree view out over the Peaks. Stretching for 30 miles or more on a clear day, it offers another excellent reason to stop.

The good news now is that the road flattens out as you leave the village and swing left on to Bonsall Lane, the glorious views continuing as you breeze downhill back into Bonsall. Time to grab that book and head for the garden, again.

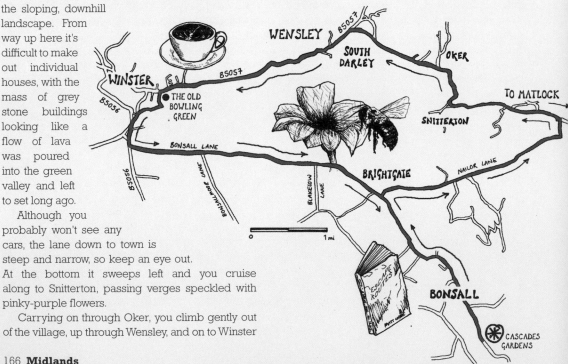

THE ROUTE

DISTANCE   12 MILES
DIFFICULTY   ○○○○
START   Cascades Gardens

Clatterway, Bonsall, Derbyshire, DE4 2AH

» Turn right from Cascades Gardens, cycle up through Bonsall and out the other side for 2 miles, until you reach a fork.

» Bear right, signposted Matlock, and stay on this road as it drops downhill, and sweeps left, through the hamlet of Snitterton.

» Continue on, through Oker, to a junction with the B5057. Turn left and continue through Wensley and on to Winster.

» When you reach Winster, take the first left (on to East Bank) and climb up out of the village, past the Old Bowling Green pub.

» At the top of East Bank, bear left at the junction and carry on to the next one – at the top of the hill.

» Bear left again, on to the B5056, then take the first left on to Bonsall Lane.

» Follow this for 2 miles, until you reach a fork at Brightside: bear right and cruise downhill, back to Bonsall.

STOP AND SEE

EN ROUTE

Matlock *Derbyshire*
Spend a couple of hours mooching around the independent shops here, or head to the park for a picnic (there's a bandstand and everything).

The Old Bowling Green *East Bank, Winster, Derbyshire, DE4 2DS; 01629 650219; www.peakparkpub.co.uk*
This grey-stone pub dates back to 1472, and since David and Marilyn Bentley took over in 1990 it's won lots of awards for serving quality beer.

OFF ROUTE

The Heights of Abraham *Matlock Bath, Derbyshire, DE4 3PD; 01629 582365; www.heightsofabraham.com*

Take a cable car from Matlock Bath and head up to a plateau overlooking the valley. From here you can take a guided tour around the labyrinthine cave systems that burrow deep into the hillside, check out an exhibition, or simply admire the view.

Matlock Bath *Derbyshire*
A 15-minute cycle ride into the valley from Bonsall brings you to this bizarre strip of fish-and-chip shops, cafés, amusement arcades, and pubs. Think Blackpool (but nicer) surrounded by green hills.

EAT, DRINK, SLEEP

Cascades Gardens *Clatterway, Bonsall, Derbyshire, DE4 2AH; 01629 822464; www.cascadesgardens.com*
Aside from the surrounding greenery at beautiful Cascades Gardens, there are four luxury rooms. Each one is subtly themed

(try the India Suite) with exotic bits and bobs that blend with original fireplaces and spacious bathrooms.
Doubles from £72 per night.

Holmefield Guest House *Dale Road North, Darley Dale, Derbyshire, DE4 2HY; 01629 735347; see www.englishretreats.com*
Book yourself into the Chatsworth Room and you can enjoy a long soak in the slipper bath that looks out over Derwent Valley. This restored house is surrounded by over an acre of gardens, has a library, and offers in-house evening meals – ensuring you'll switch off properly.
Doubles from £79 per night.

Silver Ridge *Foxholes Lane, Tansley, Derbyshire, DE4 5LF; 01629 55071; www.silverridgetansley.co.uk*
Perched on Tansley Moor, on the other side of Matlock, this former labourer's cottage dates back to 1760. The three rooms are of a high standard, and include hand-made wooden furniture, flat-screen TVs, and other careful touches.
Doubles from £90 per night.

The Riva *124 North Parade, Matlock Bath, Derbyshire, DE4 3NS; 01629 581662; www.theriva.co.uk*
A blend of olde worlde pub and modern gastro, with untreated wooden tables and high-backed leather chairs. Try the oak-smoked trout from the local smokehouse.

RENT

Middleton Top Cycle Hire *Middleton-by-Wirksworth, Matlock, DE4 4LS; 01629 823204*
You'll find a good range of mountain bikes in all sizes here, along with children's buggies and trailers. And if you fancy sharing the work, there are tandems, too. An adult's bike costs from £14 per day; proof of ID needed.

36

WHITWELL TO NORMANTON

On the waterfront in England's smallest county...

THIS ENORMOUS FRESHWATER LAKE may be man-made, but the ducks don't seem to mind one bit. There are loads of them. In fact, Rutland Water is renowned for its birdlife, with four pairs of rare ospreys nesting here each summer after flying in from their winter residence in Senegal, West Africa.

It's also a wonderful place to bring the kids, with a purpose-built cycle track ringing its way around the perimeter, which offers up rather magnificent views, wandering sheep, and as much ice cream as you can possibly eat.

After picking up some bikes from the cycle hire centre at Whitwell, you head left out of the shop and follow the smooth tarmac around a little inlet.

Already the vistas out over the rippling lake are spectacular – the sun glinting off the water as though it were topped with a sheet of diamonds, against the backlit hills on the opposite shore. A mile or so

(and a couple of cattle grids) later, you reach the dam that marks the eastern end of the lake – a huge heap of rocks that looks like it was left here long ago by some mythical giant. It's the perfect place for a family photo, with the lake stretching out behind and little sailboats bobbing about in the background.

From here you carry on around to the right, weaving your way between the many sheep that congregate on the grass lining the path, before arriving at Normanton cycle centre on the opposite shore from where you began.

The best bit is that there's ice cream here – tons of it. So order a round of 99s and head down to the waterfront, where you can sit back in the sun and watch various ducks landing chaotically nearby – in the hope of a few crumbs – all quack and splash.

Suitably refreshed, you now get to cruise along flat, smooth tarmac back the way you came, all the way to Whitwell.

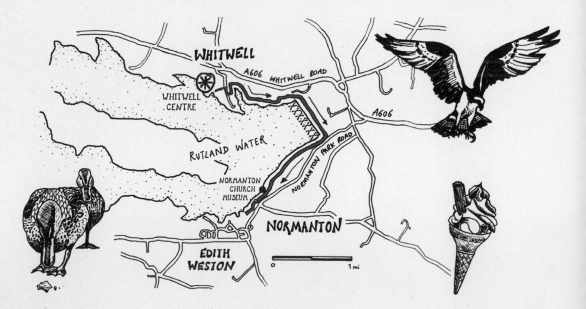

THE ROUTE

DISTANCE   7 MILES

DIFFICULTY   ⚪⚪

START   Whitwell Centre

Bull Brig Lane, Whitwell, Rutland, LE15 8BL

» Head left out of the Whitwell Centre (where you can hire bikes) to the car park's exit, then turn right into Bull Brig Lane.

» Take the first left and follow the track towards the lake. This will bend round to the left as you join the cycle path.

» Simply follow this track as it winds its way around the lake – keeping the waterfront on your right.

» After the dam at the top of the lake, the track bends right and arrives at Normanton.

» To return, just retrace your steps.

STOP AND SEE

EN ROUTE

Normanton Church Museum *South Shore, nr Edith Weston, Rutland, LE15 8RP; 01572 653026*

This evocative old building, complete with a little tower, is Rutland's best-known landmark. Eerily half-submerged on the water's edge, it houses fossilised prehistoric remains – including an Anglo-Saxon female skeleton – that will capture kids' imaginations.

OFF ROUTE

Lyndon Visitor Centre *Rutland Water Nature Reserve, Lyndon Hill, Rutland, LE15 8RN; 01572 737378; www.rutlandwater.org.uk*

The views of the lake as you arrive are worth the trip here alone. As you descend the hill, the whole of Rutland Water stretches out before you, gleaming in the sun. This world-renowned reserve attracts over 20,000 feathered friends each year – including rare ospreys from March to September, which are a spectacular sight.

The Horse and Jockey Inn *2 Saint Mary's Road, Manton, Rutland, LE15 8SU; 01572*

737335; www.horseandjockeyrutland.co.uk
This privately owned pub is a suntrap – the tables outside just what you need on a long summer's day. Even better, it's totally geared up for cyclists, with racks outside so you can lock up the bikes before enjoying a gammon steak.

The Rutland Belle *Whitwell Harbour, Rutland; 01572 787630; www.rutnet.co.uk*
See the other side of Rutland Water on a 45-minute cruise around the reservoir. Departs from Whitwell Harbour on the hour – and from Normanton at twenty past.

EAT, DRINK, SLEEP

The Finch's Arms *Oakham Road, Hambleton, Rutland, LE15 8TL; 01572 756575; www.finchsarms.co.uk*
Perched on a hill overlooking the lake, this 17th-century pub has six stylish rooms, with black wood, mocha-coloured bedspreads, and en suite walk-in showers (or roll-top baths in rooms 3, 4, and 6). The food's delicious, too – especially the apple and raspberry crumble.
Doubles from £95 per night.

Beech House *Main Street, Clipsham, Rutland, LE15 7SH; 01780 410355; www.theolivebranchpub.com*
Swish bathrooms, antique furniture, and goose-down duvets ensure total relaxation at this quiet country house, five miles from Rutland Water. Across the road is the Olive Branch pub, which has a Michelin star for dishes like white pork stew with sage and onion mash, and seasonal vegetables.
Doubles from £110 per night.

The Admiral Hornblower *64 High Street, Oakham, Rutland, LE15 6AS; 01572 723004; www.hornblowerhotel.co.uk*
Stay in one of 10 smart rooms in the restored 17th-century farmhouse behind the pub and restaurant. Sturdy wooden

furniture and oatmeal-coloured walls give off a relaxed vibe – and you're only a few steps away from a pint of real ale and roast rump of lamb on colcannon – just what you want when you're escaping the nine-to-five. Doubles from £60 per night.

RENT

Rutland Cycling *Whitwell Centre, Bull Brig Lane, Whitwell, Rutland, LE15 8BL; 01780 460060; www.rutlandactivities.co.uk*
Allegedly home to Europe's largest cycle-hire fleet, with a huge range of bikes for all ages and abilities. Tandems, trailers, hybrids, and mountain bikes… oh and there are electric bikes, too – if you're feeling lazy. Adult bikes from £15.99 per day.

HELPFUL HINT

Bring some binoculars – there's a lot to see.

NORTH WEST

37

HEBDEN BRIDGE TO TODMORDEN

Peace, tranquillity, and waterfront pubs...

ONE OF THE FIRST questions you're bound to ask when you arrive in Hebden Bridge is 'how am I going to get out of here without going uphill?' Tucked away in the Upper Calder Valley, the town is surrounded on either side by steep (and I mean *steep*) wooded hillsides, which are not really conducive to cycling – at least not the leisurely kind. But take a closer look, and you'll find that there is Another Way: the canal.

The Rochdale Canal, to be exact, and it runs parallel with the road that meanders through the town, remaining gloriously flat the whole way. Better news still is that it takes approximately 17 seconds to get to the towpath from Holme House, the rather smart B&B that lies on one of the town's side streets.

As you cruise up to the bridge and on to the waterfront, the first thing you notice is the tranquillity. Take a snap along here and you could sell it as a postcard: swans snoozing on the bank, a couple strolling arm in arm, and a statuesque narrowboat gliding silently over the water up ahead.

Half a mile later and you're outside the Stubbing Wharf pub, where groups of friends are gathered around tables, chatting in the sunshine. Bikes lean against a nearby wall (unlocked) and there's another narrowboat, moored just a few metres away ('fancy a tipple, dear?').

Further on you pass someone sitting outside their cottage, painting, and before you know it you're leaving the trappings of town life behind. The old mills and workshops that lined the water's edge a couple of miles back are replaced by the leafy frills of the hillsides.

At certain points along the way, where the towpath sweeps right or left to follow the contours of the valley, you get fleeting glimpses of the moorland that lies beyond. More than this, though: it gives you a sense of how the canal was simply carved out of this hillside back in the late 1700s.

Like many towns in this part of the world, the waterway is the reason why Hebden Bridge is here – at least in its present guise. When the area exploded with mills during the Industrial Revolution, the Rochdale was a vital supply route to major cities such as Manchester.

It's fascinating seeing the leftovers from that exciting era as you continue on along to Todmorden – workers' cottages, old mill chimneys, and, of course, locks. There are 90-odd in total, along the canal's 32 miles, meaning it's slow progress at certain points for those in boats. Not, however, for those on bikes.

After four miles of hill-free cycling, you arrive in Todmorden and peel off over the bridge, for a long lunch in the Golden Lion before heading back.

THE ROUTE

DISTANCE 9 MILES

DIFFICULTY ◐◐

START *Holme House New Road,
Hebden Bridge, West Yorkshire, HX7 8AD*

» Turn left from Holme House and turn right
when you reach the canal towpath.

» Simply follow the towpath for the next
4½ miles, to Todmorden.

» When you see the Golden Lion pub, on
the opposite side of the path, you need to
leave the towpath at the next bridge.

» To get back to Hebden Bridge, just
retrace your steps back along the towpath.

STOP AND SEE

EN ROUTE

The Stubbing Wharf *King Street, Hebden
Bridge, West Yorkshire, HX7 6LU;
01422 844107; www.stubbingwharf.com*
Sit outside this waterfront pub and watch
the narrowboats chug past on their way
to who-knows-where. If you're feeling
peckish, order some pâté on toast with
home-made chutney.

The Golden Lion *Fielden Square,
Todmorden, Lancashire, OL14 6LZ;
01706 816333;
www.thegoldenliontodmorden.co.uk*
Grab an outside table overlooking the
canal, and settle back in the sunshine to
watch the world go by. After all, it's not as
if there are any hills on the return journey...

OFF ROUTE

Hardcastle Crags *Hollin Hall, Crimsworth
Dean, Hebden Bridge, West Yorkshire,
HX7 7AP; 01422 844518;
see www.nationaltrust.org.uk*
Head up to this wooded valley, just outside
Hebden Bridge, and take a scenic walk
along rivers and waterfalls. Gibson Mill is
well worth a look, too, for a glimpse into the
lives of the 19th-century mill workers who
lived round here.

Little Valley Brewery *Cragg Vale, Hebden
Bridge, West Yorkshire, HX7 5TT; 01422
883888; www.littlevalleybrewery.co.uk*
Anyone with the audacity to brew
continental lager in the land of Yorkshire
Bitter deserves some respect – and the stuff
made by Dutchman Wim van der Spek is
not only tasty, but organic, too.

EAT, DRINK, SLEEP

Holme House *New Road, Hebden Bridge,
West Yorkshire, HX7 8AD;
01422 847588,
www.holmehousehebdenbridge.co.uk*
There's an air of calm about this swish
refurbished townhouse that makes you
feel instantly on holiday. In each of the
three rooms you'll find fluffy towels,
Gilchrist & Soames products, and flowers
and chocolates.
Doubles from £75 per night.

Kersal House *Hangingroyd Lane, Hebden
Bridge, West Yorkshire, HX7 7DD;
01422 842664; www.kersalhouse.co.uk*
Bright, airy rooms and shelves full of books
await you at Kersal House, which has an
embargo on frills and chintz. Best of all,

you're only a few minutes' walk from the
town's pubs and independent shops.
Doubles from £60 per night.

Myrtlegrove *Old Lees Road, Hebden
Bridge, West Yorkshire, HX7 8HL; 01422
846078; www.myrtlegrove.btinternet.co.uk*
Self-contained en suite room in a Victorian
grey-stone house overlooking the Calder
Valley. The owner, Maureen, grows her own
fruit, bakes bread, and makes the jams to
go on your toast in the morning. There are
some really nice walks leading straight
from the house if you over-indulge at
breakfast and need to work it off.
Doubles from £50 per night.

RENT

Blazing Saddles *35 West End, Hebden
Bridge, West Yorkshire, HX7 8UQ;
01422 844435; www.blazingsaddles.co.uk*
This friendly, family-run bike shop has
cycles to suit all tastes – from hardcore
Specialized and Trek mountain bikes
(which you can demo for £40 a day) to
more mellow Konas (£20) – which come
with helmets and repair kits. Ask nicely and
they'll suggest more rides if you're keen.

38

LANESHAWBRIDGE TO BLACK LANE ENDS

The wide-open north-west…

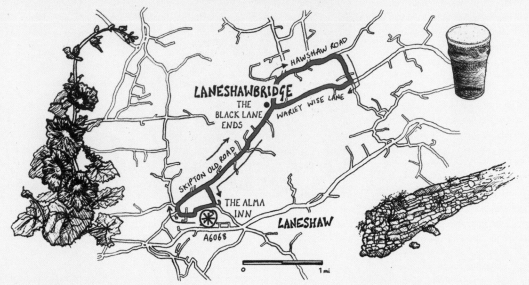

STANDING OUTSIDE the Alma Inn in Laneshawbridge, it feels as if you have the whole of Lancashire spread out below, just for you. For 10 miles or more, all that are visible are fields and moorland rising and falling towards the horizon, while the vast blue sky overhead is populated by puffy white clouds sculpted into exotic shapes by the high-altitude winds.

Down here, though, there's nothing more than a gentle breeze blowing, ensuring that you stay cool as you set off down the lane. Eyes firmly on the road (ahem), you thread your way down a slight descent between weathered drystone walls. Passing a cluster of houses, where tall pink flowers stand to attention on the verge, you reach a junction and make a right. Okay, so it's uphill – but take a look at the views! Sheep grazing away in distant pastures appear as little more than scatterings of breadcrumbs, and you can still see the Alma, too, away to your right – just a white speck among all the greenery.

Breathing in gulps of fresh Lancashire air for the next few miles, you'll eventually spot a pub on the horizon… someone must have read your mind.

On tap here at the Black Lane Ends are locally brewed Cooper Dragon ales and vistas across the vast, open landscape, so you might want to bring a spare memory card for the camera. The views only get better as you carry on up the road, until it flattens out, allowing you to glide while gazing towards the distant moorland and on towards Yorkshire.

Soon there's another slope to ascend. But whoever unfurled this lane over the top of these hills must have had one too many at the Black Lane Ends: to the tipsy eye it might look straight, but seen from the saddle it meanders drunkenly hither and thither as it summits the brow.

Nevertheless, you go on, sweeping round to the right between clumps of rust-brown bracken, before some ups and downs bring you back out opposite the Black Lane Ends again (tempted?).

Now it's payback time. From here you simply follow your tracks back to the Alma, gliding downhill for the next mile and a half with barely a turn of the pedals, before a shortcut at the end takes you back up to the pub. You may have only ridden about seven miles, but your eyes have taken in half the county.

THE ROUTE

DISTANCE   7 MILES

DIFFICULTY   ○○○○

START   The Alma Inn *Emmott Lane, Laneshawbridge, Lancashire, BB8 7EG*

» Head left out of the Alma Inn and follow Hill Lane around right, to the junction with Skipton Old Road (the first junction you come to).

» Turn right on to Skipton Old Road and keep going for 2¼ miles, passing the Black Lane Ends pub before veering right, on to Hawshaw Road.

» After ½ mile, bear right, on to Tom Lane.

» Turn right at the end, on to Warley Wise Lane.

» Follow this for just over a mile until you arrive at the junction with Skipton Old Road again: bear left.

» Continue along Old Skipton Road for a mile, until the turning for Long Lane: turn left and follow it to the end.

» Turn right on to Hill Lane, and follow it back to the Alma.

STOP AND SEE

EN ROUTE

The Black Lane Ends *Skipton Old Road, Colne, Lancashire, BB8 7EP; 01282 863070*
Even if you're impervious to the persuasion of real ales and home-made pies, the view from this place is enough to stop anyone in their tracks.

OFF ROUTE

Hawshaw Road *Colne, Lancashire*
This might involve half a mile of extra climbing, but you'll be glad to have made the effort. When you reach the fork with Tom Lane, carry straight on, along Hawshaw Road, and as you crest the hill it drops away to reveal a beautiful and clear view all the way towards Yorkshire. It's just you, the odd sheep – and nearly 360 degrees of the finest scenery the north-west has to offer.

Pendle Hill *Lancashire*
At just over 550 metres high, this is barely more than a foothill by Alpine standards – but it's the steepness that gets you. There are various routes up – all of them come with breathtaking views as standard. Look out for witches on your way up; it's famous for them here (see ride *39*, p182)…

EAT, DRINK, SLEEP

The Alma Inn *Emmott Lane, Laneshawbridge, Lancashire, BB8 7EG; 01282 857830; www.thealmainn.com*
Fireplaces and wooden beams sit happily alongside sage-green and terracotta walls in this 18th-century coaching inn. Upstairs there are nine rooms with sturdy, wood-framed beds, stone-floored en suite bathrooms, and views out to Pendle Hill – over four miles away. The restaurant serves treats like duck with crispy roast potatoes. Doubles from £80 per night.

Rye-Flatt *20 School Lane, Laneshawbridge, Lancashire, BB8 7JB; 01282 871565; www.rye-flatt.co.uk*
Within walking distance of the Alma, this cottage offers the kind of cosiness you'll be craving after a day out in the fresh northern air. There are two bedrooms to choose from, both bright and sunny, with old, stone window frames and big piles of pillows. Doubles from £50 per night.

Stone Head House *Stone Head Lane, Stone Head, Lothersdale, North Yorkshire, BD22 0LZ; 01535 630630; www.stoneheadhouse.co.uk*
Located in a hamlet made up of ancient cottages, this place, which dates back to 1596, fits right in. There are three rooms to choose from, but don't expect underfloor heating and fancy TVs; instead you get unadulterated countryside calm. Doubles from £62 per night (subsequent nights £46).

RENT

Residents at the Alma can book bikes there, free of charge. Or else visit Pedal Power (see ride *39*, p185, for details).

39

SAWLEY TO BOLTON—BY—BOWLAND

Puddle-ducks and wicked witches...

A MORE APT NAME for the Spread Eagle pub in Sawley would be 'the Waddling Ducks'. Step outside the front door and there's a whole gaggle of them hanging out on the corner, quacking away merrily. It's like a Jemima Puddle-Duck lookalikes convention.

The reason they're here – aside from the supply of free crumbs they get from the Spread Eagle's sentimental punters – is the River Ribble, which swings right past the pub and under the bridge just behind. You go over it to begin the ride, heading off into the lanes bound for Bolton-by-Bowland.

That big green blob in your peripheral vision as you glide along is Pendle Hill, which rises up out of nowhere – a challenge to all who gaze at it to grab their walking boots and have a go.

Nearly 80 years before the Salem witch trials in Massachusetts began, the villages surrounding this omnipresent mound became embroiled in a witch-hunt that resulted in a dozen locals (mostly women) going on trial accused of murdering 10 people by means of witchcraft.

Today, however, there are no signs of broomsticks or black cats as you drop down over the bridge and arrive in Bolton-by-Bowland. There is, however, a rather convenient tea room selling fresh sandwiches and tempting cakes.

Your saddlebag loaded with snacks for the road, it's time to cruise off past rows of whitewashed cottages, and swing left before the church to leave the village. For the next three miles or so you're heading upwards – though never steeply – with the views causing you to pull over and reach for the camera on several occasions.

Pendle Hill is behind you now, and as the road flattens out you're given a glimpse of what else is around. Peer out through the trees and you see Pendle's distant cousins, shrouded in heat mist about 10 miles away. What you're looking at is the Forest of Bowland – a huge area of gritstone fells and moorland that's refreshingly lacking in tourists.

It's time for some payback now, after that long, assiduous uphill journey, and it comes in the form of some satisfying descents. It's particularly good timing, too, because the road happens to open out here as you zoom downhill and bank left towards Wigglesworth, treating you to 360-degree views of open moorland.

In fact, it's a pretty cruisy run all the way back to Sawley from here, giving you a chance to click through the gears and enjoy the scenery. A couple more left turns and you're closing the loop, arriving safely back at the Waddling Ducks to find them all still loitering where you left them.

THE ROUTE

DISTANCE   15 MILES

DIFFICULTY   ⚫⚪⚪⚪

START   The Spread Eagle

Sawley, Clitheroe, Lancashire, BB7 4NH

» Go left from the pub and then left again, crossing the bridge (twice) and sweeping right, following the sign for Bolton-by-Bowland.

» Stay on this road until you cross the bridge to enter the village 2 miles later.

» Take the first left, on to Hellifield Road – signposted Hellifield.

» Stay on this road for the next 3½ miles, dropping downhill to a crossroads: turn left towards Wigglesworth.

» Cruise down this road for nearly 2 miles, to the next junction: turn left towards Bolton-by-Bowland.

» Continue for just over 4 miles, until you arrive at the next junction: turn right – on to the road back to Sawley. Now retrace your steps back to the Spread Eagle pub.

STOP AND SEE

EN ROUTE

The Village Shop & Tea Room *Main Street, Bolton-by-Bowland, Lancashire, BB7 4NW; 01200 447201, www.bolton-by-bowland.com* Stop off for a quick cuppa and some home-made cake, or buy some freshly made sandwiches and a bottle of elderflower pressé to take away for a picnic out on the road.

OFF ROUTE

Sawley Abbey *Lancashire; see www.english-heritage.org.uk* Just along the road from the Spread Eagle, this ruined Cistercian abbey dates way back, to 1148. It was eventually destroyed, like many religious buildings across the country, on Henry VIII's orders in 1536.

Walking With Witches Trail *Lancashire; see www.visitlancashire.com (click on*

'Things To Do' then 'Walking' then 'Middle Distance Walks') While you're unlikely to see any real-life wicked witches on this scenic trail beginning in the car park at Barley village (although you never know), the possibility makes a good excuse to explore the Lancashire countryside. There are two loops (of around four miles each), which take in the key sites associated with the trial – including Pendle Hill itself.

EAT, DRINK, SLEEP

The Spread Eagle *Sawley, Clitheroe, Lancashire, BB7 4NH; 01200 441202; www.spreadeaglesawley.co.uk* After a day spent pedalling amid the fresh Lancashire air, you can tuck into baked fish pie with cheesy mash, before heading up to one of seven uniquely styled rooms with flat screen TVs, L'Occitane products, and chunky sleigh beds at this puddle-duck-friendly pub.
Doubles from £80 per night.

The Coach and Horses *20 Main Street, Bolton-by-Bowland, Clitheroe, Lancashire, BB7 4NW; 01200 447202; www.boutiquedininghouse.co.uk*

This place is a lot funkier than your average village eatery. Expect high-backed chairs, patterned fabrics, and interesting dishes like goats' cheese and beetroot bread-and-butter pudding, served with Lancashire cheese 'custard' and courgette 'crumble'…
Doubles from £100 per night.

Park House *Church View, Gisburn, Clitheroe, Lancashire, BB7 4HG; 01200 445269; www.parkhousegisburn.co.uk* This Georgian country house is about three miles from Sawley, in the town of Gisburn, overlooking an 11th-century Norman church. There are seven rooms with period styling and fireplaces (go for room 8, which has a roll-top bath, too).
Doubles from £77 per night.

RENT

Pedal Power *17 Waddington Road, Clitheroe, Lancashire, BB7 2HJ; 01200 422066; www.pedalpowerclitheroe.co.uk* There's a fleet of mountain bikes to choose from, for both kids and adults of all different shapes, sizes, and abilities. A day's adult bike hire costs £24. Helmet rental costs £2 extra per day.

40

COW ARK TO BASHALL TOWN

Empty lanes, a cosy cottage, and an especially excellent farm shop...

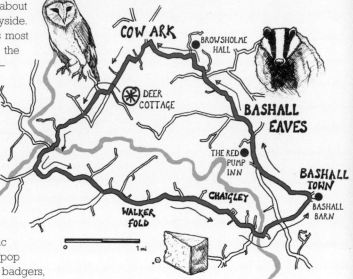

IT'S AMAZING HOW LITTLE is known about Lancashire's rather gorgeous countryside. While the Lake District next door gets most of the limelight in this part of the world, the lanes around Lancs stay blissfully empty – as you'll find out when you arrive at the bizarrely named hamlet of Cow Ark.

Secreted away in Lancashire's Ribble Valley, this place is one of several sneeze-and-you'll-miss-it settlements dotted around the River Hodder and its tributaries. At Deer Cottage, tucked away a mile or so down the lane from Cow Ark, you can sit on the small balcony on warm summer evenings and watch the eponymous creatures tiptoe round the garden. It's so wildlife-tastic here, you almost expect David Bellamy to pop out of the bushes; as well as deer, you'll see badgers, owls, and other birds of prey – the latter squawking away in the nearby fields as you pedal off down the drive and out into the lanes.

The scenery round here is dramatic to say the least. Flat fields are abruptly halted by hills that tower up in the distance – all covered with patches of auburn heather that stand out against the blue sky.

Later you drop downhill and sweep left over a bridge, crossing the rushing waters of the Hodder, before its (strangely quieter) sibling – the River Loud – joins you, flowing through the trees alongside.

It's on now towards Whalley and Clitheroe, the hills on both sides enfolding you like a giant's hug, providing shelter from the outside world. It's so quiet out here that you wonder where the crowds are the whole time – and when you'll have to start climbing. But the good news is that there are very few hills to conquer on this ride: a minor miracle in this very peaky part of the world.

A few miles further on you meet the River Hodder again, having pedalled on easily through Walker Fold and Chaigley, and as you freewheel downhill

over the bridge (stopping for a photo) it's not long before you arrive at Bashall Town. If you haven't brought lunch with you, then you're in for a treat.

Bashall Barn's farm shop sells various temptations – such as crumbly Lancashire cheeses, home-made quiche, and toffee-fudge ice cream; and from the terrace of the restaurant next door, you can look out over the lush landscape while tucking into sausage and mash... And there's still no sign of those crowds.

After lunch, it's flat, smooth pedalling for the next few miles as you pass the Red Pump Inn and climb up back towards Cow Ark. It's never particularly steep, though, and if you do fancy a rest you could always call in at Browsholme Hall for a mooch round.

Now, it's just a couple of miles between you and Deer Cottage; the road speckled with dabs of sunlight as you make your way back. It's worth checking over your shoulder as you pull into the drive, just to make sure you haven't been followed. After all, we don't want anyone finding out about this little secret...

STONYHURST COLLEGE

BOLTON-BY-Bo

LEAGRAM
2 YEAR OLD
ORGANIC
BOB'S
KNOBS

THE ROUTE

DISTANCE 11 MILES

DIFFICULTY ○○○

START **Deer Cottage** *Whitewell Road, Cow Ark, Lancashire, BB7 3DG*

» Take a left out of Deer Cottage drive.

» Turn left again at the first junction.

» Follow this road for 1½ miles, crossing the River Hodder before turning left – signed Whalley, Clitheroe, and Preston.

» Pedal through Walker Fold and Chaigley, before you reach the river again in 2¼ miles.

» Cross the bridge and continue along the lane for just under a mile until you reach a junction at the end. Turn left, following the brown sign for Bashall Barn (if you're stopping at the barn and brewery, follow the brown sign and take the next right).

» The route continues on past the barn, then the Red Pump Inn on your left, and Browsholme Hall on the right, before arriving back in Cow Ark after 3 miles.

» Go through the village and, after a mile, you'll reach Deer Cottage on your left.

STOP AND SEE

EN ROUTE

Bowland Brewery *Bashall Barn, Bashall Town, Lancashire, BB7 3LQ; 01200 443592; www.bowlandbrewery.com*
Who knows what the magic ingredients are, but with names like Sky Dancer and Headless Peg you can be sure there's something special about these ales. Tours are pretty impromptu: just show up, pay a few quid and watch the master brewer at work. You'll even get a pint at the end of it.

Browsholme Hall *Clitheroe Road, Cow Ark, Lancashire, BB7 3DE; 01254 827166; www.browsholme.com*
Pronounced 'brusom', this enormous red sandstone hall dates back to 1507 and has been owned by the same family the whole time. Having stood strong through the Reformation, civil wars, and 500 winters,

the house is a treasure trove of antiques and amazing possessions that have been collected over 14 generations.

OFF ROUTE

Riverbank Tea Rooms *The Green, Slaidburn, Lancashire, BB7 3ES; 01200 446398; www.riverbanktearooms.co.uk*
Located in a pretty village on the banks of the Hodder, this rather excellent tea room is the starting point for some great rides and walks. Maureen and Joe Clarkson rustle up packed lunches, home-cooked meals, and tempting cakes, so after a morning spent strolling along the river you can sit outside the café with a nice pot of tea.

The Inn at Whitewell *Whitewell, nr Clitheroe, Lancashire, BB7 3AT; 01200 448222; www.innatwhitewell.com*
In the 1300s this manor house belonged to the keeper of the Royal Forest, but for the last 400 years or so it's earned a reputation for good food, a cosy hearth, and a superb selection of wines. There are 23 bedrooms, too, mostly with open fires, horsehair mattresses, and views of the river.

EAT, DRINK, SLEEP

Deer Cottage *Whitewell Road, Cow Ark, Lancashire, BB7 3DG; 01995 61865; www.deercottage.co.uk*
This restored former barn is the antidote to Monday-to-Friday stress. Downstairs there are two bedrooms (a double and a single), while upstairs you'll find old beams, a smart modern kitchen, a sumptuous sofa, and a wood-burning stove. The sun shines into the cottage for much of the day and when it's clear you can see all the way to Pendle Hill, eight miles away.
From £110 per night (it's a minimum two-night stay).

Peter Barn *Rabbit Lane, Cross Lane, Waddington, Lancashire, BB7 3JH;*

01200 428585; www.peterbarn.co.uk
This converted tithe barn is surrounded by carefully planted gardens that give way to pristine countryside – and the owner, Jean, makes her own jams and muesli to serve at breakfast. If you fancy a change from cycling, there are some great walks nearby – including one across the fields to Waddington, which has three pubs.
Doubles from £64 per night.

The Red Pump Inn *Clitheroe Road, Bashall Eaves, Lancashire, BB7 3DA; 01254 826227; www.theredpumpinn.co.uk*
Forget all thoughts of home from the moment you arrive, as owners Jonathan and Martina prepare an oft-changing menu of local dishes (try the slow-roasted belly of Pendle pork), along with a choice of ales and wines. Upstairs there are three rooms with countryside views.
Doubles from £70 per night.

RENT

Pedal Power *17 Waddington Road, Clitheroe, Lancashire, BB7 2HJ; 01200 422066; www.pedalpowerclitheroe.co.uk*
There's a good range of mountain bikes on offer for £24 a day (helmets £2).

LANCASTER TO CROOK O'LUNE

Towpaths and cycle trails in the Lancashire Dales...

NOTHING IS TOO MUCH trouble for James, owner of the Ashton in Lancaster. Don't be surprised if the first thing he asks when you walk through the door is 'bacon muffin?'. Having bought the place as a wreck in January 2008, he set about conjuring up his vision of the perfect B&B. The result is a seriously stylish house with five beautiful bedrooms – each with its own look and feel, but the same (high) standard of creature comfort. Whether you choose one of the Grand rooms – with double walk-in shower or roll-top bath – or a Classic – with original fireplace, dinner-plate-sized showerhead, and underfloor heating – you'll feel extremely well looked after.

The cycling's pretty good around here, too. Lancaster is surrounded by deep green hills and winding country lanes, which begin the moment you leave the Ashton's driveway. A quick shimmy across the main road brings you on to Grab Lane, and if you glance left, over the fields, you'll see the domed roof of the rather grand Ashton Memorial poking above the trees in Williamson Park. It was built in the early 1900s by local industrialist, Baron Ashton (aka James Williamson Jnr), who kindly donated his name to quite a few places around here – including James' B&B, of course.

At the end of the lane you swing right and climb a small hill, a group of Friesian cows briefly pausing their chewing to see what all the fuss is about as you pass. Three miles later you reach Caton, calling in at the Crazy Cake Company for some unexpectedly sensible sandwiches, salad boxes, old-fashioned sweets, and (yep, you guessed it) cakes.

It's here that you hang a left on to the cycle track for a flat, smooth run along to Lancaster. Emerging from a tunnel of overhanging trees, you meet the River Lune half a mile later – a swirling mass of whisky-coloured water.

The wet, fecund smell of the river's reeds is replaced by the irresistible aroma of sizzling bacon wafting down from Woodie's café in the nearby Crook O'Lune picnic area – leading you to an unassuming little cabin serving cups of tea and sausage butties to hungry walkers.

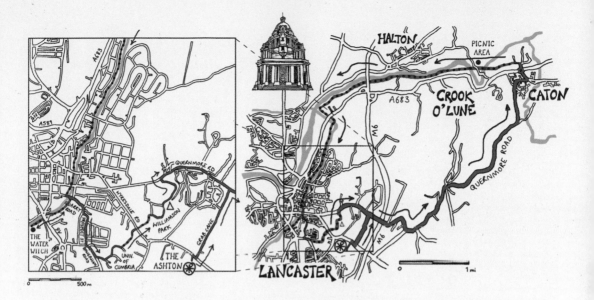

When you've had your fill, it's only a short, flat ride back to Lancaster. This last section takes you on to the aqueduct carrying the Lancaster Canal.

Deep-pink flowers and bright-green reeds line the waterside, providing visual accompaniments to the sound of your tyres crackling over the sandy trail and amorous mallards chatting up their ladies. A series of small overhead bridges later, you arrive at the Water Witch pub, where you can sit outside and watch boats chug along the canal.

And now it's only a short ride back to the Ashton, cutting through Williamson Park for a closer look at the memorial you saw earlier. By the time you get back, there's a good chance James will be waiting with yet more offers of food – and with any luck it'll be an afternoon tea this time…

THE ROUTE

DISTANCE   14½ MILES

DIFFICULTY   ◐◐◐

START   **The Ashton** *Wyresdale Road, Lancaster, Lancashire, LA1 3JJ*

» Turn right out of the Ashton's driveway and take the first left, on to Grab Lane.

» At the end of Grab Lane turn right and stay on this road for the next 3 miles, following the signs for Caton.

» Just after entering the village, turn right, on to Copy Lane.

» Turn left at the end of Copy Lane on to Brookhouse Road. Follow this to the mini roundabout: go straight over, to Station Road.

» Just before the end of Station Road follow signs for the cycle path and turn left to join it.

» Follow this for 3 miles, passing the Crook O'Lune picnic area and continuing on under two big bridges. Just after the second one, turn left on to a footpath, follow the sign for the canal towpath.

» About 40 metres along the footpath, take the steps leading up on to the aqueduct. Turn right at the top, on to the towpath.

» Follow the towpath for 2 miles, to the fifth bridge (at Quarry Road). Dismount and cross the road, rejoining the towpath on the other side, by the White Cross pub.

» Keep going, past the White Cross, with the canal on your right, to the Water Witch.

» Head back from the Water Witch the way you came, passing the White Cross pub again; turn right on to Quarry Road (which runs over the bridge that crosses the canal by the White Cross).

» Follow Quarry Road for under ¼ mile (it turns into Dale Street); pass 3 left turns, then the road sweeps left, on to Primrose Street.

» Take the next right on to Prospect Street.

» Follow this to the end then turn left on to Bowerham Road.

» Take the second left, into the grounds of the University of Cumbria campus.

» Bear left, towards the sports centre, past the five-a-side football pitch, and out to the junction opposite Williamson Park.

» Cross over into Williamson Park and bear right, up the hill to the Ashton Memorial.

» Continue past the memorial and down the hill to exit the park, then turn right on to Quernmore Road.

» Follow this for ½ mile before turning right on to Grab Lane and following it to the end. The Ashton is ahead of you, on the right.

STOP AND SEE

EN ROUTE

Crook O'Lune *Lancaster, Lancashire*
Standing on the edge of the picnic area, you'll see the River Lune meandering between the fields of grazing cows while the dale hills rise up in the distance. It's no wonder this place is featured in paintings by Turner and in an elegy by Thomas Gray...

The Water Witch *Canal Tow Path, Aldcliffe Lane, Lancaster, Lancashire, LA1 1SU; 01524 63828; www.thewaterwitch.co.uk*
Housed in former stables beside the canal, this is an ideal place in which to celebrate your arrival back into Lancaster. Ask to sample some of the ales it's famous for.

The Ashton Memorial *Williamson Park, Lancaster, Lancashire, LA1 1UX; 01524 33318; www.williamsonpark.com*
Take a stroll through the peaceful paths and gardens and look down on the city from the omniscient dome-topped Ashton Memorial.

OFF ROUTE

Morecambe Bay *Lancashire*
Just five miles from Lancaster city centre, this beautiful bay is packed with wildlife, walks, and modern art. Green fields give way to the famous mudflats, where the tide can arrive at the rate of a galloping horse.

EAT, DRINK, SLEEP

The Ashton *Wyresdale Road, Lancaster, Lancashire, LA1 3JJ; 01524 68460;*
www.theashtonlancaster.com
More like a boutique and boutique hotel, than a B&B, this is the sort of place you dream about after a stressful week at work. Owner James is a whizz in the kitchen – whipping up home-made soups, mouth-watering deli boards, and filling evening meals. He'll even make a packed lunch for your ride if you ask nicely. Doubles from £128 per night; add around £30 per person for a three-course evening meal with wine.

The Sun Hotel *63–65 Church Street, Lancaster, Lancashire, LA1 1ET; 01524 00006; www.thesunhotelandbar.co.uk*
Located in the centre of town, this 300-year-old coaching inn has 16 smart rooms with exposed-stone walls, flat-screen TVs, and stylish modern furniture. The pub has a good selection of cask ales, delicious wines, and tasty meals, and during the day it's the kind of place where people call in for coffee and a read of the papers. Doubles from £72 per night.

Old Station House *25 Meeting House Lane, Lancaster, Lancashire, LA1 1TX; 01524 381060*
Charmingly chintzy, conveniently located by the station, and really friendly (thanks to owner Andrea), this used to be the stationmaster's cottage – back when stations had masters and not managers. There are six rooms, free parking, and wi-fi. Doubles from £60 per night.

RENT

Leisure Lakes Bikes *103 Penny Street, Lancaster, Lancashire, LA1 1XN; 01524 844389; www.leisurelakesbikes.com*
There are six Specialized bikes to choose from – three for boys, three for girls. Each one comes with panniers, helmets, and puncture-repair kits, with prices ranging from £6 an hour to £15 for 24 hours.

42

ARNSIDE TO LEIGHTON HALL

Delicious food, dramatic hills, and views out across the bay…

YOU DON'T EVEN HAVE to go outside the B&B to get a breathtaking view in this part of the world. Sitting in the lounge at Number 43 in Arnside, cup of tea in hand, you've got Morecambe Bay stretched out before you – so smooth that it's tempting to stroll across the water to the Lake District's hills on the other side. On a clear day you can see for over 40 miles from here – all the way to the Old Man of Coniston, one of the most iconic peaks of the lot.

Number 43 is one of those swanky B&Bs with all the trimmings of a 5-star hotel. Owner Lesley has a platter of cold meats, pâtés, and cheeses waiting when you arrive, which can be washed down with organic wines (no hangover!). The stylish rooms feature sumptuous linen, posh products, and gadgets galore – including a Bose CD player.

The landscape around Arnside was made for cycling; one minute you're on the waterfront, the next you're out in the lanes. Wobbling off from Lesley's place, with the bay on your left, you see swans gliding silently alongside you and sailboats silhouetted out on the water. Further along you pass a parade of twee shops including the Bake House café and pizzeria, and Laura Lee's Café – tempting you to stop and snack before you've barely got going.

Once you're out into the lanes, though, you see craggy hillsides rising up in the distance – scenic reminders that you're skirting the edge of the Lake District – and soon you're pedalling along through woodland with the earthy aroma of leaf litter and pine hanging in the air.

In a couple of miles you can freewheel down to Yealand Redmayne (not much more than a strip of cottages lining the road), which slips imperceptibly into Yealand Conyers, where you round the corner to arrive outside the New Inn. There's a dish of pan-fried crevettes with citrus salad waiting, which sets you up for the cheeky post-lunch climb.

It's a bit of a biggy, but you could always get off and stroll – halfway up there's a clearing in the old oak trees, where you can see the valley floor tiled in various shades of green.

A mile or so later you come upon the entrance to Leighton Hall and duck on to its driveway, cruising up to the rather magnificent country house. Don't be fooled by its crenellated grey walls: they were a 'modern' addition, added around 1825 (the main part of the house dates back to 1246).

When you've filled up with tea and taken a nose around the place, the route carries on through the grounds and out the other side, dropping downhill, to Leighton Moss Nature Reserve. From here it's only a few miles back to Arnside – where you can enjoy another installment of that pristine view over the bay.

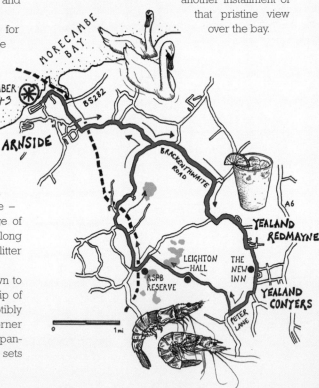

THE ROUTE

DISTANCE   11 MILES
DIFFICULTY   ○○○○
START   Number 43

The Promenade, Arnside, Cumbria, LA5 0AA

» Bear right from Number 43 and follow the waterfront.

» Just over a mile later, it sweeps left and leads you to a level crossing.

» After another mile you reach a junction: turn left towards Yealand Redmayne.

» Follow this road for 1½ miles to a junction: bear left towards Yealand Redmayne.

» Go through the village and on to Yealand Conyers, passing the New Inn and turning right ¼ mile later, on to Peter Lane.

» Climb for about a mile until you see the entrance for Leighton Hall on your right.

» Go through the grounds to the other side (about 1¼ miles) and turn left at the exit.

» Turn right at the bottom of the hill, and follow the road for nearly 2 miles, until you see a sign for Arnside: turn left.

» You're now on the same road to Arnside that you emerged from earlier. Continue along it, back over the level crossing, and bear right to reach Arnside's waterfront.

STOP AND SEE

EN ROUTE

The New Inn *40 Yealand Road, Carnforth, Lancashire, LA5 9SJ; 01524 732938*
Enter the bar on your left and you're greeted by copper table tops, an old fireplace, and a menu featuring filling classics like beef and ale pie. Try one of the Robinsons beers, too.

Leighton Hall *Carnforth, Lancashire, LA5 9ST; 01524 734474; www.leightonhall.co.uk*
Forget those stuffy old country houses where you daren't breathe for fear of being told off. This is a real family home, where you're free to sit on the chairs, stretch out on the lawn, and even play a tune on the piano. There's a great tea shop here, too.

Leighton Moss Nature Reserve
Carnforth, Lancashire; 01524 701601; see www.rspb.org.uk
Red deer, marsh harriers, and bearded tits are just a few of the species that you're likely to see here. Kids and adults alike will love the nature trail that takes you along reed beds and a coastal lagoon.

OFF ROUTE

Arnside Knott *Lancashire*
Take a walk along the promenade and over to Arnside Knott – the moss-covered limestone rock that rises out of the flatland surrounding the town. Climb to the top for great views if you're feeling energetic.

EAT, DRINK, SLEEP

Number 43 *The Promenade, Arnside, Cumbria, LA5 0AA; 01524 762761; www.no43.org.uk*
The moment you arrive here there's an almost audible 'fisss' as the stress leaves your body. After handing you a glass of wine (or hand-made ginger ale) Lesley, the owner, will show you to your room. There are six to choose from – plus two suites – or if you fancy coming with a group of friends you could book up the whole place and get it stocked with gourmet food. Doubles from £55 per night.

Grisedale Farm *Leighton, Carnforth, Lancashire, LA5 9ST; 01524 734360; www.grisedalefarm.co.uk*
If you're looking to really get away from it all, then come here. Located along the lane from Leighton Hall, this 17th-century farmhouse has two rooms (a double and a twin), period furniture, zero light pollution, and freshly laid eggs for brekkie. Doubles from £70 per night.

Ye Olde Fighting Cocks *The Promenade, Arnside, Cumbria, LA5 0HD; 01524 761203; www.fighting-cocks.co.uk*
Built over the site of an old cock-fighting pit (hence the name), this cosy pub looks out over the bay. Old-fashioned-cosy rather than contemporary-cool, the rooms have period features including four-poster beds and chandeliers, and wonderful views to the Lake District. Downstairs you can get a good home-cooked meal before curling up by the fire with a drink. Doubles from £72 per night.

The Big Chip Café *1 The Promenade, Arnside, Lancashire (yep, not Cumbria), LA5 0HF; 01524 761874; www.arnsidechipshop.co.uk*
This award-winning chippy serves up tasty fresh haddock, plaice, fishcakes, and other seafood treats. Slap on the salt and vinegar before washing it down with a can of fizzy pop – you've earned it after all that cycling.

RENT

Leisure Lakes Bikes *103 Penny Street, Lancaster, Lancashire, LA1 1XN; 01524 844389; www.leisurelakesbikes.com*
A fleet of six Specialized bikes (three gents; three ladies) are available from £6 an hour to £15 for 24 hours. Each one comes with panniers, helmet, and puncture-repair kit.

YORKSHIRE

43

COLTON TO BOLTON PERCY

Award-winning food, a riverside pub, and a country-garden tea room...

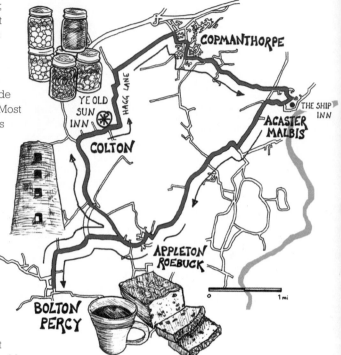

DON'T BE FOOLED by first impressions; there's a lot more to Ye Old Sun Inn at Colton than meets the eye. With its whitewashed walls and red-tiled roof it looks conventional enough from the outside, but wander round the back and you'll find an old-fashioned deli selling slices of cake, home-made pies, traditional lemonade, and other treats. Most of them made by Ashley McCarthy, who runs the pub, shop – and smart B&B next door – with his wife, Kelly. Since taking over in 2004, they've won heaps of awards for their food, so there's a good chance you'll be loosening your belt by the end of the weekend. Just as well you brought the bike...

After picking up some deli delights you head left out of the pub and on to surprisingly flat lanes. The popular perception of Yorkshire is that it's all hills and dales, but out here in the low-lying Wolds you won't see an incline all day.

The first couple of miles involve an easy spin along to Copmanthorpe, where you wiggle through a few side streets and out the other side into open countryside. The wide, expansive fields seem to go on forever – more akin to those in Suffolk – and on the horizon you can see trees bowing from the pressure of holding up the sky.

Half a mile later you nip over a crossroads and thread your way to Acaster Malbis for a pint at the Ship Inn. Sat beside the River Ouse, it was a favourite with barge crewmen in the 19th century, who'd stop here on their way upstream to York. Just inside the entrance to the pub you'll see the old hatch where the landlord used to serve the river-men their meals.

From here you head on to Appleton Roebuck, passing newly harvested fields in summer; the hay bales scattered like pieces on a giant chessboard. If you're still feeling thirsty, call in at the Shoulder of Mutton on the village green, but the route takes you on through the village and left for Bolton Percy.

Aside from the fact that it's got a cool-sounding name, the other reason to come here is D'Oyly's, an excellent farmhouse tea room. It's belonged to the Houseman family for over a century, and as you cruise around the last corner the sound of clinking teacups announces your arrival. This is the kind of place you dream about on hot summer days when you're stuck in the city; tables are scattered around the sun-drenched garden and sparrows bounce about on the lawn looking for crumbs while the owner, Vicky, keeps everyone topped up with tea.

After eating your own bodyweight in cake, you've just got two more miles to work off the calories before you get back to Colton, where Ashley will no doubt be cooking up a feast at the pub. Best work those pedals a bit harder then...

THE ROUTE

DISTANCE 13 MILES
DIFFICULTY ◐◐
START Ye Old Sun Inn

Colton, Tadcaster, North Yorkshire, LS24 8EP

» Turn left out of Ye Old Sun Inn and follow the lane for 2½ miles, to the next junction.

» Turn right here, on to Manor Heath, and follow it along to Copmanthorpe. After less than ¼ mile, Manor Heath bends left and becomes School Lane.

» At the next junction, turn right, to pass the Royal Oak pub on your left.

» After passing two 'No Entry' roads on your left, then St Giles Way, look out for a sign for Acaster Malbis, directing you left, on to Station Road.

» Station Road becomes Temple Lane (just after you pass St Giles Way again, on the left); keep following Temple Lane, over the railway bridge, to a crossroads after a mile.

» Go straight across, following the sign for Acaster Malbis.

» Follow the road around right, past Poplar Farm Caravan Park. If you want to stop at the Ship Inn at Acaster Malbis, take the next left, on to Mill Lane; otherwise, carry on for another ¼ mile until you reach the next junction.

» Turn left on to Appleton Road, towards Bolton Percy.

» Stay on this road for almost a mile, then turn right at the next junction – towards Bolton Percy.

» After 1½ miles cycle through Appleton Roebuck (passing the Shoulder of Mutton and Roebuck Inn pubs). Just before leaving the village, turn left – following the sign for Bolton Percy.

» Follow this road for just over a mile (passing the old windmill on your right and crossing the railway), and carry on until you reach D'Oyly's Tea Room at Bolton Percy.

» From here, retrace your steps back to the old windmill, turning left just before it.

» At the next junction, turn left, for Colton.

» This takes you over the railway (twice), and after 1 mile you turn right, back into Colton to Ye Old Sun Inn.

STOP AND SEE

EN ROUTE

The Ship Inn *Moor End, Acaster Malbis, York, North Yorkshire, YO23 2UH; 01904 703888*

Sit outside, near the river, and watch the odd boat glide indolently past. If you feel like a stroll, why not amble along to Naburn, on the opposite bank, pausing on the way to snack on some of those goodies you brought with you from Ye Old Sun?

Shoulder of Mutton *Chapel Green, Appleton Roebuck, North Yorkshire, YO23 7DP; 01904 744227*

Wood beams, a pool table, and probably the cheapest beer in Britain (I paid £3.07 for two pints). Take a seat out by the village green and sip the head off your ale while the occasional cyclist pootles past.

D'Oyly's Tea Room *North House, Bolton Percy, York, North Yorkshire, YO23 7AN; 01904 744354; www.doylys.co.uk*

Enjoy a leisurely flick through the Sunday papers while Vicky brings you home-made cake – straight from the Aga. If you've got time, amble along the lane to see the village church. Don't worry if you end up running late: they've got two cosy B&B rooms upstairs…

OFF ROUTE

Boat Trip to York *YorkBoat, The Boatyard, Lendal Bridge, York, North Yorkshire, YO1 7DP; 01904 628324; www.yorkboat.co.uk*

See a different side to York by a trip down the river. From the Ship Inn you can cruise the five miles or so down to the city, check out the eponymous Minster, soak up the atmosphere of the medieval houses on The Shambles, then make your way back.

EAT, DRINK, SLEEP

Ye Old Sun Inn *Colton, Tadcaster, North Yorkshire, LS24 8EP; 01904 744261; www.yeoldsuninn.co.uk*

Right next door to the pub you've got a three-room B&B with a jukebox in the hall and a hot-tub in the garden. If you're coming here with friends, why not book the whole house – and eat together in the private dining room? Owners Ashley and Kelly have got loads of suggestions about what to see and do locally.
Doubles from £80 per night.

Orchard Lodge *Mount Pleasant House, Acaster Malbis, North Yorkshire, YO23 2UP, 01904 700924; www.orchardlodgeyork.co.uk*

This Scandinavian-style wood cabin has two rooms (a double and a single) set in an orchard, where chickens wander round and you're only a short walk from the river. There's a high-spec kitchen with cooker, dishwasher, and more, and a large lounge area with flat-screen TV. Eat outside on the deck or stroll to the river.
From £340 for five nights.

Garden Cottage *The Old Vicarage, Main Street, Appleton Roebuck, York, North Yorkshire, YO23 7DG; 01904 744882; www.gardencottageyork.co.uk*

If you're coming with a group of friends then try this five-bedroom house in Appleton Roebuck. There's a huge private garden, a big farmhouse kitchen, and a lounge with a wood-burning stove.
From £650 for seven nights.

RENT

Cycle Sense *Unit 657a, Street 4, Thorp Arch Estate, Wetherby, West Yorkshire, LS23 7FJ; 01937 844068; www.cyclesense.co.uk*

There's a varied fleet to choose from here, including road bikes, off-roaders, trailer cycles, and a tandem. Adults' bicycles cost from £15 a day, with helmets.

44

KIRKBY MALZEARD TO THE DROVERS INN

A homely pub, a hidden valley, and epic views across the moors…

YOU MIGHT GET A bit of a surprise when you arrive at the Drovers Inn near Dallowgill. Placed carefully on top of a moorland hill like a proverbial ye olde cherry, it's a tad smaller than you might expect.

In fact, it feels more like you're walking into someone's lounge than into a country boozer; there's a fire crackling away quietly, a clutch of tiny tables, and the landlord, Steve, chatting in the corner with a couple of locals.

Diminutive it might be, but this place has a rather large reputation; if I'd been given a pound for everyone who'd recommended it, I'd have made more than enough to get a round in. And while the pub may be on the small side, the giant scenery outside certainly makes up for it.

The ride begins in Kirkby Malzeard – where (useless fact alert) Bing Crosby unexpectedly called in for a game of cricket, one hot August day in 1976 – taking you through the village of Laverton (think red phone box and benches by a babbling brook), and out on to smooth-cycling lanes, before you hang a right and head towards the pub.

All the while you've been climbing gently, the views expanding to give you a tantalising glimpse of what lies in store after your pint at the Drovers. From outside the pub you can see a line in the distance where the neatly parcelled fields end and the moor takes over – the purple heather running riot all over the hillsides.

All that is still to come, though. Leaving the locals to their chatting in the Drovers, you dive left down a lane that takes you back through time; grassy banks become prehistoric ferns, and you can hear water trickling over the rocks in some hidden nearby stream.

You're pedalling through a valley that the rest of the world forgot about, a world in which rabbits have time to hang around at the roadside, nonchalantly nibbling at patches of grass.

Soon you start to climb, though – with signs of life appearing in the form of the odd cottage here and there – and before long you're on that moorland you looked over while sipping a pint back at the pub.

Rabbits are replaced by sheep, put out here to keep the grass from taking over, and the view opens out for miles on all sides. On your left the land falls away into a valley and, as late afternoon turns to early evening, the temperature change causes pillows of cloud to snuggle into the gap.

Finally you make a right, and it's pretty much downhill all the way now, back to Kirkby Malzeard, and your B&B room at Cowscot House – which, incidentally, is almost the same size as the bar at the Drovers' Inn.

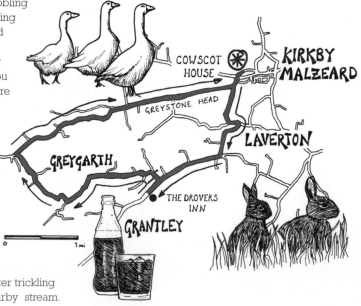

THE ROUTE

DISTANCE   8½ MILES

DIFFICULTY   ⭘⭘⭘

START   Cowscot House

Back Lane, Kirkby Malzeard, Ripon, North Yorkshire, HG4 3SE

» Head left out of Cowscot House and follow the lane until you reach the main road through Kirkby Malzeard village.

» Cross straight over this, to the grass triangle; then bear right, towards Laverton.

» After ½ mile you drop down into Laverton and turn right, to cross the humpbacked bridge (for Pateley Bridge). If you reach the red phone box, you've missed your turning.

» At the next junction, turn right towards Pateley Bridge.

» Keep on this road for a mile, until you reach the Drovers Inn.

» Come out of the pub and take the first left, signposted Dallowgill.

» As you drop downhill, the road veers sharply left – don't go straight on!

» Stay on this road along the valley and up the other side, on to the dales. After 2 miles you'll see a sign for Kirkby Malzeard as the road swings sharply right. Stay on it until you reach the junction just outside Kirkby Malzeard – and turn left for the village.

STOP AND SEE

EN ROUTE

The Drovers Inn *Dallowgill, Kirkby Malzeard, North Yorkshire, HG4 3RH; 01765 658510*

This no-frills Yorkshire pub sits on the edge of Dallowgill Moor, and is only open from 3.30pm on weekdays. So why not come up here for a late-afternoon thirst-quencher, when the sun turns the surrounding scenery golden?

OFF ROUTE

The Yorkshire Moors *see www. kirkbymalzeard.com (click on 'Footpaths')*
Ask the owners of Cowscot House, Liz and Mike, to put together a packed lunch, and then set off on foot across the moors. The most scenic spots are nearby Grewelthorpe Moor and Kirkby Malzeard Moor, where you can see all the way to the east coast on clear days – about 50 miles away.

Fountains Abbey and Studley Royal

Ripon, North Yorkshire, HG4 3DY; 01765 608888; www.fountainsabbey.org.uk
Cameras at the ready... You may find yourself getting a little snap-happy when you see the arches of this 800-year-old abbey poking above the treeline. The ruins sit on the banks of the River Skell, and after a free guided tour you could spread out on the lawns for a long, lazy picnic. If you're still keen after that, there are the Georgian water gardens to check out.

Ripon *North Yorkshire*

Spend the day in this ancient city and you can check out the 12th-century cathedral, stroll along the canal, and – if you're here on a Thursday – shop for a bargain or three at the open market, which dates back to the eighth century. When you hear the horn blowing in the square at 9pm, as it has every day for over 1,000 years, you know it's time to head home.

EAT, DRINK, SLEEP

Cowscot House *Back Lane, Kirkby Malzeard, Ripon, North Yorkshire, HG4 3SE; 01765 658181; www.cowscothouse.co.uk*
Book one of the four rooms in this converted barn and stables, and you'll wake up the next day to home-made yogurt, freshly baked bread, and recently laid eggs. Let them know beforehand, and Mike and Liz will even have an afternoon tea waiting when you get back from your ride.
Doubles from £35 per person, per night.

The Moorhouse *Dallowgill, Kirkby Malzeard, Ripon, North Yorkshire, HG4 3RH;*
01765 658371; www.moorhousebnb.co.uk
About 15 steps away from the Drovers Inn you'll find this renovated five-bedroom house with views out over the moor. As with Cowscot, you can arrange to have tea, toast, and home-made cake waiting for you when you get back.
Doubles from £80 per night.

Box Tree Cottages *Coltsgate Hill, Ripon, North Yorkshire, HG4 2AB; 01765 698006; www.boxtreecottages.com*
As the name suggests, this Grade II-listed building was once three cottages, but has now been turned into a smart six-room guest house with an acre of gardens. The centre of Ripon is only a few minutes' walk away, and Kirkby Malzeard about six miles.
Doubles from £65 per night.

RENT

Dales Mountain Biking *Dales Bike Centre, Fremington, Richmond, North Yorkshire, DL11 6AW; 01748 884908; www.dalesmountainbiking.co.uk*
Crazy as it seems, with such good cycling countryside all around Kirkby Malzeard, Dales Mountain Biking is the nearest hire facility – about 20 miles away. The good news is they have an extensive fleet of hard tails (£22 per day) and full suspension mountain bikes (£40), which come with helmets, pumps, and puncture repair kits – and there's a great little café on site (plus some superb mountain biking)…

45

EAST WITTON TO JERVAULX ABBEY

An old coaching inn and an ancient abbey, topped off with a scoop of gourmet ice cream...

WALKING INTO THE BLUE LION at East Witton is like rewinding 200 years of history. The old stone floors are worn from centuries of shuffling feet, the fireplace stained from countless roaring blazes, and the bar-top wiped down to the grain in places – by all the barmaids and men who have served up thousands of frothy pints to passing travellers down the years. The menu, however, is bang up to date.

In fact, the Blue Lion is renowned for its food, with tender chargrilled beef, melt-in-the-mouth smoked haddock fillets, and other delicious dishes served up at candlelit tables. The atmosphere is so olde worlde that you wouldn't bat an eyelid if a top-hatted coachman walked through the door – having lost his way somewhere between here and 1789.

The countryside surrounding East Witton has hardly changed since then, either – as you'll quickly realise when you head off into the lanes on your bike. Within minutes you're pootling over an aged bridge that's barely wide enough to fit a car. Its weathered stone sides are speckled with grey and yellow patches of lichen, which take decades to grow, thriving especially in places where the air is fresh.

As you continue on slowly uphill – the sound of your own breathing audible in the general hush – it isn't long before you're making a right and pedalling along a plateau, with freshly ploughed fields the colour of cocoa falling away for 10 miles or more on your left.

It's enough to get you thinking about food – chocolate ice cream, to be precise – and after another few miles of easy riding you find yourself cruising down the driveway at High Jervaulx Farm, where 35 flavours are waiting to be sampled in the café.

I've tasted a *lot* of ice cream in my time (trust me), and the creamy delights they make here definitely rival the stuff you get in Cornwall. What's more, it's all made on site, the cream coming from those cows chewing away matter-of-factly in the nearby fields.

You're barely a couple of miles away from the Blue Lion now, but there's one more place you should visit on the way home. Even by Yorkshire standards Jervaulx Abbey is old – dating way back to 1156 – and with clumps of purple flowers and bright green trees growing up between the stonework, it has all the drama of an elaborately created film set.

Nevertheless it's peaceful. Take a seat on one of the benches and all you'll hear in the parkland opposite is the occasional call of a ewe looking for her lamb... That, and hundreds of pairs of teeth nibbling at the grass. It makes you think about food all over again. Time to get back to the Blue Lion...

THE ROUTE

DISTANCE   11 MILES
DIFFICULTY   ○○
START   **The Blue Lion** *East Witton, nr Leyburn, North Yorkshire, DL8 4SN*

» Head right from the Blue Lion and follow the A6108 out of the village. After ½ mile you go over a small bridge, then turn right opposite the Cover Bridge Inn – signposted Spennithorne.

» After crossing another little bridge you carry on up this lane for about 1½ miles to a crossroads: turn right, towards Finghall.

» After 3 miles you'll see a turning on the right, signposted Jervaulx: turn right here.

» Follow this to the crossroads and go straight across, towards Jervaulx.

» You'll reach another junction after 1½ miles: for the Brymor Ice Cream shop, turn left towards Masham; otherwise turn right towards Middleham – on to the A6108.

» After ½ mile on this road you'll reach a brown sign for Jervaulx Abbey – follow this to see the ruins.

» The Blue Lion is just 1½ miles further along this road from the abbey.

STOP AND SEE
EN ROUTE

Brymor Ice Cream *High Jervaulx Farm, Masham, North Yorkshire, HG4 4PG; 01677 460337; www.abmoore.co.uk*
Rock up at this family-run farm and you'll find temptation in the form of raspberry cheesecake, fudge brownie, black cherry whim wham, and 32 other lusciously flavoured ice creams.

Jervaulx Abbey *Jervaulx, Ripon, North Yorkshire, HG4 4PH; 01677 460184;*
www.jervaulxabbey.com
Stop and savour the peace in the grounds of this ruined Cistercian monastery. Entry is free (unless you'd like to put something in the honesty box) and over the road you'll find a tea shop selling tasty fruit cake. Go on, there's always room…

OFF ROUTE

The Black Sheep Brewery *Wellgarth, Masham, Ripon, North Yorkshire, HG4 4EN; 01765 689227;*
www.blacksheepbrewery.com
Call in for a brewery tour; you'll get to sample a Riggwelter and other tasty tipples, before a leisurely lunch in the renowned bistro. By this point you'd probably rather not know that Theakston's Brewery (01765 680000; www.theakstons.co.uk) is just down the road, but if you're interested…

Middleham Castle *Castle Hill, Middleham, North Yorkshire, DL8 4QG; 01969 623899; see www.english-heritage.org.uk*
This was the castle that Richard III ('My kingdom for a horse') grew up in, and although it's in ruins these days, somehow that only adds to its character. There's a viewing platform offering sweeping views of the Wensleydale countryside.

EAT, DRINK, SLEEP

The Blue Lion *East Witton, nr Leyburn, North Yorkshire, DL8 4SN; 01969 624273; www.thebluelion.co.uk*
Aside from serving excellent food in its atmospheric bar (complete with open fire), the Blue Lion has 12 uniquely styled rooms to stay in. Go for Room 3, located in the main building.
Doubles from £89 per night.

Park House *(see Jevaulx Abbey in 'Stop and See' for contact details)*
This polished B&B, in the grounds of the abbey, was once two workers' cottages. Now one, it offers a choice of three rooms, which makes for a tough decision: look out across the parkland to the abbey ruins; or over the garden, the River Ure, and beyond? Doubles from £75 per night (including free entry into the abbey, and tea and home-made cake on arrival).

Rookery Cottage *East Witton, nr Leyburn, North Yorkshire, DL8 5SN; 01969 622918; www.btinternet.com/~njbussey/Rookery*
This whitewashed 16th-century cottage is right opposite the Blue Lion, making it handy when the need for sleep takes over after pudding. As well as two rooms (one double and one twin) there's a sunny garden out the back, where you can look out over the hills and spend a while reading your book.
Double from £65 per night.

RENT

Dales Mountain Biking *Dales Bike Centre, Fremington, Richmond, North Yorkshire, DL11 6AW; 01748 884908; www.dalesmountainbiking.co.uk*
Though fairly far away, Dales Mountain Biking is the nearest hire facility around. The good news is they have an extensive fleet of hard tails (£22 per day) and full suspension mountain bikes (£40), which come with helmets, pumps, and puncture-repair kits – and there's a great little café on site. The area surrounding the centre offers some excellent mountain biking trails to suit all abilities, too.

46

WEST WITTON TO MELMERBY

Short and steep, with some of the best views in England...

DO YOU GO FOR A Night at the Movies, Champagne, or Chocolate Heaven? It's a tough decision (and not to be taken lightly), but whichever room you choose at the Wensleydale Heifer you're in for a treat. Quite literally.

I went for the chocolate option (sorry, couldn't resist) and found bars of the stuff in the bedside table where you'd normally get a copy of the Good Book. Even in the bathroom – with its cocoa-coloured walls that look temptingly edible – there were carefully placed piles of Cadbury's where you'd usually see Molton Brown products (don't worry, they have those too). As you might have guessed, this is probably not the place to come if you're looking to lose a few pounds – but then you haven't been out on your bike yet.

Within minutes of leaving the Heifer (a Galaxy stuffed in your back pocket, just in case), you arrive at the foot of the aptly named Witton Steeps – and it's time to make another choice: ride or walk up? The good news is it's a short hill, and a few switchbacks later you're up on the top looking down over Wensleydale, far below.

A skinny little lane leads you out on to the expanse of Melmerby Moor, which blushes purple with a burst of heather flowers in the late summer sun. This has to be one of the most scenic – and least travelled – roads in England; a thin strip of tarmac takes you straight over the heath, and in all directions – for 30 miles or more – it's just empty dales.

Soon you're dropping over the other side, into Melmerby, where you make a right and carry on along the bottom of the valley to Carlton. Your reward for the climb is a well-earned pint at the Foresters Arms, where a tasty roe-deer steak with brandy-cream sauce will re-energise you.

From here you retrace your steps back out of the village, carrying on along the valley, winding your way between thick hedgerows bordered by fields. Vast shafts of sunlight pierce the clouds above, spotlighting the hillsides away to your right, before you turn your back on them and climb again.

Slowly but surely, over the next couple of miles, you pedal your way up on to Middleham High Moor, making a left at the top to cruise along the edge of Middleham Gallops. Racehorses have been thundering up and down this stretch of soft, peaty grass since 1739, when it was a full-blown racecourse, and nowadays some of Britain's best trainers still come here to test their new steeds. Listen for the rumble of hooves as you pedal along for the next mile or so, with that view of Wensleydale stretched out below you, on the right this time.

If it's starting to look familiar, that's because you're about to arrive back at the top of Witton Steeps, closing the circle. Now all that stands between you and Chocolate Heaven is a downhill run back to the Wensleydale Heifer...

THE ROUTE

DISTANCE   9 MILES
DIFFICULTY   ○○○○
START   The Wensleydale Heifer

West Witton, North Yorkshire, DL8 4LS

» Head left from the Wensleydale and take the first turning right, signposted Melmerby.

» This is Grassgill Lane and over the next ½ mile it takes you up Witton Steeps, via a series of switchbacks.

» At the summit of the hill you'll have Wensleydale below you on your left; keep going until you see another sign for Melmerby, directing you right.

» You should have the racehorse Gallops on your left now, as you drop over the back of the hill and across Melmerby Moor for the next 1½ miles, to arrive at a junction in Melmerby: turn right.

» Follow this road for ¼ mile until you reach a junction: turn right towards Carlton. After ½ mile you'll enter the village and reach the Foresters Arms on your left.

» From the Foresters Arms, retrace your steps back out of Carlton and carry on past the junction you came out of earlier. Follow this road along the bottom of the valley for 1½ miles, taking the second turning left.

» Follow this lane to the next junction: turn right towards Wensley.

» Continue along this road as it slowly bears left, taking you back up on to the hill overlooking Wensleydale. After 1½ miles you'll see a turning left; take this.

» After ½ mile you'll see the Gallops appear again on your left. Keep following this road, to emerge at the junction at the top of Witton Steeps.

» Now simply retrace your route back down the hill to the Wensleydale Heifer.

STOP AND SEE

EN ROUTE

The Foresters Arms *40–42 Carlton-in-Coverdale, nr Leyburn, North Yorkshire, DL8 4BB; 01969 640272; www.forestersarms-carlton.co.uk*

This cosy, grey-stone pub has been spruced up, but the food is as good as ever. Forget scampi and chips and think chicken in sea salt and thyme with a Dijon mustard and lemon sauce. There are two B&B rooms here, if you can't bear to leave.

OFF ROUTE

The Forbidden Corner *Tupgill Park Estate, Coverham, Middleham, North Yorkshire, DL8 4TJ; 01969 640638; www.theforbiddencorner.co.uk*

Walking around this magical garden is like being in a scene from the David Bowie movie, *Labyrinth*. You enter through a monster's mouth, with no map – just a checklist of features to look out for along the way, as you wander through hidden doors, underground tunnels, and mazes.

Vintage Bus Trip *01748 828747; see www.wensleydalerailway.com*

Take a trip back in time on a bona fide sixties bus. The bright-green single-decker runs throughout the summer and chugs its way along from Ripon to Garsdale. Why not get on at Leyburn, for the 45-minute ride over to Aysgarth Falls, where you can have lunch at the Mill Race Tea Shop (see ride 17, p223)?

Bolton Castle *nr Leyburn, North Yorkshire, DL8 4ET; 01969 623981; www.boltoncastle.co.uk*

This foreboding castle is in pretty good nick for its 600 years – despite a few scars from Civil War skirmishes. Mary, Queen of Scots stayed here in 1568, after her defeat in the Battle of Langside. The view out across the hills is rather spectacular, too.

EAT, DRINK, SLEEP

The Wensleydale Heifer *West Witton, North Yorkshire, DL8 4LS; 01969 622322; www.wensleydaleheifer.co.uk*

Aside from the 13 themed rooms, which have rather exciting bathrooms, fresh cakes, and other goodies, there's a DVD collection to choose from if you feel like unwinding after the ride (help yourself to popcorn from the machine) and a restaurant downstairs that serves up delicious fresh-fish dishes.
Doubles from £170 per night.

Capple Bank Farm *West Witton, Leyburn, North Yorkshire, DL8 4ND; 01969 625825; www.capplebankfarm.co.uk*

If you don't fancy the climb up Witton Steeps then book one of the rooms (one double and one twin) in this renovated farmhouse. You'll find it at the top of the hill (which means fabulous views over Wensleydale while you're eating your breakfast cereal)
Double from £40 per person, per night.

Stable Cottage *Main Street, West Witton, North Yorkshire, DL8 4LU; 01969 624810; www.stablecottagedales.co.uk*

How about booking into your own cosy cottage for a few days? This 18th-century stone house has a private country garden, rustic-chic bedroom, and good local food just a few steps away in the village shop. Or you could always pop along to the Wensleydale Heifer for dinner...
From £60 per night (less if staying a week).

RENT

Dales Mountain Biking *Dales Bike Centre, Fremington, Richmond, North Yorkshire, DL11 6AW; 01748 884908; www.dalesmountainbiking.co.uk*

As with rides 14, 15, and 17, Dales Mountain Biking is the nearest hire facility. The centre offers an extensive fleet of hard tails (£22 per day) and full suspension mountain bikes (£40), which come with helmets, pumps, and puncture-repair kits – and there's a great little café on site.

47

BAINBRIDGE TO AYSGARTH FALLS

The Wensleydale Tour of the Tea Shops...

TO HOT-TUB, OR NOT TO HOT-TUB? That is the (most challenging) question you'll find yourself asking during a stay at Yorebridge House in Bainbridge. Book into the Nishiki room at this stylish hotel and you can soak away an afternoon in your own private garden, wallowing in the bubbles till your toes turn wrinkly.

In fact, this whole place is a temple to getting wet. There are baths next to windows so you can lie back and look out over the dales, double walk-in showers that are big enough to host a party, and even his 'n' hers roll-tops if you're staying in 'Greenwich'. It's tempting to stick the 'do not disturb' sign on the door and go AWOL for the weekend, but that would be a real shame – because you'd miss out on a rather spectacular bike ride.

Leaving the hotel (eventually), you head off over the River Bain and out into the Wensleydale countryside towards the village of Askrigg, cycling along a wide verdant valley bordered by fields of juicy grass. Miles of drystone walling stitches them all together, and from a distance it looks as though someone has scribbled over the green hillsides with a giant grey pencil.

Soon you're pedalling up through Askrigg, calling in at Sykes House – where you can sit outside with a cuppa and look across at the old church. They do a delicious Victoria sponge here, too, which will keep you topped up for the next few miles.

Back in the eighties, Askrigg's elegant Georgian houses formed the backdrop for the TV series, *All Creatures Great and Small*, based on the adventures of Yorkshire vet, James Herriot, and it really is as idyllic as it looked on screen.

From here you head back out into the dales, the view even grander because you're on higher land. There's plenty of time to admire it over the next few miles, the road staying pretty much straight until you swing right and freewheel down to Aysgarth Falls.

After all that open space, the road narrows now as you glide along a treelined lane, twisting and turning to arrive at another river – the Ure this time. Pausing on the bridge and casting your eyes right, you'll see it tumbling towards you over the rocky staircase.

Pop into the Mill Race Tea Shop for a ploughman's lunch and then take a stroll further down the river to see the other two sections of the waterfall, before you start back. The route takes you along that wide, open valley again, on the other side this time, and in the distance Askrigg's houses appear snuggled against the hillside. It's not often you see most of your route laid out before you like this – something to think about while you're in that hot-tub back at the hotel...

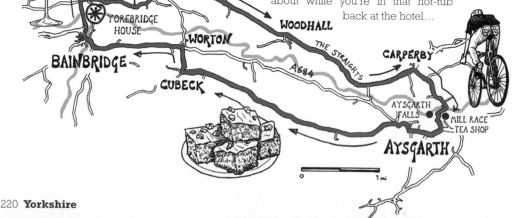

THE ROUTE

DISTANCE 12½ MILES

DIFFICULTY ○○○

START Yorebridge House

Bainbridge, North Yorkshire, DL8 3EE

» Turn right out of Yorebridge House, then go right again at the next junction, signposted Askrigg.

» Follow this road for 4½ miles (passing through Askrigg after about a mile), until you see a right-hand turning, signposted Aysgarth Falls. Turn right here.

» Follow this road all the way to Aysgarth Falls, continuing on up the hill to the next junction, with the A684.

» Turn right here, towards Aysgarth.

» Cruise to Aysgarth and go straight through the village, taking the left fork as you leave – for Thornton Rust.

» After about 3 miles you reach a junction with the A684: turn left towards Bainbridge.

» After 1½ miles you reach Bainbridge. Cycle through the village until you see a right-hand turning signposted Askrigg: turn right here.

» Now simply follow this road out of the village until you reach Yorebridge House.

STOP AND SEE

EN ROUTE

Sykes House *Main Street, Askrigg, North Yorkshire, DL8 3HT; 01969 650535; www.sykeshouse.co.uk*

This is a traditional tea shop as only Yorkshire does them, with a rather splendid selection of home-made cakes. There are two B&B rooms upstairs, so if you really fall in love with the place you can stay here.

Mill Race Tea Shop *Yore Mill, Aysgarth Falls, Aysgarth, North Yorkshire, DL8 3SR; 01969 663446; millraceteashop.co.uk*

The perfect lunch stop, in an old water mill right by the river. There's a food shop here, too, so you could always fill up your saddlebag with yummy cheeses, jams,

and chutneys and then head off to the nearby waterfalls for a picnic feast.

OFF ROUTE

Mill Gill Force *nr Askrigg, North Yorkshire; see www.waterfallsoftheyorkshiredales.co.uk*

If you fancy a walk to loosen up those legs, then how about a stroll up to Mill Gill Force? It's tucked away in the woods above Askrigg, and if you set off along Mill Lane, by the church, you'll find a footpath that takes you up there. From the waterfall you can cut across to Low Straights Lane, which leads you along to Moor Road, then back downhill into Askrigg – about three miles.

Wensleydale Creamery *Gayle Lane, Hawes, Wensleydale, North Yorkshire, DL8 3RN; 01969 667664; www.wensleydale.co.uk*

'Cheese Gromit!' If you've even an inkling of interest in cheese (let alone as much as Wallace) you'll love this place. They've been making cheese here since 1150 – that's AD not AM – and if you take a tour round the creamery you'll see how they still make it by hand, as they always have. Head to the restaurant once you've finished sampling, and order a traditional ploughman's – with a chunk of you-know-what…

EAT, DRINK, SLEEP

Yorebridge House *Bainbridge, North Yorkshire, DL8 3EE; 01969 652060; yorebridgehouse.co.uk*

This swish boutique hotel on the edge of Bainbridge has 11 unique rooms with huge beds, Bang & Olufsen TVs, and a rather extensive cocktail list.

Doubles from £160 per night.

The Apothecary's House *Main Street, Askrigg, North Yorkshire, DL8 3HT; 01969 650626; www.apothecaryhouse.co.uk*

Fancy staying in a former doctor's house? This place sits opposite the church and has three rooms to choose from – with original

fireplaces, old oak beams, and comfy beds. It's also perfectly positioned for a stroll round the village.

Doubles from £72.50 per night (minimum two-night stay).

Bottom Chapel *Station Road, Askrigg, North Yorkshire, DL8 3HZ; 01969 650180; www.bottomchapel.co.uk*

There's a choice of three rooms in this smart converted chapel, where you'll find old-fashioned iron bedsteads and – if you're in the small double – exposed stone walls and leaded windows.

Doubles from £70 per night.

RENT

Dales Mountain Biking *Dales Bike Centre, Fremington, Richmond, North Yorkshire, DL11 6AW; 01748 884908; www.dalesmountainbiking.co.uk*

This dedicated mountain bike centre has a selection of hard tails (£22 per day) and full suspension mountain bikes (£40). Each bike comes with helmets, pumps, and puncture-repair kits. They'll also recommend more rides if you're keen…

48

BROMPTON—ON—SWALE TO GILLING WEST

From lakeside to riverside with stunning scenery in between...

IT'S EARLY MORNING ON Brompton Lakes, and the only signs of life are a couple of moorhens on the bank opposite. It's going to be another scorcher of a day, and the glassy water is so still it looks as though you could step straight off the deck and glide across it.

This peaceful spot is a true wildlife magnet. Aside from those moorhens there are swans and ducks, and below the surface it's teeming with fish. Spaced out in a large semi-circle around the edge of the lake, like the private boxes you see at an intimate performance, are eight eco-friendly cabins with glass fronts. Gone are the days when 'green' was a euphemism for uncomfortable, though; these spacious pods with rounded roofs are the kind of thing you saw in sixties sci-fi films about how everyone would be living in The Future. I wish...

Inside they're awash with expensive leather sofas, flat-screen TVs, and wood-burning stoves that you can rotate in whichever direction you want. But the true beauty of this place is what's on the outside – and there's some wonderful cycling to be had in the surrounding area.

A quick cruise along the road sees you diving off left on to the narrowest of lanes, which quickly becomes a dirt track as you leave the rest of the busy world behind. Eventually even the dirt gives way to good old grass, as you join a bridleway that skirts the edge of a field. In the distance, to your right, you can hear the whirr of tyres from traffic on the A1; it's a shame they're in such a hurry – they don't know what they're missing.

A mile or so later, you're on to country lanes, cruising along the flat ground towards Gilling West. Glance left at any point and you'll see cornfields disappearing off into the distance, bordered by dark green trees and a massive blue sky overhead.

Turning left into the village, you find a perfectly placed pit-stop in the form of the White Swan pub, where a pint of Black Sheep and a home-made steak pie will stock you up on calories for the run up to Richmond.

There's nothing steep to worry about, though, and a couple of miles later you're dropping downhill through this elegant Georgian town, freewheeling over the river for an ice cream dessert at the Station.

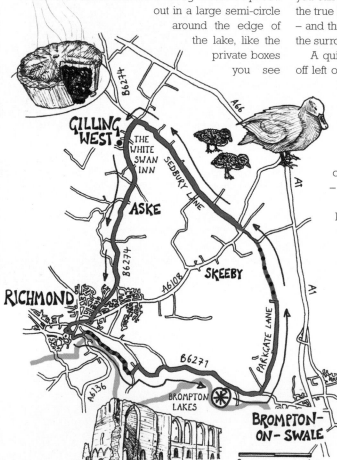

These days there aren't any trains here, just a cluster of shops that includes a bakery, a cheese deli, and a rather nice restaurant called Seasons. After the railway closed in these parts in the 1960s the building lay dormant until reopening a few years ago, and now it makes a relaxing place to hang-out en route to Brompton.

Once you've finished polishing off a raspberry pavlova tub (with real meringue bits), the route takes you along a path through the trees for a mile or so, emerging at the ruins of Easby Abbey. Even in its dilapidated state, with cuttings of blue sky visible through the ancient arched windows, this place will have you whipping out the camera to get a good shot. The old, weather-worn walls are laid out on freshly mown lawns, almost as though they've been put out for display.

When you've seen enough of the Abbey, simply climb up to the lane that takes you back towards Brompton; it's only about a mile away. And you can spend the rest of the day at the lakeside, watching those moorhens.

THE ROUTE

DISTANCE 11 MILES
DIFFICULTY ○○○
START Brompton Lakes

Easby, Richmond, North Yorkshire, DL10 7EJ
» From Brompton Lakes, head to the main road and turn right.
» After less than ½ mile turn left into Parkgate Lane and follow it to the end, until the road runs out (after roughly 1 mile).
» Take the bridleway ahead of you, and follow this across the fields until you reach a road on the other side.
» Bear left – effectively straight on – until you reach a junction with the A6108. Bear right here (again, you're basically carrying on straight), towards Scotch Corner.
» About 200 metres later bear left again, on to Sedbury Lane. This takes you to a junction on the edge of Gilling West: turn left then immediately left again.
» You're now heading through Gilling West, along the High Street. As you leave the village, the road becomes the B6274.
» When you reach the roundabout on the edge of Richmond, take the second exit.
» Follow this road down the hill, and at the next roundabout take the first exit, on to Dundas Street.
» Follow Dundas Street as it turns right, then left, dropping downhill towards the river. Take the first turning left, just past the church, on to Lombards Wynd.
» Lombards Wynd turns left shortly after you enter it; when it does this, you turn right to enter a narrow lane that quickly becomes a track through the woods – called Easby Low Road.
» Follow this for about a mile, through the trees and then a field. As you follow the right-hand edge of the field, you should see the ruins of Easby Abbey ahead of you.
» The path takes you around the edge of a private house and becomes tarmac as you come out in front of the Abbey. As it bears left, you'll see the car park ahead, to your right. Follow the road as it bends left and climb the hill to the junction at the top.
» Turn right here and follow the road to a junction with the B6271 again: turn right and the turning for Brompton Lakes is less than a mile along on your right.

STOP AND SEE

EN ROUTE

The White Swan Inn *51 High Street, Gilling West, Richmond, North Yorkshire, DL10 5JG; 01748 821123*
When you see the white walls of this homely country pub, you know you're only a minute away from a good pint and some proper fortifying grub. There's a garden out back, too, if you fancy eating alfresco.

The Station *Station Yard, Richmond, North Yorkshire, DL10 4LD; 01748 850123; www.richmondstation.com*
This atmospheric old railway station still has many of the public-transport trimmings. Among the ornate pillars and big stone windows you'll find an art gallery, a café, and a bunch of foodie shops.

Easby Abbey *North Yorkshire; See www.english-heritage.org.uk*
Tucked away at the bottom of a hill by the banks of the River Swale, this abbey was once home to dozens of monks in white robes. Poke your head into the little church here, too, and you'll see paintings dating back to the 13th century.

OFF ROUTE

Richmond Castle *Riverside Road, Richmond, North Yorkshire, DL10 4QW; 01748 822493; www.english-heritage.org.uk*
Hard though it is to believe, this omnipresent fortress dates back to 1079, when the victorious Normans went on a building spree after the Battle of Hastings. There's a photo-tastic view of the surrounding dales from the keep.

Richmond Farmers' Market *Richmond, North Yorkshire; see www.ndfm.co.uk*
From rare-breed pork to ostrich burgers and chutneys, this market has lots to make your mouth water. It takes place on the third Saturday of every month, so why not fill your shopping bags (reusable of course) and take them back to the lake for a feast?

EAT, DRINK, SLEEP

Brompton Lakes *Easby, Richmond, North Yorkshire, DL10 7EJ; 01748 850333; www.bromptonlakes.co.uk*
These waterfront eco-lodges make a cracking change from a B&B stay. There are 20 to choose from, each featuring high-spec kitchens, walk-in showers, and tons of space. And, of course, you get to sit out on the deck and watch the wildlife go about its business. Lodges from £305 for a two-night stay.

The Frenchgate *59–61 Frenchgate, Richmond, North Yorkshire, DL10 7AE; 01748 822087; www.thefrenchgate.co.uk*
The attention to detail in this place is staggering. From the specially built seven-foot-wide beds, to the showers, which are so spacious that you don't get wet while the water warms up. And just wait till you sample the food and wines… Doubles from £118 per night.

Arandale Guest House *27 Queens Road, Richmond, North Yorkshire, DL10 4AL; 01748 821282; www.arandaleguesthouse.co.uk*
This Victorian townhouse has bags of character and three smart en suite rooms – book room one, which has an old-fashioned roll-top bath. There's a hot-tub, too, which is perfect for soothing those legs before bed.

RENT

There's free bike-hire available for Brompton Lakes guests.

LAKE DISTRICT

49

BROUGH TO SANDFORD

Kings of 'your own' castle...

WITH ITS TURRETS, battlements, 15 acres of gardens, and four-poster beds, the imposing presence of Augill Castle seems to fit right in with its wild Cumbrian surroundings. Sandwiched between Scotland and the Yorkshire Dales, this whole area was once awash with forts, designed to keep the Scots from invading England. Augill, however, was not one of them.

Sure, it may have the hallmarks of medieval heritage, complete with 'arrow slit' windows and even a flag; but what you're looking at is a remarkable example of Victorian vanity – built by John Bagot Pearson in 1840 so that he could literally look down on the rest of his family. That's some ego.

In stark contrast, today the castle is owned by Wendy and Simon Bennett, who've added their own touches to the place – the odd piano here, a church pew or Indonesian blowpipe there – giving it a real 'our home is your home' atmosphere.

Head out of the driveway, however, and you only have to journey a couple of miles before you encounter the real medieval deal – or rather its ruins. The keep at Brough Castle was built in 1200, and has been battered by over 800 years of weather and several invasions. Silhouetted against the blue sky, it's a poignant reminder of Cumbria's turbulent past. Looping round through Brough and out the other side, you get a second glimpse of it, a mile or so later – this time with the Yorkshire Dales rising up in the distance beyond.

For the next few miles the lanes ripple along gently, taking you across the River Eden in Warcop, before you dive off left along a single-track lane to leave the man-made world behind as the grass tries its best to reclaim the tarmac along here. Finally you arrive at an oasis in the form of the Sandford Arms.

Its pub aside, Sandford is little more than a handful of houses surrounded by fields and high hedgerows, and the outside world seems a long, long way from here when you're sitting in the beer garden sipping a cloudy cider. The remoteness only increases as you carry on through the village and down to the River Eden, where at last the road runs out.

Pausing on the bridge, you'll see brown trout shimmying away against the flow, treading water in the hope of catching a dozy passing fly.

With no more asphalt left it's time to duck off-road, cutting across a bridleway that loops back to Warcop. You re-enter the village over Eden Bridge, which has been carrying traffic across the river since 1374. When I cycled over it, I almost expected a troll to pop its head up from beneath the red sandstone arches and demand a toll...

Safely across, you follow your tracks back to 'your' castle at Augill. Why not call Wendy and ask her to raise the flag?

THE ROUTE

DISTANCE   14 MILES
DIFFICULTY   ○○○○
START   Augill Castle

South Stainmore, Cumbria, CA17 4DE

» Turn right out of Augill Castle's drive and cycle towards the junction with the A685.

» Just before the junction, turn right on to the track that takes you through a tunnel under the main road.

» You emerge on to a little lane running parallel with the A685; follow this to the end, and take the path leading right, back to the A685. (If you want to see Brough Castle, turn left halfway along the lane and then follow the brown sign.)

» At the main road, turn left and cycle into Brough. (Stick to the path if you feel safer.)

» At the T-junction opposite the Castle Hotel, turn left on to Market Street, towards Great Musgrave.

» Take the first left, on to Musgrave Lane, for Great Musgrave. Continue for almost 2 miles, passing through Great Musgrave, to arrive at a junction: turn right, for Warcop.

» You're now on the B6259, which takes you through Warcop after 1½ miles.

» Take the first left after leaving the village, signposted Sandford.

» Turn left at the next junction, in Sandford.

» Carrying on from the Sandford Arms, follow the road through the village. The road wiggles through and out the other side, taking you across a bridge over the river, where the road ends by a bungalow.

» On your left is a gate; go through this and join the bridleway leading back to Warcop. You need to bear right across the field, going through the gate at the top of the hill.

» The bridleway takes you over the hill and between some farm buildings to the river on your left. Stay on the track, following the river, until you reach the tarmac road again.

» Bear left to rejoin the road, crossing the bridge and climbing up back into Warcop.

» Follow this road through the village, to the junction with the war memorial.

» Turn right on to the B6259, signposted Kirkby Stephen.

» Now retrace your steps back to Brough and Augill Castle, turning left when you see the sign for Great Musgrave, after 1½ miles.

STOP AND SEE

EN ROUTE

Brough Castle *Brough, Cumbria see www.english-heritage.org.uk*
Fires, sieges, marauding Scots… The red sandstone walls of this 12th-century castle have seen it all. Grab a cornet from the ice cream parlour nearby and take in the view of Cumbria and Yorkshire spread out around you. Let us know if you see anyone coming...

The Sandford Arms *Sandford, Cumbria, CA16 6NR; 01768 351121; www.sandfordarmscumbria.co.uk*
This traditional village boozer has a rich history dating back hundreds of years. Ask the landlord, Stephen, to tell you all about it while he serves up a minted lamb Henry – that's a shoulder of local lamb, marinated and oven-baked in mint gravy. Tasty.

Chofh's Tearoom *New Road, Brough, Cumbria, CA17 4AS; 01768 342800*
Treat yourself to a cuppa and a slice of cake at this cosy café, which you'll pass on the way into Brough.

OFF ROUTE

Appleby-in-Westmorland *Cumbria*
This small medieval town arranged round the River Eden has bags of atmosphere and some seriously old buildings. Check out the church, which dates back to Norman times – and the castle, too, built in the 1300s.

EAT, DRINK, SLEEP

Augill Castle *South Stainmore, Kirkby Stephen, Cumbria, CA17 4DE; 01768 341937; www.stayinacastle.com*
When was the last time you stayed in a castle – even a Victorian one? After a day out in the Cumbrian wilds, you get to take your place around the huge table in the Gothic dining hall and tuck into dishes like Cumbrian venison.
Doubles from £160 per night.

The Coach House *Eden Gate, Warcop, Appleby-in-Westmorland, Cumbria, CA16 6PL; 01768 341955; www.coachhouse-in-eden.co.uk*
This Grade II-listed converted coach house looks out over the River Eden on the edge of Warcop. There are three cosy rooms to choose from – all with oak beams, open fireplaces, and plenty of character.
Double from £56 per night.

The Tufton Arms Hotel *Market Square, Appleby-in-Westmorland, Cumbria, CA16 6XA; 01768 351593; www.tuftonarmshotel.co.uk*
This luxury boutique hotel, about six miles from Brough, has a rather superb restaurant and 22 period-styled rooms with Molton Brown products and fluffy bath robes.
Doubles from £120 per night.

RENT

Stonetrail Holidays *Street Farm, Ravenstonedale, Kirkby Stephen, Cumbria, CA17 4LL; 01539 623444; www.stonetrailholidays.com*
A range of well-maintained, modern Trek mountain bikes are available here, costing £16 a day for an adult's bike including helmet, padlock, pump, and maps. Delivery is free within a 10-mile radius.

50

RAVENSTONEDALE TO ORTON

See a different side to Cumbria…

THERE'S A COMMON MISCONCEPTION that Cumbria is all about steep hills and vast lakes – the land of Wordsworth and Turner. But once you've set off from Coldbeck House in Ravenstonedale, you'll soon realise that there's a whole other side to the landscape around here.

Here, you suddenly leave civilisation behind and emerge into the wide-open space of Ravenstonedale Moor. The drystone walls have disappeared and it's just you, your bike, and a thin strip of tarmac stretched across the purple-specked greenery.

This whole area lies to the east of the Lake District National Park – the bit that everyone thinks of as 'The Lakes'; out here the hills have been smoothed off with an artist's palette knife, rather than chiselled out of solid rock, so there are no steep shockers to climb.

Nevertheless, you're slowly gaining height, and in a few miles' time reward comes in the form of a 360-degree view across the moorland – only the odd farmhouse interrupting the scenic solitude. There are lakes out here, too – like the one you see to your left after another few miles, with its opaque, glassy 'eye' reflecting the lustrous cloud passing overhead.

All this time you've been tracing a squiggly line leading northwards, ever deeper on to the moor; but around the five-mile-mark you hang a left for Orton. It's largely downhill for the next few miles, giving you plenty of time to soak up the view, shift through the gears, and cruise easily across the unkempt land.

Civilisation soon returns, though; heathland becomes pasture, then an avenue of trees sees you into Orton. There's a surprise in store here, in the form of Kennedys Fine Chocolates, where the sweet aroma lures you in off the street. Houses are gathered around the shop in an expectant triangle, and you get a sugar rush just from ducking your head inside…

If you're after something more substantial than a pack of chocolate Brazils, there's a coffee house, too, serving home-made soups and other comfort-food staples – and the George Hotel, for classic pub fare.

Still feeling the effects of your chocolate high, you leave Orton, but avoid the moor and sweep right towards Ravenstonedale. Way out in the distance you can see the landscape beome suddenly bumpy, signalling the start of the Pennines.

But before you get anywhere near those hills you make a left to close the loop and spin back towards Coldbeck House. It is strange that Mr Wordsworth and friends overlooked this area; they didn't know what they were missing.

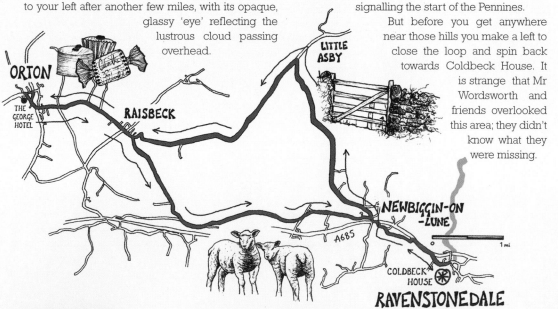

THE ROUTE

DISTANCE 17 MILES

DIFFICULTY ○○○○

START Coldbeck House

Ravenstonedale, Cumbria, CA17 4LW

» From Coldbeck House, turn right and head out of Ravenstonedale village to the junction with the A685.

» Turn left on to the A685, then take the first left into Newbiggin-on-Lune.

» Go straight through the village and out the other side, arriving back at the A685. Turn left here, then immediately right – signposted Kelleth and Great Asby.

» Follow this road for 2½ miles, out on to the moor, until you reach a junction: turn left towards Orton and Tebay.

» Follow this road across the moors, for another 2½ miles, to a junction: keep right.

» After 1½ miles, turn right at the junction, signposted Shap and Appleby.

» Within ¼ mile, you reach Orton.

» From Orton, go back to the last junction and turn left, following your route back to the earlier junction; but this time, you follow the road as it sweeps right, signposted Ravenstonedale and Kirkby Stephen.

» Stay on this road for 1½ miles, to the next junction: turn left for Kirkby Stephen.

» After passing through Kelleth, you come to the junction you passed earlier (after leaving the A685). Turn right, and at the junction with the A685, turn left.

» Take the first right and retrace your earlier route back through Newbiggin-on-Lune to reach the A685 again. Turn right; and right again, for Ravenstonedale.

STOP AND SEE

EN ROUTE

Kennedys Fine Chocolates *The Old School, Orton, Cumbria, CA10 3RU; 01539 624781; www.kennedyschocolates.co.uk*
Stop for lunch in the café; then stock your saddlebag with treats. This sweet-smelling shop sells toffees, buttons, butterflies, mice,

and much more – all covered in delicious chocolate. Forget your wallet and your taste buds are unlikely to forgive you.

The George Hotel *Front Street, Orton, Cumbria, CA10 3RJ; 01539 624229; www.thegeorgehotelorton.co.uk*
This traditional-style 'hotel' is more a pub with rooms, but the food served here is just what you need after a morning in the moorland air. Try the lamb shoulder, or the rather filling Cow Pie.

OFF ROUTE

The Howgill Fells *Cumbria/Yorkshire*
This range of grassy hills starts just along the road from Ravenstonedale and extends into Yorkshire, giving you great walking opportunities right on your doorstep if you're staying at Coldbeck House. Richard Tolley, who runs Coldbeck with his partner Belle, is also a qualified walking guide, so why not leave the bikes in the shed for a day and head out on foot?

Smardale Gill Nature Reserve
see www.cumbriawildlifetrust.org.uk
Roe deer, ravens, red squirrels, and buzzards are just some of the creatures to look out for as you stroll through the wooded slopes and green banks here. Along the way you'll cross the disused Smardale Gill viaduct, its 14 arches a striking testament to the Victorian Steam Age.

EAT, DRINK, SLEEP

Coldbeck House *Ravenstonedale, Kirkby Stephen, Cumbria, CA17 4LW; 01539 623407; www.coldbeckhouse.co.uk*
Tucked away in a quiet corner of the village, this atmospheric Georgian house dates back to 1820 – with stained glass, original fireplaces, and two acres of gardens where you can hide yourself away with a pot of tea after the ride. Doubles from £90 per night.

The Black Swan *Ravenstonedale, Kirkby Stephen, Cumbria, CA17 4NG; 01539 623204; www.blackswanhotel.com*
This friendly hotel is a real family affair, where you'll no doubt see owner Louise Dinnes behind the bar at some stage. Mum takes care of the (yummy) puddings while Dad handles the beer. And after a dinner out in the garden by the river, you've got 14 uniquely styled rooms to choose from. Doubles from £80 per night.

Orton Hall *Orton, Cumbria, CA10 3RF; 01512 435440; www.ortonhall.com*
This Grade II-listed Jacobean mansion is surrounded by seven acres of parkland and a private wood. There are four suites to choose from (sleeping between two and four), all with original features such as fireplaces, stone window frames, and wood panelling.
A two-night stay in the Naseby Suite costs from £210 for two people.

RENT

Stonetrail Holidays *Street Farm, Ravenstonedale, Kirkby Stephen, Cumbria, CA17 4LL; 01539 623444; www.stonetrailholidays.com*
Not only do these guys offer an impressive range of Trek mountain bikes, but they also dish out complimentary tea and cake if you're passing. Daily hire costs £16 for an adult bike, which comes with a helmet, pump, maps, and a padlock – and they'll even deliver within a 10-mile radius at no extra charge.

CHERRY AMARETTO
White Chocolate cream with

51

FAR SAWREY TO WRAY CASTLE

Giving the Lake-District crowds the slip…

THE IRONY OF THE Lake District is that although people come here in a bid to get away from it all, in reality you often can't move for the crowds that flock here. Head to Ambleside or Windermere in the height of summer, for example, (or winter, too, for that matter) and there are queues for the tea shops, standing room only on the pleasure boats, and people following closely on your trail when you're out for a hike. On Lake Windermere's opposite shore, however, it's a different story.

Setting off from West Vale Country House in the hamlet of Far Sawrey (just up the road from Beatrix Potter's former home), you drop downhill to the Windermere waterfront and peel off left before the ferry port to follow the shoreline. Any cars on your tail are soon left behind, most of them continuing on to catch the boat to join the crowds on the other side.

In less than a mile, tarmac turns to dirt track and the bike comes into its own. Huge old trees shelter you from any overhead droplets of rain, while the smell of moist earth hangs in the air. Nature is so rampant here, it's as if the plants are growing before your very eyes – even the rocks that line the trail are covered in a vivid green moss.

At times you're only a metre or so from the lake's edge; territorial swans keeping a beady eye on you from among the reeds as you pass. 'Noise' is limited to the occasional slap of water against the shore – the delayed reaction to an unseen boat out on the lake.

After a mile or so you emerge back on to paved road and climb uphill, away from the water, to be greeted by views out over Windermere that would have had Wordsworth reaching for his pen. In the distance, beyond the opposite shore, velvety peaks in shades of green and purple rise up to meet smudgy grey clouds; it's like looking at a super-sized watercolour painting. The best bit, though, is that you've got it all to yourself – the mainstream hordes don't tend to venture over here.

Sweeping across a shallow valley of fields, you arrive at Wray Castle a mile or so later. From a

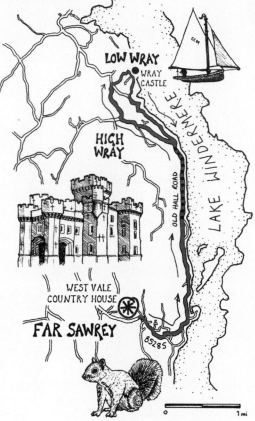

distance it looks like the real medieval deal (with turrets and arrow slits – the whole shebang), but is actually one of those lookey-likeys built in the 1800s.

The building itself is closed to the public, but the garden is accessible, so how about opening that picnic blanket and getting stuck into the packed lunch the guys at West Vale prepared for you?

Better still, if you carry on round the back of the estate and drop down to the lake again, you could stretch out on the grass and watch the sailboats gliding silently up and down. Whenever you're ready to face the outside world again, there's a path that will hook you back up to the trail leading home…

THE ROUTE

DISTANCE   10 MILES
DIFFICULTY   ○○○
START   West Vale Country House
Far Sawrey, Hawkshead, Cumbria, LA22 0LQ

» Turn right out of West Vale Country House and follow the B5285 for about ¾ mile, until you drop downhill and take the first turning left – signposted Harrowslack and the lake shore.

» Follow this side road, parallel to the lake, as it becomes a dirt track then tarmac again. After about 2½ miles you'll see a car park to the right; ignore this and carry on up the hill.

» After another mile you reach a junction: turn right towards Wray Castle and Ambleside.

» After ¼ mile, you'll reach the entrance for Wray Castle. Turn right and pedal along the drive to the castle. When you reach it, follow the driveway right, around the back of the castle, and enter the bridleway on your right, leading you down to the lake.

» Drop downhill to the waterfront and bear right, to follow the shore along past the boathouse, until you reach a path that hugs the water's edge.

» Turn left on to the path and continue along until you reach a car park after about ½ mile.

» Continue straight ahead to cross the car park and exit on the other side. You'll now rejoin the track you took earlier, and simply retrace your steps all the way back to West Vale Country House.

STOP AND SEE

EN ROUTE

Wray Castle *Hawkshead, Cumbria; 01539 447997; see www.nationaltrust.org.uk*
Built in around 1840 by retired surgeon James Dawson, the castle itself is closed to the public, but the gardens are accessible and awash with exotic trees including giant sequoias and other arboreal exotica.

There's a plan to turn the place into a hotel, so watch this space…

OFF ROUTE

Claife Heights Viewing Station *Far Sawrey, Hawkshead, Ambleside, Cumbria; see www.visitcumbria.com*
Back in the 1790s when tourism in the Lakes was just taking off, a viewing station was built looking out over Lake Windermere to Bowness on the opposite shore. It had tinted glass to accentuate the effects of different light on the landscape, but all that remains is the building's shell. Nevertheless there's a lovely walk up to it from the Sawrey Hotel (along the road from West Vale Country House), and there are plans afoot to restore it.

Lake Windermere *01539 443360; www.windermere-lakecruises.co.uk*
A cruise across Windermere's waters will give you a different perspective on the dramatic Lakeland scenery. You can choose a range of passes to suit your mood, depending on whether you want to stop off at different spots – or simply head out for a 45-minute pleasure ride.

Grizedale Forest *01229 860010; see www.forestry.gov.uk*
If you really fancy going off-the-beaten-track, this place has mountain-biking trails to suit all abilities. They're colour-coded, too – blue, red, and black like ski runs – so you won't unwittingly end up on that gnarly downhill. Unless you want to…

EAT, DRINK, SLEEP

West Vale Country House *Far Sawrey, Hawkshead, Ambleside, Cumbria, LA22 0LQ; 01539 442817; www.westvalecountryhouse.co.uk*
Owners Glyn and Dee lay on some superb breakfasts in this traditional Lakeland guest house with seven tasteful rooms. There's

no chintz in sight and you can enjoy uninterrupted views across the fields. Doubles from £90 per night.

Tower Bank Arms *Near Sawrey, Ambleside, Cumbria, LA22 0LF; 01539 436334; www.towerbankarms.co.uk*
This 17th-century pub in Beatrix Potter's home village featured in many of the writer's books, including *The Tale of Jemima Puddle-Duck*. If that's not enough to impress you, then the food should be… try the beef and ale Cumbrian stew.
Four double rooms; from £88 per night.

The Writing Room Suite, Sawrey Knotts *Far Sawrey, Hawkshead, Ambleside, Cumbria, LA22 0LG; 01539 442435; www.sawreyknotts.co.uk*
If you're coming up with friends then how about booking into this ground-floor apartment in a large country house? It's elegantly decked out with antique furniture and a marble fireplace, as well as a kitchen and dining area.
From £317 per week (sleeps up to 4).

RENT

Country Lanes *The Railway Station, Windermere, Cumbria, LA23 1AH; 01539 444544; www.countrylaneslakedistrict.co.uk*
Choose from a full range of mountain bikes, road bikes, tag-alongs, and trailers – all of which come with helmets, locks, and puncture-resistant tyres (always a bonus). From £16 per day for an adult bike.

52

LAKESIDE TO NEAR SAWREY

Ups and downs in the land of Beatrix Potter...

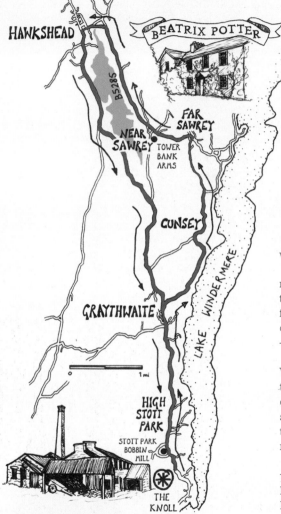

In case you didn't know, Mrs T-W was the washerwoman lead in the eponymous Beatrix Potter book published in 1905, which made her an instant celebrity – along with Jemima Puddle-Duck and Peter Rabbit, of course. The other thing you should know is that Mrs Tiggy-Winkle was a hedgehog. A real one. She was part of a menagerie that the children's author kept at Hill Top in the early 1900s, when things were a lot quieter there.

The farm is now owned by the National Trust and lies in the not-so-sleepy village of Near Sawrey – the halfway point of a scenic ride that begins at the other end of Lake Windermere.

Having jumped on your bike outside The Knoll – a B&B with all the trimmings of a boutique hotel, without the prices – you go left, along the lake's edge.

Within minutes you pass Stott Park, an old bobbin mill that did a roaring trade in the golden years of the Industrial Revolution, spitting out cotton reels for Lancashire cloth factories. You can see the mill's chimney poking above the trees before you get here – an incongruous totem pole to mass production.

Dropping downhill, now, you've got Lake Windermere on your right, and wooded hillside to the left. The Lake District really plays with your sense of scale. One minute you're looking at the vast, open stretch of Windermere, a watery coda that interrupts the flow of hills and valleys for 12 uniform miles; the next, you're diving down impossibly small lanes.

Sticking with the lake for the next couple of miles, you eventually peel off inland and climb up into the hamlet of Far Sawrey, just along the road from Beatrix Potterville, so if you're feeling thirsty the choice is A: instant gratification in the Sawrey Hotel, opposite – or B: turn left and cruise downhill to Near Sawrey, where there's a great pub just five minutes away.

I tend to opt for the latter, the Tower Bank Arms. Not only is it conveniently located just in front of Hill Top, but there's a tasty shoulder of lamb on the menu. Just don't tell us Mrs Tiggy-Winkle.

WHATEVER WOULD MRS TIGGY-WINKLE make of all this? Crowds of people trudging around Hill Top, Beatrix Potter's former home, in their muddy wellies and walking boots, dragging dirt through the house and leaving the door open (letting in the draft!).

THE ROUTE

DISTANCE   15 MILES

DIFFICULTY   ○○○○

START   *The Knoll Lakeside, nr Newby Bridge, Ulverston, Cumbria, LA12 8A*

» Turn left out of The Knoll and follow the road for 2½ miles, passing Stott Park Bobbin Mill, before forking right, for Sawrey Ferry.

» Follow this lane, running parallel with Lake Windermere, for nearly 3 miles, continuing until you reach Far Sawrey.

» Here you take the right-hand fork and climb up to the junction with the B5285 – bringing you out just opposite the Sawrey Hotel.

» Turn left and follow this road through Near Sawrey and on to Hawkshead, where you loop left in a big 180-degree arc. Follow the signs for Newby Bridge and Lakeside for the next 6½ miles – past Stott Park Bobbin Mill – to The Knoll.

STOP AND SEE

EN ROUTE

Stott Park Bobbin Mill *nr Newby Bridge, Ulverston, Cumbria, LA12 8AX; 01539 531087; see www.english-heritage.org.uk*
Believe it or not, 250 men (and boys) toiled here from 1835 to 1971, making around 250,000 wooden bobbins a week for the Lancashire mills. A guided tour gives you a glimpse into their lives.

Hill Top *Near Sawrey, Hawkshead, Ambleside, Cumbria, LA22 0LF; 01539 436269; see, www.nationaltrust.org.uk*
This is the farm that Beatrix Potter bought with the royalties from her first books. In many of the rooms it looks as though she's just nipped out for a walk – leaving sketches of her most famous characters lying around.

Tower Bank Arms *Near Sawrey, Hawkshead, Ambleside, Cumbria, LA22 0LF; 01539 436334; www.towerbankarms.co.uk*

With piles of wood stacked outside and a clock above the front door that may well be stuck on 19th-century time, this pub is like entering a (very pleasant) time warp. Cosy fires in winter, delicious food all year.

OFF ROUTE

The Lakeside & Haverthwaite Railway
01539 531594; www.lakesiderailway.co.uk
Give your legs a rest and take the steam train instead. This 3½-mile stretch of scenic branch-line takes you from Lakeside along to the nearby village of Haverthwaite. They don't make them like this any more.

EAT, DRINK, SLEEP

The Knoll *Lakeside, nr Newby Bridge, Ulverston, Cumbria, LA12 8AU; 01539 531347; www.theknoll-lakeside.co.uk*
Suave rooms, sumptuous sofas, and delicious food on tap… This quiet country house is more like a boutique hotel; think pre-dinner G&T followed by spiced parsnip and apple soup.
Doubles from £90 per night.

Low Graythwaite Hall *Graythwaite, nr Hawkshead, Ambleside, Cumbria, LA12 8AZ; 01539 531676; www.lowgraythwaitehall.co.uk*

There are five swish bedrooms in this historic country house, which once belonged to the Sawrey family. Expect DAB digital radios, locally made toiletries, and big old gardens for a post-ride stroll. Oh, and there's a heated indoor pool, too. Doubles from £90 per night.

Beechmount Country House *Near Sawrey, Hawkshead, Ambleside, Cumbria, LA22 0JZ; 01539 436356; www.beechmountcountryhouse.co.uk*
This turn-of-the-century country house has cracking views of Esthwaite Water and the surrounding hills. Stretch out in the landscaped gardens after your ride, or lock yourself away in the summer house with a good book… one by Miss Potter, perhaps? Doubles from £100 per night.

RENT

Country Lanes *Lakeside, Newby Bridge, Ulverston, Cumbria, LA12 8AS; 07748 512286; www.countrylaneslakedistrict.co.uk*
Located handily just down the road from The Knoll, this friendly hire outlet has a range of mountain bikes for all ages – along with hybrids and trailers too. Everything comes with a helmet and lock – starting from £16 for an adult's bike.

53

CONISTON TO LITTLE LANGDALE

From old-fashioned farmyard to cosy country pub…

Y OU KNOW YOU'RE IN the countryside on discovering sheds deserted; their doors left wide open and the owners nowhere to be seen… Mind you, the only likely 'intruders' at Yew Tree Farm would be one of the stray ducks waddling around the yard outside. This was the sight that first greeted me here, and with the village of Coniston miles back down the road, it was just me, the ducks, and a couple of turkeys for company.

Looking at the rickety old farm sheds and weathered walls of the house (300-years-old, if it's a day), it was as if I'd just wandered into a real-life episode of *The Darling Buds of May*. Following the instructions to 'sound your horn for attention' chalked on to the nearby blackboard, I wondered whether the Lake District's answer to Pop Larkin would appear from behind a hay bale… But instead of his whiskered face, it was Caroline Watson who responded to my polite beep. Aside from running Yew Tree with her husband, Jon, Caroline is a member of the local mountain rescue team and knows every inch of this area intimately.

So it was at her suggestion that I headed off down a slate path leading into the lush hillsides surrounding the farm…

It's not long before a babbling brook appears; time to make a right and join a narrow strip of tarmac heading uphill, with a steep rock-face on one side and a stream on the other. The further I climb, the more dramatic the landscape becomes – huge grey boulders litter the grassy verges, and prehistoric-looking ferns grow beside the drystone walls.

Craggy cliffs rise up on either side, and the day's ominous grey clouds swirl about their summits. Soon the road flattens out and the open moorland gets increasingly wild until even the tarmac can't hack it any more, giving up the ghost and reverting to a dirt track when it reaches an old disused quarry.

Although the old slate works have long since closed, a glance down at them reveals the leftovers from the decades of toil that went on here, including old rail trucks and twisted metallic branches that hang out of the rocks.

Soon it's time to plunge downhill, along an ancient bridleway that threads its way through a corridor of trees; it feels truly isolated out here and, as a brief shower passes overhead, the only sound around is the patter of raindrops on the leaves overhead – like thousands of tiny fingers drumming. But just when it seemed like I'd disappeared off the radar, civilisation appeared across the valley – a winding wisp of smoke leading from the chimney of the Three Shires Inn at Little Langdale; just a quick tiptoe across a Constable-esque ford to reach its slate floors, wood-burning stove, and frothy-topped Old Man Ale.

The trip back to Yew Tree leads cross-country, past more old mines and through the vast natural amphitheatre at High Tilberthwaite. Arriving at the farm there's no need toot a horn this time; Caroline's waiting with a rather substantial cream tea.

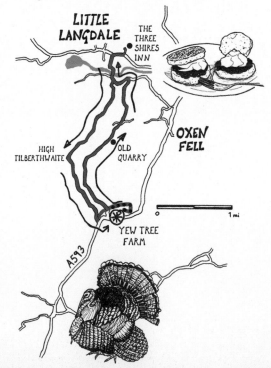

THE ROUTE

DISTANCE 7½ MILES
DIFFICULTY ⚪⚪⚪⚪
START Yew Tree Farm
Coniston, Cumbria, LA21 8DP

» Head out of the drive and turn left on to the bridleway before the road.

» Follow the bridleway until you reach the tarmac road, by the stream; now turn right.

» Stay on this road for 2 miles, climbing uphill and passing through the disused quarry and along a woodland track, before emerging on to tarmac and reaching a farm.

» Here, you follow the road around to the left (don't turn off right), dropping downhill into the valley, where you reach a ford.

» Cross the ford and follow the lane until you reach a junction at Little Langdale.

» Turn right, following the blue cycle route sign towards Ambleside.

» The Three Shires Inn is along on your left.

» From the pub, follow the route back to the ford and cross over it. But instead of going back to the road, take the first right, following the blue cycle path sign ('37').

» Continue down this track along the edge of a wood; after ¼ mile you'll pass a slate slagheap on your right; the trail follows the edge of this, so don't fork left (downhill)

» You'll know you're on the right trail, because shortly after, you reach another slagheap and climb uphill along a slate path; here you join another trail coming from the right, and keep going.

» About ¼ mile later you reach a farmyard and go straight through it to rejoin the tarmac road at High Tilberthwaite.

» Follow this road through the valley, passing through Low Tilberthwaite, until you reach a junction with the A593 about a mile later. Before you reach the actual road, turn left on to the track running parallel with it.

» This path brings you out opposite the bridleway by the stream, which you came along earlier. Simply retrace your steps back along it, to Yew Tree Farm.

STOP AND SEE

EN ROUTE

The Three Shires Inn *Little Langdale, Ambleside, Cumbria, LA22 9NZ; 01539 437215; www.threeshiresinn.co.uk*
Tucked away from the crowds in a tiny village, this traditional pub has been used by thirsty walkers since the 19th century.

OFF ROUTE

The Old Man of Coniston *Cumbria*
This 803-metre peak towers over Coniston village, keeping a watchful eye on those below. Take one of the paths up to the peak and you can do the same – the views over Coniston Water are rather spectacular.

Coniston Water *Coniston Pier, Lake Road, Coniston, Cumbria, LA21 8AN 01539 441288; see www.nationaltrust.org.uk*
Take to the lake in style, aboard the *Gondola* – a splendid Victorian steamer. Built in 1859, it was brought out of retirement and restored by the National Trust, so now you can sit back in the upholstered saloon and chug along at a civilised rate of knots.

Ruskin Museum *Coniston, Cumbria, LA21 8DU; 01539 441164; www.ruskinmuseum.com*
As the name suggests, this museum is packed with interesting artefacts from the life of the philosopher, critic, poet, and painter, John Ruskin. But there's also a fascinating exhibition dedicated to Sir Donald Campbell, who died trying to break the world water speed record on Coniston lake in 1967.

EAT, DRINK, SLEEP

Yew Tree Farm *Coniston, Cumbria, LA21 8DP; 01539 441433; www.yewtree-farm.com*
Surrounded by craggy hills, this working farm dates back three centuries. Sheep, dogs, and chickens wander round the yard, while inside it's all low-hanging beams and stone floors. Chill-out in the comfy guest lounge, where you can hear Beatrix Potter's old grandfather clock ticking in the hall, or head upstairs and stretch out on the big bed. Doubles (three in total) from £52 per night.

The Three Shires Inn *(see 'Stop and See' for contact details)*
Don't worry if you start to feel a little too 'at home' here: there are 10 comfy rooms. Doubles from £82 per night.

The Sun *Ruskin Avenue, Coniston, Cumbria, LA21 8HQ; 01539 441248; www.thesunconiston.com*
This cosy 400-year-old pub is where speed record breaker Sir Donald Campbell used to stay during his runs on Coniston Water. There are quality local dishes (try the rack of lamb) and stirring views from the restaurant; real ales in the bar; and sturdy beds and fluffy towels in the rooms upstairs. Doubles from £95 per night.

Bank Ground Farm *East of the Lake, Coniston, Cumbria, LA21 8AA; 01539 441264; www.bankground.com*
This building was the setting for Arthur Ransome's idyllic story, *Swallows and Amazons*, about learning to sail on the lake. Book a room here and have a go yourself. Doubles from £70 per night.

RENT

Grizedale Mountain Bikes *Grizedale Visitor Centre, Hawkshead, Cumbria, LA22 0QJ; 01229 860369; www.grizedalemountainbikes.co.uk*
There's a huge range of bikes here, from full-suspension beasts with disc brakes, to more sedate steeds with tag-alongs and trailers. From £25 per day; helmet £3.

54

MORESBY TO DEAN

From coastline to country lane in just a few miles…

IT'S NEVER IDEAL FACING a steep hill after a Full English breakfast. But when you're huffing and puffing your way up Ghyll Brow you'll be glad of the extra calories and, when you finally reach the top, a priceless reward greets your efforts. Whether you've pedalled up, or walked it, the prize is the same: a (ahem) breathtaking vista right out over the Irish Sea.

From up here it feels as though you're looking down at a map of England, with the contours of the coast disappearing far into the distance. Away to your right, gleaming white wind turbines swish away in the sea breeze, and behind you there's nothing but fields. Better still, it's pretty much flat going for the rest of the day.

where lunch awaits at the Royal Yew. The turquoise windowsills and whitewashed exterior give you an immediate clue that this is not your typical country pub. It's the kind of place that makes you want to run a hand over its funky-patterned wallpapers, hot chocolate-coloured walls, and exposed-brick fireplaces. What's more, instead of the usual pints of bitter and pale ale that you'd expect to find, there are beers from Belgium, China, and the Czech Republic.

But if you're after something that's brewed a little closer to home, order a Yew

Tree Ale – it's made at the pub's own microbrewery, so you can feel happy about its lack of beer miles while you savour the taste.

A few miles later you'll be feeling the urge to stop and snap again, that sea view still visible as you pass through the village of Pica and continue on to Ullock. It's here that the scenery begins to change, with steep hills rising up on the horizon, announcing the start of the Lake District National Park.

Steering clear of all that uppy-downy stuff, you leave Ullock and head on to the hamlet of Dean –

After lunch the good views continue, as you head back out of Dean and on through Branthwaite, cruising across a farm track and emerging on to the lane at the other end. Pedalling on for another few miles, breathing up the fresh scents of Lakeland air mingled with the faint smell of salt blowing in from the coast, you arrive back at Pica and close the loop.

Now comes the climax: remember that hill you climbed on the way out? This time you're going the other way – and the view is just as good…

THE ROUTE

DISTANCE   17 MILES
DIFFICULTY ◯◯◯◯◯
START   Moresby Hall

Moresby, Whitehaven, Cumbria, CA28 6PJ
» Bear left out of Moresby Hall's drive and head up to the junction with the A595. Turn left, and take the path along to the roundabout if you don't fancy the road.
» Turn right at the roundabout (taking the third exit), signposted Low Moresby.
» Climb the hill for about a mile, up through Low Moresby, to the junction at the top: turn left.
» Cycle along the top for about ½ mile, then take the first right – signposted Pica.
» Stay on this road as it passes through Pica (after a mile) and brings you to a crossroads after 3½ miles: go straight over.
» Continue on to the village of Ullock, where you reach a junction: turn right, towards Cockermouth.

» Take the first 'proper' turning, signposted Dean (not the tarmac footpath before it).
» After a mile or so you arrive at a junction in Dean – turn right. The Royal Yew pub is just along here, on your right.
» From the pub, make your way back to the last junction, and carry on past it to leave the village. After a mile, you reach a crossroads: turn left towards Branthwaite.
» Continue for almost a mile to Branthwaite, taking the first left in the village, signposted Ullock and Loweswater.
» Shortly after leaving the village you'll see a tarmac track forking right: follow this for about a mile – passing through a farm – and continuing until you reach a junction with a lane. Turn right, then take the first left – towards Gilgarran.
» After a mile you reach Gilgarran; turn left at the first junction on reaching the village.
» Follow this road on out of the village, and turn right at the first junction,

towards Distington.
» Take the first left, after ¼ mile, for Pica.
» After ¾ mile, you reach a junction in Pica: turn right, signposted Moresby Parks.
» Now just retrace your earlier steps, back through Pica towards Moresby Hall, turning left at the next junction (towards Moresby Parks), then taking the next right to drop down through Low Moresby to the coast.

STOP AND SEE

EN ROUTE

The Royal Yew *Dean, nr Workington, Cumbria, CA14 4TJ; 01946 861342; www.royalyew.co.uk*
Funky country pub (yep, there is such a thing) in the hamlet of Dean, with a rather fine selection of Belgian beers. They taste especially good with the Cumberland sausage sandwich – served with home-made onion marmalade. How very continental.

OFF ROUTE

Whitehaven *Cumbria*

Believe it or not, this Cumbrian port was the blueprint for New York (seriously). Or at least its carefully planned Georgian streets were; arranged around the harbour in a grid formation, as you'll probably notice when it comes to finding your way back to the B&B. Take a stroll around the old quayside, which dates back to 1634, then stop for a smoothie in one of the waterfront cafés. Why not bring the bike with you and cycle back to Moresby Hall along the picturesque coastal path?

Loweswater *nr Cockermouth, Cumbria; see www.nationaltrust.org.uk*
Rent a traditional rowing boat from the National Trust warden at Watergate Farm and spend a lazy afternoon rowing (or just drifting) on this glassy lake overlooked by dramatic green hills. Take a walk round the edge and there's a good chance you'll see a red squirrel or two…

St Bees Head *nr Whitehaven, Cumbria; 01697 351330; see www.rspb.org.uk*
Even if you can't tell your kittiwake from your common shag, you'll love the cliff-top walk to the bird colony viewing points, where you can see across to the Isle of Man on clear days. Keep an eye out for dolphins and the odd porpoise passing by, too.

EAT, DRINK, SLEEP

Moresby Hall *Moresby, Whitehaven, Cumbria, CA28 6PJ; 01946 696317;*

www.moresbyhall.co.uk
This Grade I-listed house dates back to 1620, with a walled garden and groomed, formal lawns out the front. It's the perfect spot for a post-ride cup of tea.
Doubles from £120 per night.

Glenfield House *Whitehaven, Cumbria, CA28 7TS; 01946 691911; www.glenfield-whitehaven.co.uk*
Owners Andrew and Margaret make you feel instantly at home in this Victorian house

that offers a choice of six rooms. And the breakfasts are to die for.
Doubles from £65 per night.

Springbank Farm Lodges *High Walton, nr St Bees, Cumbria, CA22 2TY; 01946 822375; www.springbanklodges.co.uk*
Spend a back-to-basics weekend in one of these wooden cabins on the Springbank rare-breeds farm. You can sit back on the terrace, relax, and take in the view, or head out for a burst of fine Cumbrian sea air by

heading off on a stroll along the coast.
From £300 per week (sleeping up to a total of 4 adults).

RENT

Haven Cycles *2 Preston Street, Whitehaven, Cumbria, CA28 9DL; 01946 63263; havencycles.webplus.net/homepage.html*
Choose from a range of 60 different steeds including road bikes, mountain bikes, and hybrids, for all shapes and sizes. Adults' bikes cost £15 a day.

NORTH EAST

55

HIGH KEENLEY FELL TO ALLENDALE

Riding across the top of England...

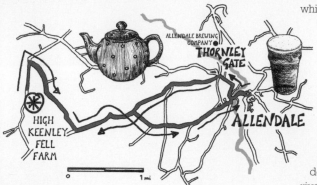

IT'S NOT EVERY DAY you get to see 50-odd miles of uninterrupted countryside in one fell swoop. So before you set off from High Keenley Fell Farm it's worth pausing on the gravel driveway for a minute to scan the horizon; you'll have an uninterrupted view across the North Pennines – all the way to the Scottish border. With not a single blip of civilisation in between.

Sure, your eyes might pick something up if you had a pair of binoculars, like the odd windswept farm sitting isolated atop a hill, but aside from those this part of the world is pretty much as nature intended.

If you can stop staring, make a right out of the farm and drift downhill. As the road falls away into the Allen Valley, all you'd need is a parachute and you'd be up, up, and away over the dales – but that fantasy is put on hold as you make a right to cruise along the top for a little bit longer.

The next few miles see you zigzagging your way across the map, heading east towards the village of Allendale. Farm buildings appear every now and again, much smaller than the ones you get in the south of England – often little more than a cottage and an outbuilding surrounded by neat parcels of land. The reason why they're so diminutive is that back in the 18th century, when many of them were built, it was the womenfolk who worked the land while the men spent their days scraping lead out of the earth in nearby mines.

Smaller farms were more manageable for these hard-working wives, who often had to dash home to attend to their household chores, on top of tilling the fields.

Around the three-mile mark you begin the descent into Allendale, the houses of the village huddled together in the valley below, as if they slipped off the hillsides at some stage. The lanes get narrower the further you descend, until you emerge at the bottom by the river. Turn right here and the road takes you uphill and into the market square, where the Allendale Tea Rooms serve up scones with cream that's as thick as the cake. You'd be advised to fill up, because the route back to High Keenley is mostly uphill.

Retracing your route out of town, you sweep round past the river and begin the steady climb back up on to the dales, to reach the farm. It's not especially steep, but it does go on for about three miles. The secret is to take it steady and stop for plenty of photo breaks; after all, it's not often that you get to take advantage of a view like this.

THE ROUTE

DISTANCE   9 MILES

DIFFICULTY   ○○○○

START   High Keenley Fell Farm

High Keenley Fell, Allendale, Hexham, Northumberland, NE47 9NU

» Head right from the farm, and then take the first right.

» Follow this lane to the next junction, about a mile away: turn left.

» Cruise along this lane, down a sharp dip and up the other side, for almost a mile – and take the first right.

» After about ½ mile, the road bends left – don't go right, it's just a dead end.

» Freewheel downhill to the next junction, then bear left – continuing downhill.

» About ¼ mile after this, take the right fork.

» At the next junction, turn left – carrying on down the hill.

» Just along from here you'll come to another junction: go right for Allendale.

» From Allendale's centre, simply retrace your steps back downhill, past the brewery and following the road as it sweeps right, past the junction you came out of earlier.

» Just over ¼ mile later, at the hamlet of Thornley Gate, you reach a multiple junction: take the second left.

» Follow this road for 2 miles and take the first 'proper' right (not a dirt track) to head back to High Keenley. .

» Now simply turn left at the end of this road, and you'll arrive back at High Keenley Fell Farm.

STOP AND SEE

EN ROUTE

Allendale Tea Rooms *Market Place, Allendale, Hexham, Northumberland, NE47 9BD; 01434 683575; www.allendaletearooms.co.uk*

This place is just what you need to power up those tired legs. Home-made cakes, quiches, and scones are served up with clinking cups of strong tea.

Kings Head *Market Place, Allendale, Hexham, Northumberland, NE47 9BD; 01434 683681*

Located at the top of the market square, about 15 steps from the Tea Rooms, this 18th-century watering hole serves traditional pub classics like ham and eggs, fish and chips, and, of course, a good selection of ales.

Allendale Brewing Company *Allen Mill, Allendale, Hexham, Northumberland, NE47 9EQ; 01434 618686; www.allendalebrewco.co.uk*

Why not stop for a tour and a tipple at this friendly microbrewery that lies by the river on the way into the village? Temptations include Golden Plover, Allendale Wolf, and Entrepreneur Ale.

OFF ROUTE

The Dales *Northumberland*

If you're staying at High Keenley Fell Farm, ask owner Caroline about the picturesque walk that takes you across the top of the dales to the old lead mine chimneys about a mile away. The mine itself was located further down the valley, in Allendale (near the brewery), and the smoke was transported through tunnels dug into the hillsides, which little boys were employed to clean. If you're keen, you can do a loop that takes you into Allendale and back to the farm – about five miles in total.

EAT, DRINK, SLEEP

High Keenley Fell Farm *High Keenley Fell, Allendale, Hexham, Northumberland, NE47 9NU; 01434 618344; www.highkeenleyfarm.co.uk*

Possibly the most panoramic views on offer from any B&B you'll stay at this year; here you can see for about 50 miles in any direction. There are three named en suite rooms to choose from, with oatmeal walls and flat-screen TVs. Opt for Cross Fell if you want all that stunning scenery visible from your bed.

Doubles from £60 per night.

Allendale Tea Rooms *(see 'Stop and See' for contact details)*

Considering the sausage, bacon, and Full English breakfasts served up by owner Wendy, you'll need to watch your waistline during a stay here. There are two en suite rooms to choose from: one twin, one double; go for the latter, it overlooks the square. Rooms from £60 per night.

Bridge End Cottage *Allendale, Hexham, Northumberland, NE47 9AA; 01434 618937; www.bridgeendcottage.co.uk*

This tastefully restored self-catering stone cottage in the village has two rooms, each boasting White Company linen and underfloor heating in the bathroom (plus a double-ended bath). And there's a wood-burning stove in the lounge. Cosy. £600 for a week.

RENT

Dale Bike Hire *Dene Croft, 35 Upper Town, Wolsingham, Bishop Auckland, County Durham, DL13 3ES; 07811 321947; www.dalebikehirenortheast.co.uk*

Choose your steed from a range of 30 bikes for all shapes and sizes – adults' cycles costing £17 per day, including helmets, pumps, and puncture-repair kits. They'll deliver too (for a small charge) and can recommend other good rides.

56

CARRAW TO SIMONBURN

Following in Roman footsteps…

WHAT MUST IT HAVE BEEN LIKE for the Roman soldiers stationed here? As you look out across the vast open space of the Pennines, it makes you wonder about the stories this ancient landscape has to tell. Only five minutes earlier you were ensconced in the comfort of Carraw B&B, before a short downhill glide along the main road saw you dive on to a bridleway and over a grassy hump, leaving the rest of the world behind. That hump, by the way, was Hadrian's Wall.

Nearly two thousand years ago a vast stone barrier was built across the top of England on the orders of the eponymous Roman Emperor. Stretching for almost 75 miles, it was designed to keep out the Picts from Scotland – and much of it is still here, up to three metres high in places. In others, however, it's now barely more than a grassy mound.

Even so, once you leave the road behind it takes little imagination to picture the scene here those two millennia ago; it probably would have been much the same as it is today. The outlook in this part of England is still pretty wild, with moorland ready to reclaim the tidy fields at any opportunity.

The bridleway takes you along the edge of this farmland-cum-heath for about a mile, getting rather stodgy in places. About two-thirds of the way down you come to a stream that cuts its way through the land, and if you stop for a second, all you'll hear is the sound of the water rushing over the rocks, and the breeze blowing through the grasses. It's not often these days that you can find moments of complete calm like this – let alone in such unspoilt open space – but if you can drag yourself away, you'll soon emerge on to a lane that takes you down to Simonburn.

It's a refreshingly easy run down to the village; you hardly have to push the pedals, and a mile or so later you're pulling up at the local tea room, where Dexter the Westie is waiting to welcome you at the gate, his tail going nineteen to the dozen.

The tea room is tucked away in a corner of the village and is one of those places that would be so easy to miss. The reward for those of us who do find it, however, is a quiet cottage garden that catches the sun, where afternoons laze luxuriously by. The village lies in a shallow valley, hidden out of sight from the rest of the world, and when you're sitting at the one of the tables, topping up your tan, it's hard to imagine that out there – somewhere – there are people stressed out and stuck in traffic.

More importantly, you're approximately four steps away from a fridge full of the finest cakes known to man – blueberry tart, lemon meringue and (my favourite) banoffi pie. After a slice or three, washed down with a ginger beer, and a quick peek at the ducks who live at the bottom of the garden, it's time to climb out of the village and make your way back up to the main road. The views expand steadily as you go, and when you reach the top, a couple of miles later, you finally see it: Hadrian's Wall. Forget the ambiguous green knoll you passed earlier; this is a whole section of stones, laid by real Roman soldiers. In front of it a few thistle flowers have sprung up rebelliously, making you wonder if they were planted by Scottish Picts who made it over the wall all those years ago…

THE ROUTE

DISTANCE   7 MILES
DIFFICULTY   ○○○
START   **Carraw B&B** *Carraw Farm, Military Road, Humshaugh, Hexham, Northumberland, NE46 4DB*

» Head right from Carraw and cruise along the arrow-straight B6318 for ½ mile, until you see the brown sign for Brocolitia Mithraic Temple up ahead. Turn left here and join the bridleway.

» Follow this for a mile, through a couple of gates and across a stream, before turning right as you join a tarmac lane at the end.

» This leads you downhill to Simonburn.

» Arriving in Simonburn 1½ miles later, you turn left just after the church for Simonburn Tea Room – otherwise, carry on past the church and take the first right to continue the route (follow the brown cycle route sign).

» The road bears sharply left after ¼ mile, but you carry straight on, up the hill.

» Half a mile further on, the road bends sharply right – but you take the left fork and continue up the hill to meet the main road.

» Turn right, on to the B6318 and cruise the last 2 miles back to Carraw.

STOP AND SEE

EN ROUTE

Simonburn Tea Rooms *The Mains, Simonburn, Hexham, Northumberland, NE48 3AW; 01434 681321; www.simonburntearooms.com*
While you'd be forgiven for being distracted by the cake selection, the tea shop's owner, Ann, whips up home-made quiches, stews, and hotpots, too – which you can wash down with locally brewed ales in the old-fashioned dining room. Wander in the garden to meet the prize-winning doves.

OFF ROUTE

Falconry Days *Lady Hill Farm, Simonburn, Hexham, Northumberland, NE48 3EE; 01434 689681; www.falconrydays.com*

Get up close and personal with eagles, owls, hawks, and falcons on a falconry experience day in the Northumbrian countryside. After being shown the basics you'll have these majestic birds of prey eating out of your hand.

The Twice Brewed Inn *Bardon Mill, Hexham, Northumberland, NE47 7AN; 01434 344534; twicebrewedinn.co.uk*
Head across the road from Carraw and join the path along Hadrian's Wall, which brings you to this welcoming pub, about 6½ miles away. Your reward for all that tramping in the fresh air is a menu full of treats like lamb shank in mint gravy.

The Roman Army Museum and Vindolanda Fort *Chesterholm Museum, Bardon Mill, Hexham, Northumberland, NE47 7JN; 01434 344277; www.vindolanda.com*
These military remains form one of the most important Roman sites in the world, and experts believe that there are around 10 forts here altogether – many of them still submerged. Aside from looking around and lapping up the history, you could have a go at discovering your own, by joining a dig.

EAT, DRINK, SLEEP

Carraw Bed and Breakfast *Carraw Farm, Military Road, Humshaugh, Hexham, Northumberland, NE46 4DB; 01434 689857; www.carraw.co.uk*
The view from the garden is reason enough to come here. You can sit outside in the sun, looking out over the North Pennines and wonder about the history buried beneath this old farmhouse. It's built on the wall's foundations, using the same stone…
Doubles from £75 per night (based on a two-night stay).

Simonburn Tea Rooms *(see 'Stop and See' for contact details)*

There are three sunny rooms to choose from (two doubles; one single), with a shared bathroom, above this rather delightful tea room. Aside from Dexter the resident West Highland Terrier, there are Aylesbury ducks wandering about the cottage garden.
Doubles from £60 per night.

Ashcroft Guest House *Lanty's Lonnen, Haltwhistle, Northumberland, NE49 0DA; 01434 320213; www.ashcroftguesthouse.co.uk*
This Victorian vicarage is surrounded by two acres of gardens that erupt into an explosion of colours each spring. There are five B&B rooms, plus a two-roomed suite, and an apartment with two more bedrooms – all en suite, with sumptuous beds and great views.
Doubles from £80 per night.

RENT

Hadrian's Wall *Twice Brewed, Northumberland, NE47 7AN; 01434 344650; see www.hadrianswall.ltd.uk*
There's a fleet of hybrids available, which will easily cope with the stretch of bridleway en route to Simonburn. Adult bikes cost £20 per day including helmet, pump, lock, and panniers.

57

MATFEN TO BELSAY HALL AND CASTLE

The B&B, the brewery next door, and the trip to a nearby castle...

DON'T, WHATEVER YOU DO, look to your right as you arrive at Matfen High House. Because it will probably spell the end of any plans you had for a bike ride.

Just across the farmyard there's a rather fine microbrewery, and the waft of hops hits you the moment you open your car door.

Assuming that you fail to resist the temptation (I did), you'll find a selection of ales waiting to be tried, with reassuringly curious names like Auld Hemp, Nel's Best, and Cyril the Magnificent – the latter named after the resident farm cat.

The strong-willed among you should head left out of the drive and on to the lane leading to Matfen village, where you'll find temptation again, a few flat miles later, in the form of the Black Bull pub. It looks out on to the green, and is a great excuse to sit, sip, and spy on the world for a while. After all, what's the hurry?

When you feel like moving on, the next right turn takes you out of the village and into the countryside. There are no surprise hills to worry about today, so for the next few miles you get to relax and enjoy the ride, cutting across a farm track and on through the hamlet of Wallridge.

Despite the lack of hills, however, you've been slowly and subtly gaining some height, which only becomes clear when you look around and see Northumbrian cornfields unfolding below you for 10 miles or more.

A brief stint along a B-road later, and you dive on to a dirt track that takes you around the back way to Belsay Hall, where you can lounge about on the grass or raise a china cup filled with a refreshing brew in the tea room. The Greek-inspired hall, with its Doric columns, looks a tad incongruous in this land of medieval castles; but don't fret if you're feeling the need for some turrets and battlements – Belsay Castle is only a short stroll away and it has the full works.

When you're ready to hit the road again, a quick pootle back down the track is all it takes; you then make a left on to the main road and keep pedalling for four easy miles, until you reach Stamfordham. From here a wiggly lane takes you to the turning for Matfen High House B&B; when you smell those hops you'll know that you're nearly there...

BELSAY HALL AND CASTLE

WALLRIDGE

BLACK HEDDON

B6309

INGOE

B6309

FENWICK

HEUGH

STAMFORDHAM

MATFEN

THE BLACK BULL

MATFEN HIGH HOUSE

0   1 mi

THE ROUTE

DISTANCE   19 MILES
DIFFICULTY   ○○○
START   Matfen High House

Matfen, Corbridge, Newcastle upon Tyne, NE20 0RG

» Head left out of Matfen High House and follow the lane for 2 miles. After less than a mile you'll pass a left turning, signposted Hexham; ignore this and follow the road around to the right (marked 'unsuitable for heavy goods vehicles').

» At the first junction you come to (after 2 miles), turn left, signposted Corbridge. This takes you into Matfen.

» Take the next right (after the Black Bull, opposite the green), signposted Ryal/Ingoe.

» After 1½ miles turn right towards Ingoe.

» Shortly after, you sweep right, by a quarry; ¼ mile after this, look out for the tarmac track leading off left – and take this.

» Follow this track for less than a mile as it takes you around a farmyard and brings you out across fields, to meet a lane running left to right: turn right here.

» Stay on this road for about 2 miles, following signs for Belsay and Wallridge.

» After passing through Wallridge you reach a crossroads: go straight over.

» A mile later you reach a junction with the B6309: turn left towards Belsay.

» Just along the road you'll see a track on your right. Take this and follow it, through a farm and past a small wood, before turning left at the grass triangle, towards Bellsay Hall and Castle.

» Shortly after, you need to follow the track round to the right, bringing you out in front of the castle.

» From the castle, retrace your steps back to the B6309 and turn left.

» Follow this for about 4 miles, passing through Heugh, to reach Stamfordham. Stay on the B6309 as you ride through the village and you'll come to a junction: turn right – towards Corbridge.

» This road wiggles for about 1½ miles, until you reach a right-hand turning: take this and cycle the mile or so back to Matfen High House.

STOP AND SEE

EN ROUTE

High House Farm Brewery *Matfen, Newcastle upon Tyne, NE20 0RG; 01661 886192; www.highhousefarmbrewery.co.uk*
Steven Urwin has won a barrel-load of awards since he started producing ales about eight years ago. Take a tour round the visitor centre and try guessing the secret of his success (I think it's the fact that he grows his own barley).

The Black Bull *Rose Cottage, Matfen, Newcastle upon Tyne, NE20 0RP; 01661 886330; www.theblackbullatmatfen.co.uk*
This traditional village pub provides a great excuse for an early pit-stop, with its various ales on tap and tables outside that catch the sun.

Belsay Hall, Castle, and Gardens
Belsay, nr Morpeth, Northumberland, NE20 0DX; 01661 881636; see www.english-heritage.org.uk
Between the Greek-columned hall with its regular contemporary art exhibitions, the surrounding gardens, and the 14th-century castle (don't miss the view from the top of the tower), there's enough here to keep you out of the saddle for a good few hours.

OFF ROUTE

Aydon Castle *nr Aydon Road, nr Corbridge, Northumberland, NE45 5PJ; 01434 632450; see www.english-heritage.org.uk*
This fortified manor house has seen off pillages by Scots, seizure by English rebels, and several centuries of attacks by the Northumbrian frost. It's still one of the finest houses you'll see for a long time.

EAT, DRINK, SLEEP

Matfen High House *Matfen, Corbridge, Newcastle upon Tyne, NE20 0RG; 01661 886592*
There are four rooms to choose from in this weathered old farmhouse (two twins, two doubles), my favourite being the 'double en suite', which has an adjoining bathroom where you can enjoy a soak in the sun while looking out over the farmyard. Ask owners Jenny and Struan to recommend some places to see – they know the area inside-out and are super-friendly. Doubles from £70 per night.

Bog House *Matfen, Newcastle upon Tyne, NE20 0RF; 01661 886776; www.boghouse-matfen.co.uk*
Don't be put off by the slightly unfortunate name; this place is homely, peaceful, and ensconced in countryside that'll have you snapping away with the camera. Rosemary whips up delicious evening meals (locally sourced, organic, and all that jazz) and you can ring ahead to discuss what you'd like. Doubles from £90 per night.

The Bay Horse Inn *Stamfordham, Newcastle upon Tyne, NE18 0PB; 01661 886244; www.bay-horse-inn.com*
This cosy hotel, pub, and restaurant offers a choice between six rooms, and boasts a chef who's worked at Gleneagles and other fancy eateries. After a day of cycling and a freshen up, you can tuck into a loin of red deer with cabbage and smoked bacon jus. Doubles from £75 per night.

RENT

The Bike Place *Station Garage, Kielder, Northumberland, NE48 1EG; 01434 250457; www.thebikeplace.co.uk*
There's a range of mountain bikes available here, from full-suspension downhillers, to trailer bikes for the kids. Adult cycles from £20 per day.

58

ALNHAM TO THROPTON

Discover the Northumbrian wilds...

THE HAMLET OF ALNHAM takes 'ye olde' to a whole new level. Forget any of the whitewashed, wood-timbered cuteness you get down south; parts of the church here date back to Saxon times, when life in this area of England was a little on the wild side. Rather like the scenery.

Alnham lies about eight crow-flying miles from the Scottish border, and attacks by Lowland chieftains were not uncommon in those days. Tempting though it is to cruise out of Alnham Farm and head straight off into the countryside, it's worth stopping; there are clues to this tumultuous past hidden down a side lane.

A quick detour down Salters Road – so called because it was once a main trade route for taking salt to Scotland – brings you to the church, which historians date back to the 1100s. What's more, if you peer through the trees next door you'll spy a mini fortified tower with walls that are two metres thick; it was built to keep the vicar safe from roaming Middle-Age outlaws.

Leaving Alnham, you hit the lanes and skirt the edge of the national park, where even the farmland looks untamed.

Thropton is the lunch destination, and the route there takes you through a bunch of villages with Dickensian-sounding names – Netherton, High Trewhitt, and Snitter – while views of the distant Cheviot Hills (marking the border with Scotland) accompany you all the way.

After five miles and only a couple of junctions, you reach the Cross Keys pub and hang a right into Thropton, arriving outside the Three Wheat Heads. In comparison to most places round here, this friendly pub is positively 'new-build' – a mere 300 years old. Unlike Alnham, though, it shows no signs of a fortified past; just old oak beams and shelves decked out with kitsch china teapots and painted plates.

After an Aberdeen Angus steak, you head back into the lanes again, climbing up steadily through Cartington and Lorbottle. Glance over your left shoulder in late summer to see the hillsides carpeted in purple heather, the shadows of overhead clouds giving the flowers a velvet-like sheen.

After sweeping left at Callaly, you cruise through the trees as the sun flickers between the branches. Back in the sanctuary of Alnham Farm, you can watch the last of the rays start to melt behind the hills, a glass of chilled white in your hand. How very civilised.

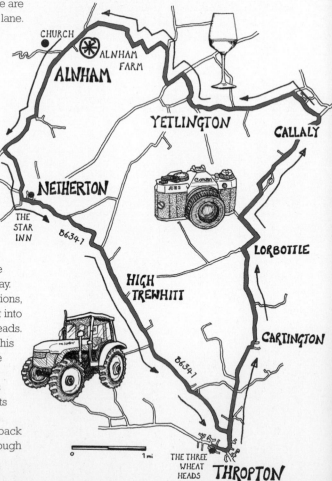

Alnham Farm
Holiday Cottages

Tel: (01669)
630210

www.alnhamfarm.co.uk

THE ROUTE

DISTANCE 18 MILES

DIFFICULTY ○○○○

START **Alnham Farm** *Alnham,*
Whittingham, Northumberland, NE66 4TJ

» Head left from Alnham Farm and follow the lane for just over a mile, where it bends sharply right at Scrainwood Farm, signposted Netherton and Rothbury.

» Sweep left ½ mile later, following the sign for Netherton (ignore the blue cycle route sign pointing straight on).

» At Netherton, turn left, towards Thropton.

» Stay on this road for over 4 miles. Pass through Snitter to reach a junction: turn right, signposted Thropton.

» At the next junction, beside the Cross Keys pub, turn right, towards Harbottle, and follow the B6341 into Thropton. The Three Wheat Heads is ¼ mile along, on your left.

» From the pub, retrace your steps back to the Cross Keys and turn left. But instead of turning left again (for Netherton), carry on past the junction you emerged from earlier and follow the sign for Whittingham.

» Stay on this road for the next 4½ miles, passing through the hamlets of Cartington and Lorbottle, before arriving at Callaly. Here you turn left, towards Yetlington.

» At the next junction, turn left for Yetlington.

» When you reach Yetlington, turn right towards Netherton.

» Turn left at the next junction, still following signs for Netherton.

» At the next junction, turn right for Alnham.

» Turn left at the next junction, continuing towards Alnham.

» The road now twists and turns for just over a mile until you reach the next junction: turn left towards Alnham; Alnham Farm is about ¼ mile along the road on your left.

STOP AND SEE

EN ROUTE

The Star Inn *Netherton,*
Morpeth, Northumberland,
NE65 7HD; 01669 630238
Step inside this old village pub and you'll feel like you're entering an 18th-century time warp. The landlady, Vera, was born here after her family took it over in 1917. There's one beer (straight from the cask) and bags of down-home atmosphere – enough to persuade CAMRA to recommend the place in their guide for the last 35 years…

The Three Wheat Heads *Thropton,*
Morpeth, Northumberland, NE65 7LR;
01669 620262; www.threewheatheads.com
Sit back in the beer garden overlooking the Simonside Hills while the chef flexes his skills to prepare your plate of salmon – straight from the nearby River Coquet.

OFF ROUTE

Cragside *Rothbury, Morpeth,*
Northumberland, NE65 7PX; 01669 620333;
see www.nationaltrust.org.uk
From a distance this place looks like a Swiss chateau, with its Gothic arches, creeping ivy, and backdrop of dense forest. Built by the Victorian inventor, Lord Armstrong, it's packed full of gadgets and is powered by hydroelectricity; leave time to check out the gardens.

The Breamish Valley *Ingram Visitor Centre,*
Ingram, Alnwick, Northumberland, NE66 4LT;
www.northumberlandnationalpark.org.uk
Grab a picnic and head to the village of Ingram, where you can stretch out by the river or go for a paddle. The visitor centre has maps detailing some great local walks along the valley that will take you to ancient hill forts.

EAT, DRINK, SLEEP

Alnham Farm *Alnham, Whittingham,*
Northumberland, NE66 4TJ; 01669 630210;
www.alnhamfarm.co.uk
This farmhouse, on the edge of Alnham,
has two tranquil rooms (one twin; one double) with period furniture, and a huge sunny garden that's made for afternoon lounging and flicking through the papers. If you'd prefer self-catering, there's a three-bedroom cottage and two-bedroom gatehouse, too.
Rooms from £80 per night.

Blacksmith's Cottage *Alnham, Alnwick,*
Northumberland, NE66 4TN; 01669 631184;
www.blacksmiths-cottage.co.uk
If you're coming here with a bunch of friends why not book into this renovated old blacksmith's cottage? There are three bedrooms, bathrooms with underfloor heating, and plenty of space in which to store the bikes.
Three-night stays from £75 per night for the whole cottage; seven-night stays from a total of £525.

The Orchard House *High Street, Rothbury,*
Northumberland, NE65 7TL; 01669 620684;
www.orchardhouserothbury.com
This chic Georgian townhouse in the centre of Rothbury makes a stylish base for your weekend, with Egyptian cotton sheets, goose-down duvets, and rather gorgeous bathrooms. There are suites available, too, giving you plenty of space in which to relax after the ride – and you're just down the road from the country lanes.
Doubles from £99 per night.

RENT

Tomlinson's Café and Bunkhouse
Bridge Street, Rothbury, Northumberland,
NE65 7SF; 01669 621979;
www.tomlinsonsrothbury.co.uk
These guys have a fleet of mountain bikes for all shapes and sizes, costing £20 per day for adults, including helmets. They also have a cool café serving fresh local food – so why not treat yourself to a huge slice of cake when you get back?

59

CRASTER TO ALNMOUTH

Coffee-coloured sand, craggy cliffs, and lungfuls of salty fresh air...

YOU MAY FIND IT slow-going along the coastal path from Craster to Alnmouth. Not because it's particularly difficult cycling, you understand; it's just that every few minutes or so you find yourself reaching for the camera, as yet another craggy cove reveals itself.

Anyone who's ever doubted Britain's ability to do gorgeous coastline should come out here and take a peek. With its pristine ribbons of sand, dramatic cliffs silhouetted against the sky, and blue-green water stroking the shore, it rivals anything you'll find on the American seaboard or the north of Denmark. And that's even *before* the sun comes out.

The ride begins in the small fishing village of Craster, where lobster pots are stacked up on the quayside, and the aroma of smoked fish hangs in the air. Folk have been catching and curing kippers here for centuries – even exporting them to the royal household – and today you still occasionally see brightly coloured boats with their cargo of catches chugging in and out of the harbour, harassed by hungry gulls.

Heading up the hill from this sleepy village, through the castellated entrance arch that spans the lane (no passport necessary), you make a left on to the coast road and set off towards Alnmouth. It's easy pedalling all the way, until you peel off on to the cliff-top path and

that camera starts burning a hole in your pocket. Off to your left it feels as though you've got the entire North Sea pooled out for your viewing pleasure, with hundreds of whitecaps breaking in the distance, like flashing smiles.

The sound of the waves stays with you for the next few miles now, accompanied by a gentle rustle of the breeze through the cornfields on your right, as you skirt along this edge of England.

Of course, there are plenty of temptations to stop you dead in your tracks – a stretch of fudge-coloured sand here, a collection of sedimentary rockpools there – and at one point you cross a small stream that feeds the sea. Soon enough, though, you're back on tarmac for the run along to Alnmouth.

Three miles later, and you're sweeping downhill to arrive on the high street, where lunch is being served at the Sun Inn. Its custard-coloured exterior puts you in a bright mood before you've even met the warm landlady, Mel.

And after one of her filling hot roast beef baguettes, you've got the whole afternoon to while away on the nearby beach.

Fingers crossed you still have some space left on that camera…

THE ROUTE

DISTANCE   16 MILES
DIFFICULTY   ○○○
START   Sea Breeze Cottage
1 Heugh Road, Craster, NE66 3TJ

» Head left out of Sea Breeze Cottage, then take the first right and cycle up the hill out of Craster. Continue to a left-hand turning, for Alnwick. Turn left and cruise through the castellated archway, up to the next junction.
» Turn left here, following the blue cycle route sign towards Alnmouth.
» Follow this road for 1½ miles, parallel with the coast, until you see it sweeping right. Here you veer off left along the dirt track – effectively straight on along the coast.
» After about 2 miles the coastal path turns to tarmac and brings you to a junction at Boulmer: continue straight on, following the blue cycle route sign for Alnmouth.
» After 2 miles take the first left for Alnmouth.
» Over the next mile you drop downhill to the edge of Alnmouth. Go straight over the roundabout to enter the town.
» From Alnmouth, simply retrace your route back to Boulmer (over the roundabout, right at the junction and past the golf course) to join the coast path back to Craster.

STOP AND SEE

EN ROUTE

Alnmouth Beach *Northumberland*
If you thought the coast that accompanied you from Craster was picturesque, wait until your eyes catch a load of this... There are three expanses of golden sand to choose from, my favourite being the stretch south of the river, which is wilder and a little quieter. If you're feeling energetic, how about a stroll along to the village of Amble?

The Sun Inn *Northumberland Street, Alnmouth, Northumberland, NE66 2RA; 01665 830983; www.sun-inn-alnmouth.co.uk*
A friendly local couple (Bren and Mel) runs this village pub in the heart of Alnmouth

(Bren's grandparents ran it before him). If you're feeling full after the Craster salmon in white wine sauce, or good old scampi and chips, then why not check in to one of the four upstairs rooms?

OFF ROUTE

Dunstanburgh Castle *Northumberland, NE66 3TT; 01665 576231; see www.english-heritage.org.uk*
Stroll along the coast from Craster and you'll see the evocative ruins of this 14th-century castle looming large on the horizon. It was begun in 1313 as a status symbol by the rebellious Earl Thomas of Lancaster, who was promptly executed by order of King Edward II for his efforts.

Howick Hall Gardens *nr Howick, Alnwick, Northumberland, NE66 3LB; 01665 577285; www.howickhallgardens.org*
If you fancy a change from all that Heritage Coastline, take a sidestep inland to these peaceful gardens. There's a wetland, woodland walks, flowerbeds crammed with colour, and, of course, the obligatory tea shop. Keep your eyes peeled for the resident red squirrels.

EAT, DRINK, SLEEP

Sea Breeze Cottage *1 Heugh Road, Craster, Northumberland, NE66 3TJ; 07599 423718; www.seabreezeholiday.co.uk*
A coastal footpath runs right outside this sunny seafront cottage. There are three bedrooms and an upstairs 'viewing room', where you've got sweeping 180-degree views along the coast to Dunstanburgh Castle (wait till you see the sunsets). Inside you'll find underfloor heating, a rather fancy kitchen, and other delightful touches. From £505 for seven nights.

Craster Tower Apartments *Craster, Alnwick, Northumberland, NE66 3SS; 01665 576674; www.crastertower.co.uk*

Book the top floor of this 15th-century Grade-II country house, owned and built by the Craster family. There are four big rooms with original features, fab views, and a woodland walk down to the Jolly Fisherman pub in the village whenever you're ready... From £939 for seven nights.

The Old Rectory *Howick, Alnwick, Northumberland, NE66 3LE; 01665 577590; www.oldrectoryhowick.co.uk*
Located just 400 metres from the sea, between Craster and Alnwick, this large family home is surrounded by spacious gardens – and a croquet lawn. There are four rooms (two doubles, two twins) and a family suite, making it ideal if you're bringing the whole gang. King-sized double from £75 per night (based on a two-night stay).

RENT

Pedal Power *Unit 6, Coquet Enterprise Park, Amble, Northumberland, NE65 0PE; 01665 713448; www.pedal-power.co.uk*
There's a fleet of hybrids to choose from, along with tandems, tag-alongs, child seats, and trailers. Adult bikes cost £14 per day with helmet, pump, lock, and repair kit.

60

NORTH SUNDERLAND TO BAMBURGH

An old church, an ancient castle, and one huge beach...

W HEN YOU'RE CURLED UP on the sofa at
St Cuthbert's House in North Sunderland,
it's hard to imagine that once a local
congregation gathered here to worship.

Named after the Northumbrian patron saint –
whose name also appears on the locally brewed
bottles of beer served with dinner – St Cuthbert's
House first opened its doors to churchgoers in
1810, but closed them for the last time in 1998,
when Jill and Jeff Sutheran bought it as their family
home. They've managed to transform the place into
a sumptuous B&B, complete with an upstairs pulpit
overlooking the nave – sorry – 'guest lounge'.

While it's tempting to just sit around and soak
up all this fascinating architectural detail, there's a
whole series of lanes out there to explore. And the
route couldn't be simpler: you leave St Cuthbert's
House, turn right, and just keep on going.

For the first two miles or so you can ease back
in the saddle, staying on the same road, which
wiggles its way south-west, from 'three o'clock' to
'five o'clock' on this circular route.

The lanes around here are refreshingly flat; the
only uphill bits being the humpbacked bridges you
cruise over to cross a couple of railway lines. The first
of these tracks is disused nowadays, but was built
in the late 19th century for transporting fish from
nearby Seahouses harbour to Chathill, where it was
transferred to the East Coast Main Line bound for
London. So important (and lucrative) was the fishing
industry around here at the time, that the fishermen
funded the project themselves.

Carrying on through Newham, you're surrounded
by farmland as far as the eye can see, with the sky
stretched tightly towards the edge of the Cheviot
Hills, way off in the distance. After a few miles, you're
coasting up outside the Apple Inn at Lucker, where a
hand-pulled pint will be yours in a matter of minutes.

From here you're only a short ride away from
lunch in Bamburgh, passing through 'ten o'clock'
and on to 'eleven' as you pedal your way around this

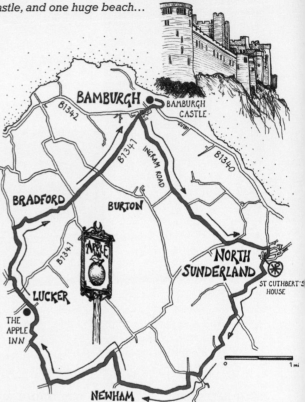

clock-face of lanes. The first you see of the historical
seaside town is its castle looming up ahead, perched
ominously on its black basalt nest.

For centuries Bamburgh was the frontier between
English rule and Scottish ambition, and defended
against multiple raids throughout the Middle Ages.
Today it makes for a fascinating walk through
medieval history, as you tread the worn stone floors
of the keep and stare out over the North Sea, across
which those Vikings travelled to launch their attack.

Thankfully the beach is much safer these days – a
huge expanse of golden sand where you can stretch
out with a book or explore the rockpools for a few
hours. And, when you've had enough sea air, it's only
a short return ride to the sofa at St Cuthbert's House.

THE ROUTE

DISTANCE 15 MILES
DIFFICULTY ○○
START St Cuthbert's House

192 Main Street, North Sunderland,
Seahouses, Northumberland, NE68 7UB

» Head right from St Cuthbert's House and
follow the blue cycle route sign to stay on
the same road for 2 miles – to a T-junction:
turn right, towards Newham.

» About 400 metres later, you turn left on
to a tiny lane, signposted Newham.

» At Newham turn right, towards Lucker.

» At the next junction turn left, for Warenford.

» About a mile later you reach a crossroads
(having crossed over the railway line): turn
right, towards Lucker.

» Just over a mile later you arrive in Lucker
(you'll see the Apple Inn on your left).

» Carry on past the pub, to the memorial:
bear right to leave the village.

» At the next junction, bear left. Shortly after,
the road bends sharp left – go straight on.

» At the next junction, turn right and carry
on for another ⅓ mile, crossing the railway
again before another junction, where you
turn right towards Bradford.

» After passing through Bradford, you come
to a junction: bear left, on to the B1341.

» Stay on this road all the way to Bamburgh,
following the signs, to arrive at the castle.

» From the castle, retrace your route, and at
the Victoria Hotel turn into Ingram Road.

» After 2½ miles, turn left, following the
blue cycle route sign for Seahouses.

» Stay on this road to a T-junction on the
edge of North Sunderland: turn right.

» At the next junction, turn right – St
Cuthbert's House is just along, on your right.

STOP AND SEE

EN ROUTE

The Apple Inn *Lucker, Belford,*
Northumberland, NE70 7JH; 01668 213450
This quiet village inn serves up a selection
of real ales and a mean Sunday roast.

Otherwise food is only served on
Wednesday to Saturday evenings so you'll
need to pop back if you want to eat.

Bamburgh Castle *Bamburgh,*
Northumberland, NE69 7DF; 01668 214515;
www.bamburghcastle.com
This was once one of the most powerful
places in all of England, where monarchs
plotted the future of the country, and
Republicans attacked in 1464. Explore the
medieval kitchen, which used to feed a
small army of inhabitants.

Bamburgh Beach *Bamburgh,*
Northumberland
Kick off your shoes and stretch out your
toes on the cool white sand of this Blue Flag
beach. Sprint to the shore and jump about
in the waves, or pick up some papers for
a lazy, sun-kissed afternoon.

OFF ROUTE

Inner Farne Island *Billy Shiel's Boat Trips,*
4 Southfield Avenue, Seahouses,
Northumberland, NE68 7YT, 01665 720308;
www.farne-islands.com
Hop aboard the good ship *Glad Tidings* for
a 2½-hour cruise to Inner Farne, where that
man St Cuthbert spent much of his life
living in a cave. Check out the 14th-century
church here, built in his honour, and see
the island's resident colonies of puffins,
guillemots, and grey seals.

EAT, DRINK, SLEEP

St Cuthbert's House *192 Main Street, North*
Sunderland, Seahouses, Northumberland,
NE68 7UB; 01665 720456;
www.stcuthbertshouse.com
This 200-year-old former Presbyterian
church has been converted into a luxury
B&B with six rooms boasting enormous
beds. Owners Jeff and Jill are keen cyclists,
and aside from whipping up gourmet
breakfasts and arranging in-room

massages, they'll also recommend some
splendid local rides.
Doubles from £90 per night.

The Greenhouse *5–6 Front Street,*
Bamburgh, Northumberland, NE69 7BW;
01670 515501;
www.thegreenhouseguesthouse.co.uk
If you're staying for a week or more, why
not book into this four-bedroom house in
the centre of Bamburgh? You'll find home-
made jams, fair-trade teas, and a bottle of
wine chilling in the fridge when you arrive.
Seven-night stay from £450.

Wynding Down Cottage *20 The Wynding,*
Bamburgh, Northumberland, NE69 7DB;
01670 511162; www.wyndingdown.co.uk
This 18th-century converted stable and
hayloft is just three minutes' walk from the
beach, with its own private garden, which
has views across the cricket pitch to the
castle. There are three rooms (two doubles
and a single with bunks) and a huge
kitchen, where you can cook up a storm.
From £450 per week (self-catering).

RENT

Boards and Bikes *The Smithy, Swinhoe,*
Chathill, Northumberland, NE67 5AB;
07563 040195; boardsandbikes.co.uk
Choose from a range of rather swish
Specialized mountain bikes, with adult
hire costing £20 a day. This includes
helmets and locks.

INDEX

Index 287

CREDITS

AUTHOR ACKNOWLEDGEMENTS

Before I go, I'd just like to thank a few people who helped me out along the way. First of all my wife, Maria, for her patience and enthusiasm – I couldn't have done this without you. I'd also like to thank my editor, Sophie, for her calmness; Harriet for the fabulous maps; Jonathan and the whole gang at Punk for the opportunity to turn my idea into reality. Thanks, too, to my agent, Borra, for her wise words; my assistant, Ben, for his help with the research; Julian for the gorgeous photos – and Jonny Boy for stepping in with some additional shots, and invaluable assistance for Jules.

Other people who made a huge difference along the way include James Gray at the Ashton in Lancaster (can't wait to go back!), who also provided the bottom right-hand photo on p192; Lesley Hornsby at Number 43 Arnside for her late-night deli-board; Decima and David Noble at Cross o'th' Hill Farm for their hospitality and brilliant suggestions; Barbara and Rob at Guiting Guest House for the packed lunch and banter – and everyone else who opened their doors (and maps) for me en route.

Finally, thanks to Danny Holroyd and the boys at On One for helping me out in my hour of need – when both my bikes got stolen. From my house. While I was in… Anyway, all's well that ends well.

We hope you've enjoyed reading *Escape Routes* and that it's inspired you to hop on your bike and get out into the English countryside. The routes, 'stop and see', 'eat, drink, sleep', and 'rent' places featured are a personal selection chosen by the author. None of these places has paid a fee for inclusion, nor was one requested, so you can be sure of an objective choice of rides and recommendations, with honest descriptions.

Finally, if you know of a route that you think should be included, please send an email to enquiries@ punkpublishing.co.uk explaining the route and why it's so special, as well as some of the places worth stopping off at along the way. We'll credit all useful contributions in the next edition, and senders of the best emails will receive a complimentary copy.

ABOUT *ESCAPE ROUTES*

Researched and written by:	Matt Carroll
Photographed by:	Julian Hanton
Hand-drawn maps by:	Harriet Yeomans
Publisher:	Jonathan Knight
Managing Editor:	Sophie Dawson
Front Cover and Styling:	Michael Harrison
Design:	Kenny Grant
Research:	Ben Cooper
Additional photography:	John Burrell
Proofreaders:	Leanne Bryan, Jessica Cowie
Editorial Assistant:	Harriet Yeomans
Marketing:	Shelley Bowdler
Published by:	Punk Publishing, 3 The Yard, Pegasus Place, London, SE11 5SD
Distributed by:	Portfolio Books, 2nd Floor, Westminster House, Kew Road, Richmond, Surrey, TW9 2ND
England Map (page 6):	©MAPS IN MINUTES™/ Collins Bartholomew 2011

The publishers and author have done their best to ensure the accuracy of all information in *Escape Routes*. However, they can accept no responsibility for any injury, loss, or inconvenience sustained by anyone as a result of information contained in this book.

Punk Publishing takes its environmental responsibilities seriously. This book has been printed on paper made from renewable sources and we continue to work with our printers to reduce our overall environmental impact.